IT HAPPENED TO ME

Series Editor: Arlene Hirschfelder

Books in the It Happened to Me series are designed for inquisitive teens digging for answers about certain illnesses, social issues, or lifestyle interests. Whether you are deep into your teen years or just entering them, these books are gold mines of up-to-date information, riveting teen views, and great visuals to help you figure out stuff. Besides special boxes highlighting singular facts, each book is enhanced with the latest reading lists, websites, and an index. Perfect for browsing, there are loads of expert information by acclaimed writers to help parents, guardians, and librarians understand teen illness, tough situations, and lifestyle choices.

1. *Epilepsy: The Ultimate Teen Guide,* by Kathlyn Gay and Sean McGarrahan, 2002.
2. *Stress Relief: The Ultimate Teen Guide,* by Mark Powell, 2002.
3. *Learning Disabilities: The Ultimate Teen Guide,* by Penny Hutchins Paquette and Cheryl Gerson Tuttle, 2003.
4. *Making Sexual Decisions: The Ultimate Teen Guide,* by L. Kris Gowen, 2003.
5. *Asthma: The Ultimate Teen Guide,* by Penny Hutchins Paquette, 2003.
6. *Cultural Diversity—Conflicts and Challenges: The Ultimate Teen Guide,* by Kathlyn Gay, 2003.
7. *Diabetes: The Ultimate Teen Guide,* by Katherine J. Moran, 2004.
8. *When Will I Stop Hurting? Teens, Loss, and Grief: The Ultimate Teen Guide to Dealing with Grief,* by Ed Myers, 2004.
9. *Volunteering: The Ultimate Teen Guide,* by Kathlyn Gay, 2004.
10. *Organ Transplants—A Survival Guide for the Entire Family: The Ultimate Teen Guide,* by Tina P. Schwartz, 2005.
11. *Medications: The Ultimate Teen Guide,* by Cheryl Gerson Tuttle, 2005.
12. *Image and Identity—Becoming the Person You Are: The Ultimate Teen Guide,* by L. Kris Gowen and Molly C. McKenna, 2005.
13. *Apprenticeship: The Ultimate Teen Guide,* by Penny Hutchins Paquette, 2005.
14. *Cystic Fibrosis: The Ultimate Teen Guide,* by Melanie Ann Apel, 2006.
15. *Religion and Spirituality in America: The Ultimate Teen Guide,* by Kathlyn Gay, 2006.
16. *Gender Identity: The Ultimate Teen Guide,* by Cynthia L. Winfield, 2007.

ACTIVISM

THE ULTIMATE TEEN GUIDE

KATHLYN GAY

IT HAPPENED TO ME, NO. 47

ROWMAN & LITTLEFIELD
Lanham • Boulder • New York • London

Published by Rowman & Littlefield
A wholly owned subsidiary of The Rowman & Littlefield Publishing Group, Inc.
4501 Forbes Boulevard, Suite 200, Lanham, Maryland 20706
www.rowman.com

Unit A, Whitacre Mews, 26-34 Stannary Street, London SE11 4AB

British Library Cataloguing in Publication Information Available

Library of Congress Cataloging-in-Publication Data

Names: Gay, Kathlyn.
Title: Activism : the ultimate teen guide / Kathlyn Gay.
Description: Lanham : Rowman & Littlefield, 2016. | Series: It happened to me
    | Includes bibliographical references and index.
Identifiers: LCCN 2015030148| ISBN 9781442242937 (hardback : alk. paper) |
    ISBN 9781442242944 (ebook)
Subjects: LCSH: Youth—Political activity—Juvenile literature. | Social
    action—Juvenile literature.
Classification: LCC HQ799.2.P6 G389 2016 | DDC 320.40835—dc23 LC record available at
http://lccn.loc.gov/2015030148

♾™ The paper used in this publication meets the minimum requirements of American
National Standard for Information Sciences—Permanence of Paper for Printed Library
Materials, ANSI/NISO Z39.48-1992.

Printed in the United States of America

To activists whose long-term efforts
help make the world a better place to live.

Contents

Acknowledgments

A ctivists from diverse backgrounds and age groups have shared their stories and comments about their participation in advocacy for or against numerous socioeconomic, environmental, and other causes. I am grateful for all the anecdotes, information, and heartfelt accounts. A special thanks to Nissa Beth Gay for her help in locating activists for interviews and to those who responded to questionnaires. They have helped make this book possible. Thank you.

WHO ARE ACTIVISTS?

....

"I love the idea of learning and then putting it to use. I want to major in social activism [in college]. I've always been the person trying to help people. I just want to do something that's meaningful."—high school senior Natalie Strohm, comment to reporter in 2014[1]

Hundreds of thousands of Americans are vigorous advocates—activists—for or against a social, political, economic, or environmental cause. They may stand on street corners with handwritten signs. They often march carrying banners. They lobby politicians or corporate officials. They write letters or post messages on the Internet. Sometimes they commit acts of civil disobedience—defying laws to further their particular issue. In some cases, they may clash with people who vehemently disagree with them.

Activists are represented in varied age groups, ethnicities, and geographic locations. They take on such issues as abortion, civil rights, global warming, human trafficking, toxic waste, jobs, and other causes. Young people play an especially important role in the realm of activism. Twenty percent of the U.S. population is between the ages of ten and twenty-four, and their "involvement is essential to disrupt the status quo and build a smarter, healthier and more peaceful world," according to the Youth Activism Project.[2]

Consider Ketorah Brewster, a high school senior in 2014 and teen activist in Boston, Massachusetts. Ketorah was a member of the Youth Jobs Coalition that advocates for teens wanting and needing jobs. "Having a job is like having a voice," Ketorah told a reporter. "Taking away a job from someone who wants to work hard is like taking away their voice and their ability to advocate for themselves."[3]

Tara Holmes, communications and marketing manager at Future 500, who works to bring corporations and activists together to solve social and environmental problems, pointed out that she had never considered herself an activist. However, in an article for Truth-Out.org, she wrote, "It took me some time to realize that the 'small, simple' actions I was taking against oppression in my own daily life, even if simply raising an important issue with my friends, family and

Activists are likely to march and carry banners such as these.

colleagues, added up to more activism than I thought. . . . In fact, I came to realize that we're all activists to varying degrees; it just depends on how you look at it. After all, who hasn't at some point in time in some small way stood up against injustice—especially when it becomes personal?"[4]

No government agency has provided estimates of the total number of activists in the United States, but innumerable diverse organizations claim anywhere from dozens to thousands of individual advocates advancing their causes. For example, in 2014 the Youth Rights Movement had ten thousand members nationwide; tens of thousands of teenagers across the United States participated in Students Working Against Tobacco (SWAT); Kids Against Animal Cruelty (KAAC) had more than fifty thousand members, fans, and supporters.

Numerous youth are involved in a coalition known as BAMN (By Any Means Necessary). The coalition is "a primarily student- and youth-based organization of leaders in our schools and communities committed to making real the promises of American democracy and equality," according to its website. BAMN campaigns to build an "integrated civil rights movement that will unite black and brown, gay and straight, to win full freedom and equality for all." The coalition is also "fighting to defend public education, to defeat budget cuts for education, to

A Post from the Past

The American Youth Congress (AYC) organized in 1935 and was composed of young people from all across the United States. AYC met once each year until 1940—the year it convened on the White House lawn. Its purpose was to advocate for youth rights and to discuss the problems facing youth during the 1930s. A primary focus was the draft, which required young males at age eighteen to sign up for the military. At the time, eighteen-year-olds were not considered legal adults until age twenty-one. At its peak in 1939 (at the beginning of World War II), AYC claimed more than 4.5 million members with over five hundred affiliated organizations nationwide.

On July 4, 1936, the AYC issued a *Declaration of the Rights of American Youth*, which noted in part, "We declare that our generation is rightfully entitled to a useful, creative, and happy life, the guarantees of which are: full educational opportunities, steady employment at adequate wages, security in time of need, civil rights, religious freedom, and peace." The *Declaration* also proclaimed "the right of freedom from toil for all children for whom labor can only mean physical and mental harm. We therefore demand the abolition of child labor with full and adequate maintenance for needy children."

Noting that war preparations were under way "by those who profit by destruction," the AYC declared, "we oppose this war and its trappings of militarized youth and mounting armaments. We do not want to die! We assert our right to peace and our determination to maintain peace."

The *Declaration* concludes, "We the young people of America, reaffirm our right to life, liberty and the pursuit of happiness. With confidence we look forward to a better life, a larger liberty and freedom. To those ends we dedicate our lives, our intelligence and our unified strength."[a]

Youth may volunteer to help serve meals at a soup kitchen sponsored by their religious community or civic group and later become antihunger activists.

defend public jobs and public services, to win college financial aid and citizenship for undocumented immigrant students, and to make every school, college, city, municipality and state a sanctuary for undocumented immigrants."[5]

Preparing for Activism

During their middle and high school years, students often volunteer for short periods of time, participating in projects for civic, religious, environmental, or political organizations, which can plant the seeds and prime them for long-term activism. School recycling is a popular volunteer project that may lead to activism in antipollution efforts. Students who clean up seashores or riverbanks on a weekend may eventually become active in conservation campaigns.

Volunteering and activism seem to be the same thing, but there are differences. University of Southern California professor Nina Eliasoph, author of *The Politics of Volunteering* (Polity Press, 2013), explained in an interview that "volunteers can become activists when they confront a problem that requires more than changing the world one person, light bulb or diaper at a time." Eliasoph pointed out, "Many early 20th century social reformers . . . began as volunteers, but painfully discovered that to help young children whose parents took them out of school to earn money, just helping each child one at a time was not enough. If

Many teens get their start in activism by running for school council offices.

the kid stopped working, the family might go homeless. The volunteers had to become political activists when they realized that if they pushed for legislation to raise the minimum wage and outlaw child labor, parents would make enough money, their kids wouldn't have to leave school at age 10 and could enjoy America's promise as the land of opportunity."[6]

Teenager Chelsey Zane of Potomac, Maryland, who was a senior at Winston Churchill High School in 2014, is an example of how volunteer efforts led to activism. In 2012, Chelsey and her parents "volunteered to read stories to sick children staying at The Children's Inn at the National Institutes of Health in Bethesda," according to a report in *Bethesda Magazine*. "That's when the Potomac teen met a girl from Ohio with a rare form of cancer. Inspired by how much The Children's Inn had helped her new friend, Chelsey created an after-school club at Winston Churchill in the girl's honor. The club, Friends of Friends in Need, is dedicated to supporting local and national charities and counts about 15 students as members." Chelsey continued her activism by seeking donations of funds and goods from retailers like Giant and Starbucks. On one of her projects she wore a costume "as Glinda the Good Witch from *The Wizard of Oz* for a dinner she organized for families staying at The Children's Inn," *Bethesda Magazine* reported.[7] The magazine honored Chelsey along with nine other students citing them as its "Extraordinary Top Ten Activists for 2014."

Another Top Ten Activist was Anna Collishaw of Bethesda. When Anna was a sophomore at Walter Johnson High School, "she got involved with International

Partners, a Silver Spring nonprofit that facilitates trips for local teens to aid poor villages in northern El Salvador." Anna made several trips to El Salvador and helped with such projects as building a water storage tank.[8]

Still another honoree was Richie Yarrow, also of Bethesda. His activism began at Richard Montgomery High School where he was part of the student government association. Richie went beyond that, becoming an advocate for students, who he argued "are the greatest stakeholders in Montgomery County public schools." Their "input is quite crucial to making sure school is run for students."[9]

One Drinking Straw at a Time

Sometimes activism is prompted by a personal experience. That was the case with Milo Cress of Colorado, who turned thirteen in 2015. He began the Be Straw Free campaign when he was only nine years old. It was prompted when he was in a restaurant with his mother, O'dale Cress, who wondered aloud why straws were handed out with every drink. Not that he was "anti-straw"—he just realized that, when not needed, providing them would be wasteful. And further, it would be ecologically damaging, because when thrown away, plastic straws do not disintegrate easily.

Milo talked to the restaurant owner who agreed to give customers a choice. From then on, Milo and his mom became activists. They traveled from Colorado to the western United States, Australia, and Europe. Milo explained his campaign about overuse of plastic drinking straws to restaurateurs, students, and civic groups. According to the campaign, 500 million disposable straws are used in the United States each day, "enough disposable straws to fill over 46,400 large school buses per year."[b]

Milo's campaign alerts people to the fact that they do not need a straw every time they order a drink at a restaurant—it is a waste of resources, he argues, and plastic straws pollute the environment. He urges restaurant owners to ask people if they want a straw. Given a choice, many customers simply opt not to use a drinking straw. He told a reporter in Washington State that being straw free "is a small step for each restaurant but a huge step for the planet."[c]

When twelve-year-old Milo visited Washington State in 2014, he spoke to students at numerous schools. One of the schools was Port Townsend High School, where he told his audience: "Here's the thing: The planet is not a place that kids will inherit at some point far off into the distant future. . . . We live here right now, and we share this planet already."

Milo explained to a Port Townsend reporter that he "didn't think anyone would want to listen to what a kid has to say, but I found that being a kid can be an advantage. . . . Both kids and adults love to hear about and participate in projects that were started by kids."[d]

When There Is Dissent

Not all activists are honored with awards or see positive results from their actions. When working for a controversial cause, they may face dissension from opponents. Activists take sides in debates—both pro and con—over such issues as free speech, gun rights and gun control, abortion, animal rights, human rights, immigration reform, workplace issues, creationism versus evolution, and foods genetically modified by scientists using biotechnology techniques. Some debates will be described in later chapters in this book.

One issue that has riled certain activists over the years is the use of names and logos of professional sports teams that are considered offensive to Native Americans, such as the name for the professional football team in the nation's capital: Washington Redskins. Opponents of the name point out that the "R-word," as they call it, once referred to the bloodied scalps, or "redskins," that U.S. soldiers showed off after killing Native Americans for a bounty. It is a racist term, opponents insist, pointing out that no sports team would be named Blackface or use derogatory names for other ethnic groups. Supporters of the Washington team name claim it honors Native Americans whom they respect for their fierceness and bravery.

Legal action was taken on this issue by the U.S. Patent and Trademark Office on June 18, 2014, canceling the Washington team's six federal trademark registrations for its logos. That same action had already been taken in 1999, was appealed, and then overturned in the team's favor. Subsequently, in 2006, five young Native Americans filed a challenge to the appeal, which resulted in the U.S. Patent and Trademark 2014 trademark judicial ruling stating that "based on the evidence properly before us . . . these registrations must be canceled because they [are] disparaging to Native Americans." However, that does not legally ban the racist name and it can still be used. Team owner Daniel Snyder, as he has done for years, defiantly declares that the Redskins name will never change.

A similar situation involves the Cleveland Indians baseball team and its Chief Wahoo logo, which depicts a grinning, red-faced cartoon with a feather headband. Protesters want the team name and logo replaced. Supporters believe the name and logo are long-standing traditions and should be maintained.

Along with professional sports teams, dozens of schools across the United States have used or are using names and logos offensive to Native Americans. After much community debate, some schools have made changes. One of them is Port Townsend High School in Washington State. For more than eight decades the school called its team the Redskins, but in 2012 students, teachers, and coaches formed a study committee regarding the divisive and derogatory use of the name and determined to select a new name. In June 2014, Redhawks became the official team name with a fierce-looking bird—a red hawk—as the logo.

Another high school—this one in Lancaster, New York—also dropped the Redskins mascot and logo for its lacrosse team. Native American students in three other districts said they would boycott lacrosse games because of the offensive name. Some students and alumni objected to any change in the mascot or logo. But in March 2015, the school board voted to begin a process to replace the Redskins name.

A confrontation about a Native American nickname for its sports team hit the University of North Dakota (UND) campus in May 2014. A group of UND students appeared to deliberately provoke a protest from an activist American Indian student group on campus. The protest was sparked because of "blatantly racist T-shirts" worn by some students during a Spring Fest. The offensive T-shirts included the phrase "Siouxper Drunk," along with a Native American in a feathered headdress—an old, no longer used UND logo. The T-shirts also depicted two beer mugs with the mascot drinking from a beer bong. According to news reports, one hundred to two hundred Native Americans and supporters from tribes in the area took part in a protest March for Change. They demanded that university officials include "sensitivity training for incoming students and a total ban of the old Fighting Sioux nickname and logo on campus." Protesters also demanded that UND get a new nickname and logo. In response the university president pledged to work with the American Indian student group to try to find "a resolution that is satisfactory, within the rules of law."[10]

The Fight for LGBT Rights

For decades, activists have campaigned for LGBT (lesbian, gay, bisexual, and transgender) rights—the same rights granted to heterosexual people. They have been frequently harassed or physically attacked and even murdered by others who are adamantly antigay. As one sign brandished by an antagonist said, "No Special Laws for Fags."

A survey by the Human Rights Campaign (HRC) found that "LGBT men are 20 percent more likely to experience verbal harassment and 17 percent more likely to experience physically aggressive harassment than men who are not gay, bisexual, queer or transgender." And "LGBT youth are twice as likely to experience verbal harassment, exclusion and physical attack at school as their non-LGBT peers. Among LGBT youth, 51 percent have been verbally harassed at school, compared to 25 percent among non-LGBT students."[11]

However, some students actively support gay rights by taking part in a national Day of Silence, which occurs every April. Hundreds of thousands of students participate to demonstrate that many LGBT people have no voice and must keep their sexual preferences secret. These LGBT supporters distribute cards at this event explaining the meaning of their silent protest:

> Please understand my reasons for not speaking today. I am participating in the Day of Silence, a national youth movement protesting the silence faced by lesbian, gay, bisexual and transgender people and their allies in schools. My deliberate silence echoes that silence, which is caused by harassment, prejudice, and discrimination. I believe that ending the silence is the first step toward fighting these injustices. Think about the voices you are not hearing today. What are you going to do to end the silence?[12]

Day of Silence opponents conduct their own protests. In Oregon, for example, four Oregon City High School students wore T-shirts with the statement "Gay Is Not OK" and "Gay Day Is Not OK."[13] In other instances, parents have urged their children to stay home or walk out of school on the Day of Silence.

A 2014 HRC research report titled *Growing Up LGBT in America* surveyed LGBT youth and includes numerous statistics. The report notes,

> The deck is stacked against young people growing up lesbian, gay, bisexual, or transgender in America. Official government discrimination or indifference along with social ostracism leaves many teens disaffected and disconnected in their own homes and neighborhoods. . . . It is critical that we get a better understanding of the experiences, needs, and concerns of LGBT youth.
>
> This groundbreaking research among more than 10,000 LGBT-identified youth ages 13–17 provides a stark picture of the difficulties they face. The impact on their well-being is profound, however these youth are quite resilient. They find safe havens among their peers, online and in their schools. They remain optimistic and believe things will get better.[14]

In its survey, the HRC also asked questions about the future and found that LGBT youth often described a high degree of optimism, frequently at similar levels as their peers. However, this optimism declined markedly compared to their peers when asked if they could achieve those dreams in the communities where they currently live. The most vivid example is that 83 percent of LGBT youth believe they will be happy eventually, but only 49 percent believe they can be happy if they stay in the same city or town.[15]

A feature in *The Daily Beast* in 2014 also suggested some optimism: "Unlike ever before, most Americans have openly gay friends, colleagues, and family members, and most approve of same-sex relationships. Young people are overwhelmingly gay-friendly, leaving little doubt which way the trends are going."[16]

About LGBT Trends

While there is no doubt that activists have helped bring about positive changes for gay rights, the path has been long and grueling. A gay rights organization was begun in Chicago, Illinois, in 1924, but few other organizations appeared until the 1950s and 1960s. One example was a lesbian rights organization, the Daughters of Bilitis, established in San Francisco in 1955. It became a national organization in 1956. Transgender groups formed in the following years.

In June 1969, the so-called Stonewall Riots occurred. Police raided the Stonewall Inn, a gay bar in New York's Greenwich Village, and a fight ensued with its patrons, which continued over a three-day period. That confrontation transformed what had been a small number of activists to a widespread gay rights movement for equal rights and acceptance.

During the 1970s in Miami, Florida, gay rights activists convinced legislators to pass a civil rights ordinance making discrimination based on sexual orientation illegal in Dade County. But a Christian fundamentalist group headed by singer Anita Bryant campaigned against the law. A special election was held and the ordinance was overturned by 70 percent of the voters—a huge defeat for the gay rights movement.

In 1977, San Francisco Mayor George Moscone appointed an openly gay man, Harvey Milk, to the Board of Permit Appeals. But because of opposition, the mayor fired him after five weeks. Milk ran for San Francisco's Board of Supervisors and won the election in 1978. However, Milk and Moscone had enemies. They were assassinated by Dan White, another San Francisco city supervisor, who had recently resigned and wanted his job back.

Some progress for gay rights came about from the 1980s through the 1990s. In 1982, for example, Wisconsin outlawed discrimination based on sexual orientation. The U.S. Supreme Court in 1996 overturned a Colorado amendment that denied gays and lesbians protections against discrimination. Between 2000 and 2015, states began to recognize and legalize same-sex unions. As of April 2015 same-sex marriages were legal in thirty-seven states with other states likely to overturn their bans.

At the end of April 2015, the U.S. Supreme Court heard arguments for and against same-sex marriage. Attorneys for both sides presented their cases regarding whether homosexual couples have a constitutional right to marry in every state rather than just those that have lifted their bans. The High Court ruled on June 26, 2015, that same-sex couples in all fifty states had the right to marry.

A Family of Activists

Van and Nancy Harrington, conservative parents of nineteen-year-old Zachary (Zach or Zack) in Oklahoma, became gay, lesbian, bisexual, and transgender (GLBT) activists after their son committed suicide on October 5, 2010. A week earlier Zach had attended a council meeting in Norman, Oklahoma. Like other gay teens, Zach was rallying to pass a proclamation making October GLBT history month in Norman. (In other parts of the nation, recognition events may use the term *LGBT*, or lesbian, gay, bisexual, transgender.) Although the Norman council approved the proclamation in a 7–1 vote, a nasty debate followed.

According to an October 2010 article in the *Normal Transcript*, "Some of those who opposed the proclamation claimed that members of the GLBT community would use it to infiltrate the public school system, essentially allowing the 'gay lifestyle' to become a part of the curriculum. . . . Numerous residents also claimed the Bible was their guiding light, citing the ancient text as their primary reason for opposing the proclamation and the GLBT community in general."[17]

Although it is not possible to pin Zach's suicide on the city council meeting alone, it was likely a factor in his depression, knowing his own community thought he was shameful, based on his gender and sexual preferences. His older sister Nikki Harrington told Morgan Welch at Dot429.com, "When he was sitting there, I'm sure he was internalizing everything and analyzing everything . . . that's the kind of person he was. I'm sure he took it personally. Everything that was said."[18] His father, Van, agreed as did Zach's brother, Austin.

Nancy Harrington, Zach's mom, posted her thoughts on HuffingtonPost .com: "As we sought answers to why [Zach] had taken his life, we discovered some revealing anthologies—personal diaries he had written. We soon realized how much he had struggled. His views were much more complex than we knew. He clearly grappled with reconciling his own sexuality with opposing views in the community, particularly the anti-gay religious view." The Harrington family also learned well after Zach's suicide that he was HIV-positive.

Our hearts were broken again when we realized the pain he must have felt when he did not think he could share this information with us. As much as my family tried to vocalize our concerns about LGBT kids in our community, we were stymied at every turn. We attempted to speak out publicly at a League of Women Voters forum in the city council's chambers, but we were not permitted to express our opinions. I personally wrote a heartfelt letter to our local newspaper, the *Norman Transcript*, and the editor refused to publish it. I felt betrayed. I felt our community was being let down.[19]

The entire family became involved in telling Zach's story by not only speaking out against homophobia, but also by allowing a film crew to make a documentary. For more than three years the crew followed family members around to create *Broken Heart Land*. Directed by siblings Jeremy Stulberg and Randy Stulberg, the film premiered in mid and late June 2014, first in Norman and Oklahoma City, then at the worldwide Frameline Film Festival in San Francisco, California. It was also broadcast on PBS World Channel's 2014 season of America ReFramed. Nancy Harrington's "hope is that this film reaches other teens and their families who might be struggling with the same issues. . . . I want other parents to let their children know that regardless of their sexual orientation, their gender identity, and especially their HIV status, they are loved, supported, and valued."[20]

What Activism Has Accomplished

As noted, activists may face passionate dissenters. Such confrontations can be discouraging and contribute to burnout. Some may question: Why go on if you cannot successfully communicate the worthiness of your cause? Still, in general, dedicated activists do not give up. Most activists say they are participating in positive efforts for society. They believe that they can make a difference and have decided to be part of a solution to a problem. Ideally they want to bring about change for the betterment of a small group or large population or the entire planet. Because of activism, some important transformations have occurred in the United States.

One major change involved child labor and had a major impact on the lives of young children from five years old to teenagers who were working in unhealthy, unsafe conditions during the Industrial Revolution of the 1800s and early 1900s. In those days, manufacturers hired children because they were agile, easily managed, and cheap labor. At the time, few activists were pressuring for childhood education, which had little value to working-class people. However, a broad-based reform group, the National Child Labor Committee (NCLC), formed in 1904 and investigated charges of child labor abuse. In 1908 NCLC issued a report that included dramatic photographs by Lewis Hines clearly illustrating the wretchedness of young children working in textile mills, coal mines, canneries, and other industries. The NCLC report was widely circulated in the United States and prompted activists to protest child labor. Activism helped pressure federal legislators in 1938 to pass the Fair Labor Standards Act, which bans young children from workplaces and limits the hours minor teens can work when school is in session. Along with NCLC's efforts to end child labor, the committee worked to provide free, compulsory education for all children.[21]

Activists have also helped bring about significant changes for women's rights. During earlier times, women were not allowed to vote or own property. But due to the efforts of hundreds of thousands of activists, women earned the right to vote in 1920 with the passage of the 20th Amendment to the U.S. Constitution, which states, "The right of citizens of the United States to vote shall not be denied or abridged by the United States or by any State on account of sex." Women's rights groups, feminists, and other activists also have helped women move out of the household and achieve major positions in government and industry.

Civil rights activists have a long history in the United States, from efforts of the 1700s and 1800s to end slavery to campaigns against racial segregation in the 1950s. *Brown v. Board of Education* (1954) overturned legislation that allowed "separate but equal" facilities for black students and helped establish integrated schools. The High Court decision in *Brown* set the stage for major civil rights activities of the 1950s and 1960s, plus legislation such as the Civil Rights Act of 1964, the Voting Rights Act of 1965, and the Fair Housing Act of 1968.

Changes in the U.S. military are the result of activism over decades. Although African Americans have served in every U.S. war, they were not always welcomed and were usually segregated from whites. They were accepted in the American Revolutionary War, but later, in the War of 1812, the federal government and some states refused to allow African Americans and Native Americans to serve in the U.S. Army, Marine Corps, or state militias. Rules regarding who could serve in the military changed repeatedly from the 1800s to the 1900s. Citizen protests, pressure on government, and demands of war influenced changes in regulations. Currently, there are "minimum qualifications for serving in the U.S. Armed Forces. Some qualifications are required by all five branches of the military. According to Military.com,

- You must be a U.S. citizen or resident alien.
- You must be at least 17 years old (17-year-old applicants require parental consent).
- You must (with very few exceptions) have a high school diploma.
- You must pass a physical medical exam.[22]

Successful Youth Activism

While media note the accomplishments of activism, especially when celebrities are involved, the efforts of young people sometimes are downplayed. There is no doubt, however, that youth activism is thriving and successful. One impressive organization is Urban Roots, a group of young people who work on a 3.5 acre organic farm near Austin, Texas, to grow food for the city's hungry people. The nonprofit What Kids Can Do sent freelance writer Abe Louise Young to learn about Urban Roots' activities. Fifteen-year-old member Nikki told her, "We grow garlic, chives, rainbow chard, tomatoes, cherry tomatoes, squash, cucumbers, melon, okra, eggplant, basil, edamame beans, sorrel, zinnias, and other

Now You Know

Women were barred from the army in the American Revolution, although a few females were able to disguise themselves as boys and fight in some battles. But in later wars women demanded change and were allowed to serve in the U.S. Army, primarily as nurses. During World War I, young women, some of them teenagers between the ages of sixteen and nineteen, joined the Army Signal Corps where they operated switchboards and connected generals with their soldiers. Women were formally recognized as part of the military in the 1940s and served in the Women's Army Corps. By the 1960s and 1970s, they served alongside men in the Vietnam War but were barred from the front lines. In 2013, the Pentagon lifted the ban on women serving in combat.

flowers. . . .You have to take care of every plant differently. You have to know when their season is, and rotate them so you don't tire out the soil. A lot of weeds will come up if you don't keep up with it."[23]

Mathew, another teen participant, added, "We just pull the weeds, we don't use any chemicals. We use fish emulsion for fertilizer, and attractor crops—those are crops that attract the bees so they pollinate, and attract the bugs to keep them from going after the other crops, like tomatoes." He also explained why he got involved with Urban Roots: "I've always lived here, so I wanted to give something back to my community." After harvesting their crops, the group donates some of the produce to food banks and poverty relief organizations. They also sell fruits and vegetables at farmers markets that provide access to people with little or no access to fresh food. "I've been twice to the Food Bank and three times to the Farmer's Market," Mathew reported. "I like that we get to meet new people and talk about something that we worked really hard for. From the Food Bank they bring the produce to Meals on Wheels, and the people are really sweet and really thankful. They don't have transport to go get food, so they are really glad that it gets brought to them."[24]

Many success stories about youth activism can be found on Youth Activism Project's website (http://youthactivismproject.org/success-stories/). Some of the stories under the heading "Putting Passion into Action" have inactive links. Nevertheless, the site provides descriptions of numerous activism projects such as environmental protection, education reform, voting rights for youth, racism and discrimination, drug abuse, and violence. Current stories appear on the organization's blog (http://youthactivismproject.org/blog/).

Other organizations that describe successful youth activism include

- Project RACE, which advocates for multiracial identity on school and government forms and classification of all children equally, and provides a place for multiracial youth to express themselves.
- Seattle Young People's Project, "a youth-led, adult supported social justice organization that empowers youth (ages 13–18) to express themselves and to take action on the issues that affect their lives," according to its website (sypp.org).
- Advocates for Youth (www.advocatesforyouth.org) is a website where teens and young adults can promote honest, factual discussions about sexuality, sexual rights, and sexual health information and services.

Whether working with an organization or going forward alone, youth from preteens to young adults often spark action for change. In other words, they take seriously the old motto "Don't Just Stand There, Do Something!" On the following pages, activists share more—much more—of what they do or have done.

YOUTH RIGHTS PROMOTERS

∙∙

"No Taxation without Representation"—a motto on a placard carried in 2013 by
a teen activist campaigning for lowering the minimum voting age to sixteen

Activists for youth rights are likely to be members of such organizations as Advocates for Youth, which has a long list of issues that teens address. These issues include abortion, contraceptive access, sex education, teen pregnancy, violence and harassment, and more than a dozen other concerns. Belinda, one person on Advocates' website, said, "I choose to be a youth advocate because I believe in taking a stance. It's important to have a say in the policies that affect you." Eric, another participant, explained why he is involved: "When Boston College moved to thwart my organization's distribution of condoms on-campus due to conflict with the Church, I realized how important the issue of comprehensive healthcare is to all students, regardless of a student's religion."[1]

Activist youth also are involved in the National Youth Rights Association (NYRA) founded in 1998. NYRA is registered in Maryland but has members in all fifty states. NYRA works on numerous projects regarding youth, such as protecting student rights and lowering the minimum age for voting. Another organization that engages youth is Amnesty International USA. In Amnesty campaigns, high school students have lobbied legislators for immigrant rights in Denver, Colorado; walked for women's rights in Miami, Florida; participated in New York City's Pride parade; and demonstrated against torture in other cities.

Dozens of teens are part of the Teen Activist Project of the New York Civil Liberties Union. They advocate for freedom of speech and religion, racial justice, immigrants' rights, students' rights, and LGBT rights. Every state has a chapter or affiliate of the American Civil Liberties Union (ACLU) that encourages student activism by offering high school seniors the opportunity to apply for a Youth Activist Scholarship for their first year in college. To apply for a scholarship, students must explain their commitment to civil liberties, free speech, and equality in their communities. ACLU confirms the commitments and awards several scholarships each year.

ACLU Defends Youth

In addition to its scholarship program, the ACLU assists youth and adults seeking to legally defend or maintain their civil rights. In 2011, for example, the ACLU of Ohio was instrumental in helping openly gay teenager Zach King, who was frequently bullied at Unioto High School in Chillicothe. One instance of a classmate severely beating and injuring him was videotaped and shown online, spreading and providing the basis for a lawsuit. The ACLU of Ohio represented King and his mom, who sued the Union-Scioto school district, saying that "school officials 'fostered an atmosphere' that permitted the bullying of LGBT students while disregarding his reports of harassment." The school board settled the lawsuit for $35,000 but admitted no wrongdoing. King has since become an activist, sharing his story with numerous groups, and in 2012 was part of a 2012 ACLU panel discussion about bullied LGBT students. Afterward he told a reporter, "It's empowering to do this, to share my story with other people. . . . And I hope they will learn, and one day there will be a lot less bullies than there are now."[2]

In another youth rights situation, the ACLU and the ACLU of Pennsylvania acted in 2013 on behalf of a transgender student, Issak Wolfe, who attended Red Lion Area Senior High School. Wolfe was a high school senior at the time and

Young people like these may be involved in campaigns to protest discrimination against LGBTQ youth.

Watch This Flick!

Bully, a 2011 movie released on DVD in 2013, sparked activism across the United States. The film depicts the lives of five bullied children and their families during the 2009–2010 school year in Georgia, Iowa, Texas, Mississippi, and Oklahoma. Parents of two bullied students who committed suicide are strong activists in support of the documentary. So is teenager Katy Butler of Ann Arbor, Michigan.

Katy Butler was instrumental in helping to spread information about *Bully*. Katy, a lesbian, was a target of bullies when she was in middle school and classmates learned about her sexual orientation. She recalled for the *Daily Beast*, "Kids . . . walking down the hallway, calling me names, pushing me against walls and into lockers, knocking my books over. Horrible things like that. Their favorite name to call me was definitely 'fag'—that was used a lot. Also: 'dyke.' They ended up slamming my hand into my locker one day and breaking my finger."[a]

After seeing *Bully* in early 2012, Katy began her activism in support of the film, which the Motion Picture Association had rated R because of the "F-word" bullies used in a brutal attack on a student. Due to the rating, teens under seventeen years old were theoretically blocked from seeing the film unless accompanied by a parent. But Katy started an online petition to get the rating changed to PG-13 so that younger children would see and understand the damage bullying can do. "These are real people, telling their real stories," Katy said in an interview with the *Washington Post*. "I think it could create a big change, and it could potentially save lives if kids are allowed to see it."[b]

After hundreds of thousands of Americans signed a petition in support of *Bully*, the Motion Picture Association in April 2012 changed the rating to PG-13. Activists were delighted and encouraged. They hope the film will be widely shown in public schools nationwide.

---

asked to run for prom king. He had repeatedly asked the principal of the school to list him on the ballot by his male name. Instead Principal Mark Shue listed him as a candidate running for prom queen—along with Wolfe's female given name—and also "threatened to bar Wolfe from attending the prom with his girlfriend," according to ACLU's report. "Wolfe's girlfriend, Taylor Thomas, posted

> ### It's a Fact
>
> The U.S. Census Bureau reported that in 2012 the population of the nation was almost 314 million. Of those millions, 25.5 percent were persons under eighteen years old.[c]

a message on Facebook and created an online petition supporting him." Shue then pressured Thomas to withdraw the petition, insisting she would not be allowed to attend the prom unless she complied. That threat prompted Wolfe to call the ACLU, whose staff attorney sent the school district a letter demanding Wolfe's right to the gender identity he chose.

"I never had an issue with my school about accepting me for who I am, so I was shocked and humiliated when the ballots came out and they had me listed as the wrong gender," Wolfe told ACLU. "To do that with no warning, and then try to intimidate us into keeping quiet, is degrading and hurtful."

The ACLU and ACLU of Pennsylvania prevailed on behalf of Wolfe. Issak and Taylor were allowed to attend the prom.[3]

Should the Legal Drinking Age Be Eighteen?

In 1984, the U.S. Congress passed the National Minimum Drinking Age Act, and all states set their legal age for purchase or public possession of alcohol to twenty-one. The penalty for noncompliance is loss of federal highway funds. But some activists have been campaigning for an even lower minimum legal drinking age (MLDA)—eighteen.

The NYRA, for example, argues, "When you are 18 you are judged mature enough to vote, hold public office, serve on juries, serve in the military, fly airplanes, sign contracts and so on. Why is drinking a beer an act of greater responsibility and maturity than flying an airplane or serving your country at war?" On its website, the NYRA points out that

> the drinking age is a highly visible symptom of our current anti-youth culture. The National Youth Rights Association does not feel this is an issue primarily about alcohol; rather it is an issue about equality, honesty, respect, discrimination and freedom. . . . Americans of all ages, races, genders, and ethnicities deserve equal respect, and they deserve the right to make their own choices in life. Youth deserve nothing less. So whether it is choosing to drink a beer, choosing to stay up late, or choosing the

Teenage drinking raises pro and con issues about the minimum legal age for alcohol consumption.

next President, NYRA feels society must respect and honor the choices of young people in an equal, fair and honest way.[4]

The question of whether to lower the MLDA has stirred controversy across the United States. Proponents contend that since people are legally adults at age eighteen, they should be treated as such and enjoy the rights of adults. Supporters also point out that the legal drinking age has not stopped teenagers from drinking. On ProCon.org, "opponents of lowering the MLDA argue that teens have not yet reached an age where they can handle alcohol responsibly, and thus are more likely to harm or even kill themselves and others by drinking prior to 21. They contend that traffic fatalities decreased when the MLDA increased." Most Americans—more than 75 percent—oppose lowering the drinking age.[5]

A Lower Voting Age?

An issue that has high priority for some student activists is lowering the minimum voting age. For decades the minimum legal voting age in the United States was twenty-one. Throughout World War II (1939–1945) and later with America's involvement in the Vietnam War during the 1960s and 1970s, activists campaigned to lower the minimum age to eighteen. They used the slogan "old enough to fight, old enough to vote," arguing that the government drafted young men to fight and possibly die for their country, but denied them the right to the ballot. Across the nation, citizens increasingly supported an amendment to the U.S. Constitution to lower the voting age. In March 1971, Congress passed the Twenty-Sixth Amendment; in July three-fourths of the states ratified it, and then President Richard Nixon signed it into law.

The amendment states, "The right of citizens of the United States, who are eighteen years of age or older, to vote shall not be denied or abridged by the United States or any State." The federal minimum voting age is still eighteen, although some states allow seventeen-year-olds to vote in primaries if by Election Day they will be eighteen.

For years, young people have been campaigning to lower the voting age to sixteen or seventeen. There was a major effort in Lowell, Massachusetts, in 2011. Teenagers organized the Lowell campaign to allow seventeen-year-olds to vote in city elections; they raised funds, urged citizens to vote, and lobbied lawmakers. "When you're 17, that's when most of us are seniors," Carline Kirksey, one of the youth leaders of the campaign, told an *American Prospect* reporter. "You have more adult responsibilities. You can join the military. You can be tried as an adult in court."[6] The campaigners argued they should have a voice in the local politics because it affects their education and lives. However, the student campaign did not convince the Massachusetts secretary of state, who declared lowering the voting age was unconstitutional. Activists have continued their efforts.

Another teen campaign in Takoma Park, Maryland, brought some success. Teens advocated for the right to vote in city elections at the age of sixteen. They carried signs saying "No Taxation without Representation," a slogan American colonists used in the 1700s. The colonials protested taxes imposed on them by the British, who did not allow their colonists a vote in the British Parliament. Modern-day Takoma Park activists in 2013 pointed out that they pay taxes on their earnings, are allowed to drive at sixteen, and thus they should have the right to vote in their municipal elections. The Takoma Park council agreed (six to one) and lowered the voting age for city elections to sixteen. The 2013 election for council members and mayor "was the first time in history that the franchise had been extended to residents under the age of 18," according to the *Washington Post*.[7]

Free Speech

Along with advocating for a voice in elections, student activists campaign for free-speech rights guaranteed by the U.S. Constitution. The First Amendment states, "Congress shall make no law respecting an establishment of religion, or prohibiting the free exercise thereof; or abridging the freedom of speech, or of the press; or the right of the people peaceably to assemble, and to petition the Government for a redress of grievances." The freedom of speech clause for some students means the right to take part in protests on high school and university campuses, read whatever books one chooses, wear some nontraditional clothing at school functions, or participate in other actions deemed free speech.

Consider a young Canadian First Nations teenager Tenelle Starr. Her school prevented her from wearing a shirt with the words "Got Land? Thank an Indian" on it. But her shirt became a popular item when businessman Jeff Menard, a member of Pine Creek First Nation, first saw the phrase on a hoodie in the United States. In 2012, he began creating T-shirts and hoodies with "Got Land?" on the front and "Thank an Indian" on the back. He started selling them in Winnipeg, Manitoba, and Saskatoon, Saskatchewan.

In early January 2014, thirteen-year-old Tenelle wore a pink hoodie with the slogan on it to her Saskatchewan school. Officials told her to take it off or turn it inside out. The words, they deemed, could offend someone. The next day Tenelle did not wear the hoodie, but she later appeared at the school wearing it, which created a controversy. A story about Tenelle and her sweatshirt made news, and later "meetings between the school and leaders of the Star Blanket First Nation led to an understanding that Tenelle's sweatshirt, and its message, were acceptable after all," CBC News reported. Tenelle and Idle No More—a movement to protect indigenous agreements and land and water—began encouraging people to make or buy the shirt with the slogan because it "supports our treaty and land rights," Tenelle said.[8]

Because of Tenelle and her hoodie controversy, Menard's sales have soared. He began selling sweatshirts on his Facebook page, and according to a report in the *Toronto Sun*, orders came from around the globe. "I had people calling me from Baltimore [Maryland]. . . .Who knows what the final numbers are going to be," he said.[9]

Another type of free-speech incident occurred on the University of California–Santa Barbara (UCSB) campus. It involved feminist studies professor Mireille

---

! Now You Know!

- Most First Nations have treaties with the Crown (Canadian government). These are formal agreements, which in their view, gives them all title and all rights to their land forever. Private ownership of land is totally alien to First Nations people. The Canadian government, however, disagrees. Officials contend that land should be privately owned and used for farming, mining, or other individual purposes.

Miller-Young and some UCSB students, who confronted a dozen pro-life supporters, members of Survivors of the Abortion Holocaust from Thomas Aquinas College. On March 4, 2014, the pro-life group, who did not have administrative permission to do so, put up posters with bloody and gory images of late-term abortions and handed out antiabortion flyers. Miller-Young, along with some UCSB students, demanded that the group tear down the signs. Miller-Young grabbed one of the placards and, along with her students, went into a nearby building, followed by the antiabortionists.

An antiabortion leader, twenty-one-year-old Joan Short, a student at Thomas Aquinas, called 911 to report a stolen sign, and Short's sixteen-year-old sister, Thrin, filmed the incident. According to a news report,

> As Miller-Young and the students boarded an elevator, Joan said that Thrin repeatedly blocked the door with her hand and foot and that Miller-Young continually pushed her back. Miller-Young then exited the elevator and tried to yank Thrin away from the door while the students attempted to take her smartphone. "As Thrin tried to get away, the professor's fingernails left bloody scratches on her arms," Joan claimed. The struggle ended when Thrin relented, Miller-Young walked off, the students rode up in the elevator, and officers arrived to interview those involved.[10]

The story did not end there. The antiabortion group charged the professor with vandalism, battery, and robbery. Police followed up to investigate and learned that Miller-Young had destroyed the poster, which she freely admitted. A UCSB student, who wanted to remain anonymous, explained that Miller-Young is "pregnant, so she's very sensitive to horrifying images" such as the ones the antiabortionists displayed. "That group posted on Christian websites about the professor, and she's been getting a lot of hate mail. People are calling her a baby killer, saying she looks like she's from a safari because she's black and from Africa, that she's going against Rule of God. . . . She's tried to show hate mail to police, but no one's helping her so she's just talking with her defense attorney."[11]

According to the student newspaper *Daily Nexus*, the incident prompted a campus debate on "whether or not Miller-Young's actions are legally considered a restriction of free speech." In the opinion of legal expert William Creeley with the Foundation for Individual Rights in Education (FIRE), the antiabortion "images are protected speech, protected by the First Amendment, however distasteful, shocking or offensive they may be to some or most viewers." Creeley added, "Taking down the signs, if the signs have been permissibly placed on campus, is an act of vandalism and also an act of censorship, so we would oppose those kinds of vigilante responses to protected expression, regardless of content of expression."

The antiabortionists, however, had not obtained permission to place their signs. And a UCSB group "set up a petition on change.org addressed to Chancellor Yang and other members of the UCSB community that requests a statement of solidarity with Miller-Young and greater restrictions on content that may be traumatic to students or trigger unwanted reminders of past experiences."[12] The petition had more than 1,900 signatures by July 1, 2014. As of that date no other action had been taken by the administration.

Free-Speech Zones

For decades, some colleges and universities have set up free-speech zones—restricted demonstration areas for students who want to express their political opinions, social views, or religious beliefs. "An overwhelming majority of colleges and universities across the country deny students the rights they are granted under the First Amendment or institutional promises," according to FIRE. "Every year, FIRE reads through the rules governing student speech at more than 400 of our nation's biggest and most prestigious universities to document the institutions that ignore students' rights—or don't tell the truth about how they've taken them away."[d]

On HuffingtonPost.com, FIRE's president Greg Lukianoff described how students at eleven universities fought restricted free-speech zones such as the one at the University of Cincinnati (UC) in Ohio. There, in 2012, "Chris Morbitzer and his campus chapter of Young Americans for Liberty (YAL) . . . sought permission to gather signatures across UC's campus for a time-sensitive, statewide 'right to work' ballot initiative." Not only did the school deny their request, but also "UC told Morbitzer that if they saw anyone from YAL gathering signatures outside of the school's tiny and restrictive 'free-speech zone,' they would call campus security and the group members could be arrested." The zone comprised just 0.1 percent of campus, required registration with the university ten working days in advance, and permitted only one speaking event at a time. Morbitzer was dismayed that he might not gather many signatures if he was confined to the free-speech zone so he took a bold step: With the help of FIRE and Ohio's 1851 Center for Constitutional Law, he sued his school. In response, United States District Judge Timothy S. Black held that UC's policy was a violation of the First Amendment and "cannot stand."[e]

A U.S. Supreme Court Decision

On June 26, 2014, the U.S. Supreme Court ruled on a First Amendment right that involved antiabortion protesters in *Eleanor McCullen et al. v. Coakley, Attorney General of Massachusetts et al.* (2014). The decision rescinded a Massachusetts law that set the area where protesters could gather outside an abortion clinic. That legal limit was a response to violence at reproductive health care clinics and was meant to protect not only providers but also clients who were harassed and sometimes physically attacked. The "buffer zone," as it was called, made it a crime to stand within thirty-five feet of an entrance or driveway to any reproductive health care facility. In a unanimous decision, the High Court ruled that the buffer zone was overly broad and limited free speech in public places like sidewalks that traditionally have been open for speech activities; thus the law was unconstitutional. The government's ability to regulate speech in such locations is "very limited," the Supreme Court declared. But its decision did not prevent states from passing less restrictive laws to protect people entering and leaving abortion clinics.

However, the antiabortion activists sued Miller-Young, and in August 2014 she appeared in a Santa Barbara court and pleaded no contest to misdemeanor charges of stealing and destroying an antiabortion sign and pushing and scratching a protestor. Judge Brian Hill sentenced Miller-Young to three years' probation, one hundred hours of community service with a Quaker group, and ten hours of anger-management classes.

Banning Books

An issue that frequently riles student activists is banning books. Teachers or school administrators may pull particular books from school shelves or reading lists because some educators, parents, or others in a community consider those books inappropriate for students to read. But student activists often have adamantly disagreed.

A case of book banning made news headlines in February 2012, when Arizona's superintendent of public instruction ordered the Tucson Unified School District to remove books about Mexican Americans from classrooms. The state had passed a new law in 2010 banning ethnic American studies on the grounds that studying about ethnic or racial groups was biased and presented injustices that promoted hatred and racism toward Anglos. Under the law, books about Mexico and Mexican Americans were considered ethnic studies and therefore banned. If the district did not remove the books it would lose millions of dollars in state funds. The prohibited books were *Critical Race Theory* by Richard Delgado and Jean Stefancic; *500 Years of Chicano History in Pictures* edited by Elizabeth Martinez; *Message to Aztlan: Selected Writings* by Rodolfo "Corky" Gonzales; *Chicano! The History of the Mexican American Civil Rights Movement* by F. Arturo Rosales; *Rethinking Columbus: The Next 500 Years* edited by Bill Bigelow and Bob Peterson; *Occupied America: A History of Chicanos* by Rodolfo F. Acuña; and *Pedagogy of the Oppressed* by Paulo Freire. The latter two titles are texts used in university studies nationwide.

After the books were taken away, news stories about the ban incensed people in various parts of the nation. In St. Paul, Minnesota, for example, a Central High School student, Ekeylie Lee, told a reporter, "It's wrong for one ethnicity to have the upper hand, wrong for one to be able to express themselves and the others not be able to." Another student, Shevell Powell, put it this way: "We need to learn about every culture. . . . We should not ban Latino culture. We need to learn more about it."[13]

Protests—wherever they took place, especially in Tucson—apparently had an effect. So did a federal court order to restore the studies that were required under an old desegregation law. In 2013, the school board revived the program. One of the students who had protested the 2010 legislation outlawing ethnic studies was Kim Dominguez. She spoke on National Public Radio's *Morning Edition* in July 2013 and was hopeful about the new program. "I think the new classes have the potential to provide the same kind of services and support that Mexican-American studies provided. . . . I would not be here right now if it was not for Mexican-American studies, it totally transformed my life and opened up new possibilities."[14]

Another book banning occurred in Meridian, Idaho, in 2014. Brady Kissel, a seventeen-year-old student at Junior Mountain View High, and several booksellers gave away copies of Sherman Alexie's *The Absolutely True Diary of a Part-Time Indian*. The award-winning novel has been repeatedly praised as an honest depiction of teen life, and its free distribution took place on World Book Night in a Meridian park on April 23, 2014. World Book Night is celebrated in April each year and is meant to encourage the love of reading, especially for folks who are not regular readers.

Earlier in April, some parents at Brady's school had complained about the *Diary*'s offensive language and declared it was anti-Christian. The book was removed from the tenth-grade reading list. However, "Kissel had gotten 350 signatures for a petition to protest the book's removal from the reading list, which she showed the school board at the meeting on April 2 at which 'Diary' was banned," according to a news story in the *Christian Science Monitor*. Two book supporters in Washington State, Sara Baker of Seattle and Jennifer Lott of Spokane, "learned of the incident and started a fundraising drive to buy enough copies of 'Diary' for the 350 students who had signed Kissel's petition." They bought the copies through a Meridian bookstore called Rediscovered Books.[15]

On World Book Night, Brady and her bookseller friends handed out copies to the students who had petitioned to keep it on the reading list. But someone called the police to request that the giveaway be stopped because the book was given to students without their parents' permission. The police found nothing wrong with the distribution of the books. After author Alexie's publisher heard about the incident, the company sent another 350 copies to Rediscovered Books to be given free to any student who requested a copy.[16]

A Post from the Past

In Des Moines, Iowa, during the 1960s, a group of students took part in their own form of free speech. Students met in December 1965 at the home of sixteen-year-old Christopher Eckhardt, who attended Roosevelt High School, to plan a way to protest the Vietnam War and to show support for a truce. The students and adults at the meeting decided to wear black armbands throughout the holiday season. When the school officials learned about the plan, they quickly created a policy stating that students wearing armbands would be asked to remove them, and if they refused, they would be suspended.

Christopher and another student attending junior high school, Mary Beth Tinker, wore their armbands to their respective schools and were sent home. The following day, fifteen-year-old John Tinker, Mary Beth's brother attending North High School, also wore a black armband, which resulted in his suspension. The students did not return to school until after New Year's Day, when they had originally planned to end their protest.

In 1966, on behalf of their minor children, parents sued the school district for violating the students' free-speech rights. The district court declared that the policy of the school officials was a reasonable form of school discipline and was needed to prevent disruption. The plaintiffs appealed the case, which eventually the U.S. Supreme Court heard in November 1968.

In February 1969 the justices in a 7–2 decision found in favor of *Tinker et al. v. Des Moines Independent Community School District et al.*, noting that "the school officials banned and sought to punish petitioners for a silent, passive expression of opinion, unaccompanied by any disorder or disturbance on the part of petitioners. There is here no evidence whatever of petitioners' interference, actual or nascent, with the schools' work or of collision with the rights of other students to be secure and to be let alone. Accordingly, this case does not concern speech or action that intrudes upon the work of the schools or the rights of other students." The High Court also declared, "Students in school as well as out of school are 'persons' under our Constitution. They are possessed of fundamental rights which the State must respect, just as they themselves must respect their obligations to the State. In our system, students may not be regarded as closed-circuit recipients of only that which the State chooses to communicate. They may not be confined to the expression of those sentiments that are officially approved. In the absence of a specific showing of constitutionally valid reasons to regulate their speech, students are entitled to freedom of expression of their views."[f]

Attire—"Rights" and "Wrongs"

Activists often express their views by wearing T-shirts, hats/caps, or other apparel with slogans such as "Epilepsy Awareness," "Green Peace," "American Indian Movement," "Stop Gun Violence," "Don't Tread on Me," "Don't Blame Me. I Voted for _____. (fill in the blank)," "Question Authority," "Fight the Power," "Stand for Something," and hundreds of others. The reality is that millions of people wear slogans of some type. But the question is: Do public school students from the elementary level through twelfth grade have the right to wear some types of shirts, arm/head bands, head coverings, or other apparel with slogans? If there ever was an "it depends" answer, this would be it.

From state to state and school to school, clothing and grooming guidelines are ever changing, depending on what students, parents, and school officials believe is appropriate. Legal experts say that school boards can create and enforce dress code programs within their districts, *if* student attire or grooming interferes with class work, creates disorder, or disrupts educational programs.

Some schools do not allow students to wear shirts bearing the names of professional sports teams; or shirts with antiwar messages or a National Rifle Association logo; or clothing that depicts lewd, sexually explicit, or indecent drug use; or other messages deemed disruptive. A school may also prohibit any kind of message on a student's T-shirt.

School dress codes may have little to do with slogans. For example, a school may forbid "skimpy clothing"—short shorts—for girls and drooping pants for boys. Or clothing associated with gangs. Or shaved heads. There also are rules for hairstyles and jewelry, such as forbidding hair longer than shoulder length for boys or banning oversized, dangling earrings for girls.

Students can challenge dress and appearance codes if the codes violate their First Amendment rights. An important factor for violations is whether the policy is fair. "A school cannot, for example, prohibit clothing that supports one political party while allowing support of another. This type of ban would be a deliberate attempt to eliminate a specific message and therefore violates the spirit of the First Amendment. If a school district can show that political discussions are disruptive to the learning environment, it is allowed to ban any clothing that expresses any political sentiment," states Kimberly Yates on SeattlePI.com.[17]

What about religious attire? The American Center for Law and Justice (ACLJ) says, "A school may not censor student expression because of its religious content unless the school can demonstrate that the speech falls within one of a few narrow exceptions (e.g., the speech causes material disruption, violates the rights of others, is vulgar, or advocates illegal conduct)."[18]

The Civil Rights Division of the U.S. Department of Justice explains on its website:

> Individual student expression may not be suppressed simply because it is religious. For example, the Division filed a friend-of-the-court brief in the case of a group of Massachusetts high school students who were suspended for handing out candy canes to other students with religious messages attached. The court agreed that the students' First Amendment rights had been violated.[19]

In another case, a group of Muslim high school students in Texas alleged that while other student groups had been allowed to meet during lunch periods, their request for space to kneel and say midday prayers during lunch period was denied. The Civil Rights Division reached a settlement agreement with the school in May 2007 allowing students to meet in a designated space in a common area outside of the cafeteria.

The Civil Rights Division also notes that "schools may not discriminate against students who wear religious clothes or head coverings." The Civil Rights Division intervened in the case of a Muslim girl who was told that she could not wear a headscarf required by her faith to school. The Division brought the suit against the school for enforcing a "uniform policy in an inconsistent manner. The case was settled by consent decree in May 2004."[20]

Just because students have First Amendment rights does not mean that they can easily exercise those rights in regard to school dress and appearance codes. Parents may have to file lawsuits on behalf of minors and that can be expensive. Sometimes, when parents or organizations like the ACLU make known their intention to sue, school officials may change their policies. Perhaps activism that prompts negative publicity can help. Yet, there is no certainty. In general, suing a school district is an uphill battle, but many activists think it is worth the climb.

3

ADVOCATES FOR TEEN GOOD HEALTH

....

"When enough people say, '[abusing drugs] isn't OK—you shouldn't be doing that,'
it can make an impact."—teenager Broderick Topil commenting to a reporter in 2014[1]

When news stories describe teens and health issues, they often focus on the teens with such social problems as abusing alcohol and other drugs, bullying, eating disorders, or other concerns. But teenagers also take part in positive efforts to prevent destructive ways of life. They are activists for teen good health.

Campaigning to Stop Alcohol Abuse

One of the most widely publicized efforts is preventing alcohol and illegal substance abuse among teenagers as well as adults. Some teens participate in Alateen programs, part of the Al-Anon organization that works worldwide to help rehabilitate family members who abuse alcohol and other drugs. Although teens themselves may not be addicted, they receive support for dealing with negative fallout because of alcohol and drug abuse in the family. Some teens tell about their experiences with Alateen on a YouTube video titled "What Do Older Teens Say about Alateen—How Alateen Helps," uploaded in March 2013. All of the teens on the video are anonymous and only part of their faces are shown, as is the policy of Alateen. One girl whose mother is in a relationship with an alcoholic said, "Alateen has taught me it is not my battle. And I don't need to take part in it. . . . I can just go on and work on myself and become a better person."[2]

A young man said, "[Alateen] definitely changed my life. It taught me how to trust people again. . . . I had extreme trust issues. . . . I was extremely depressed and extremely angry. . . . The program showed me that within the walls of the meeting I could say whatever I wanted. I would not be judged for it." One teenage girl said, "Without [Alateen] I don't think I would be the strong and positive person that I am today. . . . I can trust people now."[3]

Other groups involve teen activists against underage drinking, in spite of or in opposition to the National Youth Rights Association campaigns to lower the legal drinking age from twenty-one to eighteen. Some teens are part of the nationwide Red Ribbon campaign, a student-led prevention effort. Red Ribbon Week occurs every October in all fifty states. Schools that take part in Red Ribbon Week hold events that include depictions of simulated car crashes due to drunk driving and speakers who talk about how drug abuse has negatively impacted their lives. In Alma, Kansas, Bailee Henry, a senior at Wabaunsee High School whose school has participated in Red Ribbon events, thinks the campaign helps. She told a reporter for the Kansas *Capital-Journal*, "It makes an impression, especially during Red Ribbon Week, because they [students] get the message from lots of different viewpoints." Broderick Topil, a junior at Eudora High School, agreed. In his opinion, teens who attend Red Ribbon events hear a "second voice," which "makes them rethink their decision [about drug use]. When enough people say, 'That isn't OK—you shouldn't be doing that,' it can make an impact."[4]

The Centers for Disease Control and Prevention (CDC) reported that "in 2010, there were approximately 189,000 emergency room visits by persons under age 21 for injuries and other conditions linked to alcohol. . . . Alcohol is the most commonly used and abused drug among youth in the United States, more than tobacco and illicit drugs, and is responsible for more than 4,300 annual deaths among underage youth." CDC lists the consequences of alcohol abuse:

- School problems, such as higher absence and poor or failing grades.
- Social problems, such as fighting and lack of participation in youth activities.
- Legal problems, such as arrest for driving or physically hurting someone while drunk.
- Physical problems, such as hangovers or illnesses.
- Unwanted, unplanned, and unprotected sexual activity.
- Disruption of normal growth and sexual development.
- Physical and sexual assault.
- Higher risk for suicide and homicide.
- Alcohol-related car crashes and other unintentional injuries, such as burns, falls, and drowning.
- Memory problems.
- Abuse of other drugs.
- Changes in brain development that may have lifelong effects.
- Death from alcohol poisoning.[5]

A Post from the Past

During the late 1700s, Americans drank excessively—at home, at work, at social events, wherever alcoholic beverages were available. In fact, alcohol was considered healthier than water, which was often contaminated and caused deadly diseases. Drinking alcohol became such a problem that an organized effort against the sale and use of alcoholic beverages began.

The American Temperance Society, which was founded in 1826, was part of that movement. At first, their objective was moderation in drinking, but that soon changed to "total abstinence from intoxicating drinks. . . . A national political party, the Prohibition Party, was established in 1869 to work toward this goal. Also important to the movement were the Woman's Christian Temperance Union (WCTU), founded in 1874, and the Anti-Saloon League, founded in 1895. The crusade against alcohol was dramatized by Carry Nation, who became famous at the turn of the century for wrecking saloons with a hatchet."[a]

Activists in the temperance movement successfully petitioned for the Eighteenth Amendment to the U.S. Constitution, which prohibited the manufacture, transport, and sale of alcohol. The amendment took effect in 1920, ushering in a period known as Prohibition. But many people opposed prohibition and campaigned for another amendment. In 1933, the Twenty-First Amendment passed, repealing national prohibition.

Efforts to Stop Drug Abuse

Along with alcohol abuse, illicit drug abuse among teenagers "can increase their risk for injuries, violence, HIV infection, and other diseases," according to the CDC.[6] Government agencies like the CDC and the National Institute on Drug Abuse (NIDA) have many programs and materials to help youth overcome drug abuse. Some of the drugs that are commonly abused include tobacco, heroin, cocaine, methamphetamine, some cough and cold medicines, mescaline, inhalants, codeine, oxycodone HCL, and anabolic steroids. The effects of these and other drugs are listed on NIDA's website.[7]

Every year NIDA surveys eighth, tenth, and twelfth graders to measure their use of and attitudes toward drug, alcohol, and tobacco use. The 2013 survey, titled Monitoring the Future (MTF), found that marijuana use by adolescents has been on the increase since about 2000, due to the changing perceptions of the drug. "Young people are showing less disapproval of marijuana use and decreased perception that marijuana is dangerous." MTF reported that "in 2013, 7.0 percent of 8th graders, 18.0 percent of 10th graders, and 22.7 percent of 12th graders used marijuana in the month before the survey; up from 5.8 percent, 13.8 percent, and 19.4 percent in 2008." Other findings in the report showed that drugs such as synthetic marijuana (also known as Spice or K2) and herbal mixtures laced with synthetic chemicals are of concern. In addition, "nonmedical use of prescription and over-the-counter medicines remains a significant part of the teen drug problem. In 2013, 15.0 percent of high school seniors used a prescription drug nonmedically in the past year."[8]

Fourteen-year-old Jordyn Schara of Reedsburg, Wisconsin, was so concerned about prescription drug abuse that she started programs to collect unwanted prescription and over-the-counter medicines as part of a Prescription Pill and Drug Disposal (P2D2) program. In 2010, her effort "helped collect over 900,000 pounds of drugs across the country that are now out of the hands of young children and teens. The program is quick and anonymous," she explained. "I merged my program with my mentor's national program and it has now grown and spread to over 22 states. Currently, Illinois has a P2D2 law on their books and I am working to enact a similar law for Wisconsin."[9]

The P2D2 law in Illinois was enacted with the help of high school students from Antioch and Pontiac. They lobbied state legislators in support of a bill to provide funds for pharmacies and police and fire departments to collect unwanted medications and educate the public about the dangers of not properly disposing of medication and drugs. The Illinois legislature passed the law in March 2011.[10]

Anabolic Steroid and Performance-Enhancing Drug Abuse

The use of anabolic steroid drugs is illegal unless prescribed for medical reasons. Doctors may prescribe steroids to reduce swelling from disease or injury; to treat delayed puberty, anemia, and osteoporosis; and to treat men who do not produce enough testosterone. Anabolic steroids are synthetic substances similar to the natural male hormone testosterone. They are known scientifically as anabolic-androgenic steroids. *Anabolic* refers to muscle building, while *androgenic* refers to increased male characteristics.

When anabolic steroids become news, they usually are the subject of illegal use by professional athletes. Activists waste no time in condemning the practice of using steroids to enhance sports performance. Much less attention is given to teenagers who want to improve their appearance or athletic prowess. The U.S. Food and Drug Administration reported that among U.S. high school students, an estimated 4.9 percent of males and 2.4 percent of females have used anabolic steroids at least once in their lives. That means 375,000 young men and 175,000 young women have ingested steroids.[11] Steroid use can endanger teen health and can even lead to fatal heart attacks and suicide.

The Taylor Hooton Foundation (THF) of McKinney, Texas, has become a leader in advocacy against abuse of anabolic steroids and other appearance- and performance-enhancing drugs such as the human-growth hormone and dietary supplements that contain banned substances. The THF was formed in memory of Taylor E. Hooton, the seventeen-year-old son of Donald and Gwen Hooton. Taylor committed suicide in 2003 due to quick withdrawal of anabolic steroids.

Taylor was a high school student athlete, a popular baseball pitcher at Plano West Senior High School near Dallas, Texas. His coach suggested that he gain weight to increase his strength. Since his baseball team members were already taking steroids to beef up, Taylor did the same. The results were a puffy face, acne on his back, bad breath, and sometimes violent outbursts (called "roid rage"). Donald Hooton recalled that the symptoms added together indicated steroid use. A therapist recommended that Taylor quit, which he did "cold turkey." Without the steroids, Taylor became deeply depressed, and his parents believe that led to his suicide. The Hootons established THF soon afterward, and Taylor's brother Don Hooton Jr., an athlete and former baseball pitcher in college, joined the foundation as vice president of education. In a 2014, Don recalled,

> When I lost my younger brother, Taylor . . . I was in college and he was in high school. He was my best friend; losing my best friend made me want to spread the message. I saw the steroid use in the college I attended along with the others in the area—saw that it was a problem and there was a need to educate. So . . . if I could just reach that one person or save that one person's life, I consider it a success.[12]

Hooton pointed out that the "average beginner age" for steroid abuse "is 15 years old." He added,

> Our surveys tell us that the fastest growing user group for anabolic steroids is girls in high school, many of them who aren't in sports and don't work out—they are using strictly for image purposes versus performance

purposes. Photoshopped bodies in magazines aren't realistic but the media portrays that is glamour and girls want that.

With the performance-enhancing supplements or over-the-counter supplements, which are now spiked, some kids don't even know what they are taking when they buy supplements. This means added caffeine, diuretics, or methamphetamine to the supplements. Recently some [youth] were tested and had traces of Viagra. Millions of kids are doping and don't even know it.

Hooton, VP of education for the Taylor Hooton Foundation, travels to numerous events, presenting antiabuse programs at schools and before major league baseball and football players. Major league baseball is a primary sponsor of the foundation. When speaking to young people, he said the foundation challenges them "to take part in the All Me League . . . where a young adult signs up to live a PE free lifestyle, sign a pledge, and do things the right way"—that is, get in shape without performance-enhancing drugs and play "clean."

Campaigns to Stop Tobacco Use

Cigarette smoking by high school students has declined since 1997, but other forms of smoked tobacco are becoming popular. The use of hookah water pipes and small cigars has raised public health concerns, the NIDA reported. "In 2013, 21.4 percent of 12th graders had smoked a hookah at some point in the past year, an increase from 18.3 percent in 2012, and 20.4 percent had smoked a small cigar."[13]

One student campaign to end tobacco use began in 1998 in Florida, and since then thousands of Florida teens have joined the fight. They form SWAT (Students Working Against Tobacco) teams that visit grade schools and middle schools. They serve on community groups that push for tougher regulations regarding tobacco use and discuss these issues with legislators. SWAT's mission is "to mobilize, educate and equip Florida youth to revolt against and de-glamorize Big Tobacco. SWAT is a united movement of empowered youth working towards a tobacco free future," according to its website.[14]

SWAT members in Florida explained why they are involved: "I am passionate about fighting against corporate tobacco and showing my peers the industry's deceit. Being able to represent SWAT youth is an honor," wrote Magi L. on the SWAT website. Alex T. says, "[I am] passionate about this issue because both myself and my sister have asthma. . . . Personally, I have had to witness family members affected by this addiction and do not want to see anyone suffer in that way." Robert P. wrote, "SWAT has given me use of a voice that can save future generations of youth from becoming addicted to tobacco." And Raekwon W.

noted, "So far, the achievement in SWAT that I am most proud of is helping to get a resolution discouraging the sale of flavored tobacco in my county."[15]

Teens in Oklahoma, citing Florida's success, also organized SWAT teams. In other states, teens take part in such programs as Kick Butts Day and the American Lung Association's Teens Against Tobacco Use (TATU).

Kick Butts Day is a global campaign that engages students from across the United States. More than one thousand events across the nation were held in March 2014. The website for the national campaign (http://www.kickbuttsday .org/events) shows events planned for each state and Washington, DC.

Campion College in Jamaica, Wisconsin, held its fifth annual event in 2014. It was "designed to empower youth activism and included presentations and displays in the school's auditorium, which highlighted the dangers of smoking

Smoking Stats

The U.S. Department of Health and Human Services (HHS) issued a report in 2014 declaring that "every day, an estimated 1,315 people in the United States die because of smoking. For each of those deaths, at least two youth or young adults become regular smokers each day." A fact sheet on the report states:

- Smoking rates among adults and teens are less than half what they were in 1964; however, 42 million American adults and about 3 million middle and high school students continue to smoke.
- Nearly half a million Americans die prematurely from smoking each year.
- More than 16 million Americans suffer from a disease caused by smoking.
- On average, compared to people who have never smoked, smokers suffer more health problems and disability due to their smoking and ultimately lose more than a decade of life.
- The estimated economic costs attributable to smoking and exposure to tobacco smoke continue to increase and now approach $300 billion annually, with direct medical costs of at least $130 billion and productivity losses of more than $150 billion a year.[b]

In spite of signs like these that appear in countless places across the United States, they don't necessarily stop smoking, so activists often join campaigns to encourage people to quit using tobacco.

tobacco." Seventeen-year-old Melissa Lalah explained to the newspaper *Gleaner*, "We are trying to get everybody educated and make them aware that if they have problems with smoking in their surroundings and the school, then they need to speak up against it because it is not only harmful to themselves, it's harmful to everyone around them."[16]

On Kick Butts Day in Juneau, Alaska, Lauryn Guthrie, a ninth grader at Thunder Mountain High School, told *Healthy Living Southeast* magazine that she got involved in 2014 because "younger kids smoke and they're not supposed to. I want to show them what can happen." A fifth-grade cousin who was with Lauryn at the high school said she knew classmates who were already smoking.[17]

TATU is an American Lung Association program that teaches students ages fourteen to seventeen nationwide to mentor youngsters about the dangers of smoking. At the college level, "tobacco-free policies are a growing trend . . . across the United States. Today there are approximately 431 colleges and universities that are 100% tobacco-free, and more join the list every year!" according to the American Lung Association.[18]

Healthy Food

Americans generally do not associate youth with healthy food. The media focus is on teens and junk food, eating disorders, obesity, and increases in sugary soda

From preadolescents to college students, activists sometimes grow and sell vegetables as part of their efforts to
encourage healthy eating.

consumption. But many young people from preadolescents to college students are
healthy food activists. They take part in numerous projects. Sometimes they grow
and sell vegetables and fruits to encourage healthy eating; or they conduct campaigns for healthier food and beverage offerings in school cafeterias and vending
machines; or they take part in educational programs about nutritional foods and
share the information with their peers.

   In Chicago, about twenty students from varied high schools in the city addressed the Chicago Board of Education in 2010 about the schools' food service.
In a speech to the board, Teresa Onstott, a sophomore at Social Justice High
School, described the "sickening pizza, chicken sandwiches and nachos" the
district serves each day and urged the board not to renew the contract for the
company providing the food. The students suggested alternatives such as schools
growing some of their food.[19]

However, when the menu choices changed in 2011, students rejected the healthy foods. CBS News in Chicago said that students complained the "new pizza products with tougher crusts were 'overly tangy and tomatoey'" and canned pears tasted 'like wet toilet paper.'" A processed chicken patty appeared to be the only food that students liked.[20]

Activists help in campaigns to provide healthy foods in so-called urban food deserts—low-income neighborhoods that do not have grocery stores or supermarkets offering fresh produce and healthy food options. The U.S. Department of Agriculture (USDA) says that more than 23.5 million Americans live in food deserts in such cities as Chicago, New York, Detroit, New Orleans, Atlanta, and San Francisco. Food deserts also can be found in rural communities where residents have to travel thirty to forty miles to get to a grocery store.

Nineteen New York students who have been activists for healthy food call themselves Teens for Food Justice, a team "with a strong and passionate commitment to civic leadership." They worked throughout 2013 to "maintain a classroom hydroponic farm at Bedford Stuyvesant New Beginnings Charter School" in New York. Students installed a "classroom 'greenhouse,' which is capable of growing an abundance of leafy greens and vine crops." Their first harvest was in January 2014. The students "receive the training, skills and confidence to lead local community outreach and educational programming on . . . such critical topics as shopping and eating well on a food assistance or limited budget, healthy recipe preparation . . . fitness training, sustainable practices such as recycling and composting, and basic nutritional training."[21]

A nationwide campaign sponsored by the Case Foundation developed Youth L.E.A.D. (YL) for food justice in South Florida. Founded in 2010, "YL educates, empowers, and employs low-income teens of color to adopt healthier and sustainable eating habits while working to increase access to healthy foods and green spaces in their communities." According to YL's website, the program empowers youth to become "changemakers"—activists—who "address the root causes of health disparities and climate change in their own communities by supporting and maintaining local, sustainable, healthy food systems. In the process, youth also earn job and life skills along with a stipend and a weekly supply of local produce."[22]

GMOs

A long-standing debate over healthy food involves genetically engineered (GE) plants and animals commonly known as genetically modified organisms (GMOs). Scientists create GMOs in laboratories by removing desired genes from a species of plant or animal and transferring them to other species. For example, some food crops like corn and soybeans are modified to resist or kill harmful bacteria, insects, and viruses.

Although modern scientists use high-tech (biotechnology) methods to create GMOs, farmers have been modifying plants and animals for thousands of years through cross-breeding and cross-pollination. A wide range of plants originated in the wild, but early people were able to improve on vegetables and fruits by selecting the best seeds or vegetative parts and planting them during each growing season.

Over the centuries, scientific developments have made it possible for many food crops and animals to be modified in some way. Currently, the majority of foodstuffs sold in the United States and other countries contains some genetically altered ingredients. The exceptions are organic foods grown in family or school gardens or on commercial farms. To be certified and sold as organic, the foods must be produced according to strict guidelines set by the U.S. Department of Agriculture. Organic meats, poultry, eggs, and dairy products cannot come from

Foods labeled and sold as organic must be produced according to strict USDA guidelines.

animals fed antibiotics or growth hormones. Fruits and vegetables must be grown without chemical pesticides and fertilizers.

Organic items sold in supermarkets and natural food stores can be expensive, however, so most Americans choose conventionally produced foods. In other words, most of us consume genetically engineered foods, ranging from fresh produce and meats to processed foods like cereals and snacks. Supporters argue that genetically engineered foods are not only safe, they are also designed to grow in areas of the world with dry and unfertile land and help prevent starvation and provide needed nutrients.

Opponents claim that GMOs can create unsuspected and potentially serious health problems (severe allergies, for example) in people who consume modified foods. Critics also strongly object to the fact that giant agribusinesses like Monsanto, DuPont, Syngenta, Bayer, BASF, and Dow Agrosciences control a large portion of global food production. The focus is primarily on Monsanto, the world's largest seed company, which produces patented GE seeds called Roundup Ready (RR). The RR crops resist the herbicide (weed killer) called Roundup, a Monsanto product. So farmers who plant RR crops and use Roundup herbicide know their plants will survive. And Monsanto will profit from both the seeds and herbicide.

The catch is that farmers who buy RR seeds must sign a legal agreement to plant them for only one year. For the next planting season, farmers must buy new RR seeds. They risk infringing on Monsanto's patent if they collect seeds from their harvest and plant them, as farmers worldwide have done for centuries. Many farmers cannot afford to buy these seeds every year. In opposition to GMOs, some small farmers have joined together to create seed collectives. Instead of relying on Monsanto seeds, these farmers keep and exchange their non-GMO seeds and plant them in fields separate from GMOs.

Most resistance to GMOs, however, has been in the form of demonstrations. Since 2012, activists in cities around the world have organized a March Against Monsanto in protests patterned after the Occupy Wall Street movement against wealth inequality. Numerous activists campaign against Monsanto because of the corporation's past development of dangerous pesticides like DDT (banned by the U.S. government in 1972), Agent Orange (an herbicide used during the Vietnam War that later caused diseases among U.S. veterans and their families), and the cancer-causing PCBs (polychlorinated biphenyls).

Activists against Monsanto carry banners and signs with "No GMO" slogans and demands that food labels identify GMOs in products. In Oxnard, California, teenagers from nearby Thousand Oaks went after school to their first official protest in 2012, chanting "Hey, hey, ho, ho, we've got a right to know." Seventeen-year-old Heather Power-Gomez, one of the protesters, told a reporter, "In biology class, we learned about genetically modified organisms and how they can affect your body. . . . [Scientists] can change the genetic structure of [crop seeds] so your body doesn't know how to react."[23]

Despite protests, scientific studies on the effects of GMO crops continue, and some scientists speak out to counter protesters. In addition, the editors of *Scientific American* noted in the September 2013 issue of the magazine, "The American Association for the Advancement of Science, the American Medical Association and the National Academy of Sciences have all unreservedly backed GM crops. The U.S. Food and Drug Administration, along with its counterparts in several other countries, has repeatedly reviewed large bodies of research and concluded that GM crops pose no unique health threats. Dozens of review studies carried out by academic researchers have backed that view."[24]

In a follow-up blog in *Scientific American* online, chemist Ashutosh Jogalekar made this point: "Every time you oppose a GMO you are also opposing the very real benefits that GMOs have brought over the last three decades to some of the poorest parts of the world. I always find it depressing to hear citizens of developed countries railing against the supposed evils of GMOs from the luxury of their air-conditioned living rooms while a farmer in the developing world would likely donate an arm for a GMO crop if it's going to bring him greater yields and put food on his family's table. Let us spare a thought for those who cannot afford to make the choices that we make when we voice our opinions with so much passion."[25]

Advocating for Teen Sexual Health

Teen activists are raising awareness about sexual health and advocating for comprehensive sex education, which "includes age-appropriate, medically accurate information on a broad set of topics related to sexuality including human development, relationships, decision making, abstinence, contraception, and disease prevention," according to a SIECUS (Sexuality Information and Education Council of the United States) fact sheet. In the council's words, the programs

- provide young people with the tools to make informed decisions and build healthy relationships;
- stress the value of abstinence while also preparing young people for when they become sexually active;
- provide medically accurate information about the health benefits and side effects of all contraceptives, including condoms, as a means to prevent pregnancy and reduce the risk of contracting STIs [sexually transmitted infections], including HIV/AIDS;
- encourage family communication about sexuality between parent and child;

- teach young people the skills to make responsible decisions about sexuality, including how to avoid unwanted verbal, physical, and sexual advances; and
- teach young people how alcohol and drug use can effect responsible decision making.[26]

Research findings reported by the National Campaign to Prevent Teen and Unplanned Pregnancy show that

> two-thirds of the 48 comprehensive programs that supported both abstinence and the use of condoms and contraceptives for sexually active teens had positive behavioral effects. Specifically, over 40 percent of the programs delayed the initiation of sex, reduced the number of sexual partners, and increased condom or contraceptive use; almost 30 percent reduced the frequency of sex (including a return to abstinence); and more than 60 percent reduced unprotected sex. Furthermore, nearly 40 percent of the programs had positive effects on more than one of these behaviors. For example, some programs both delayed the initiation of sex and increased condom or other contraceptive use. No comprehensive program hastened the initiation of sex or increased the frequency of sex, results that many people fear. Emphasizing both abstinence and protection for those who do have sex is a realistic, effective approach that does not appear to confuse young people.[27]

As noted, reasons for comprehensive sex education are numerous, but some parents and school personnel insist on abstinence-only-until-marriage programs. Yet these programs seldom work. Even teens who sign a pledge not to have sex until marriage sometimes ignore their agreement.

Abstinence-only also ignores LGBT individuals, as a Parma, Ohio, teenager Danny Sparks noted. Danny told Advocate.com in 2010 that his mandatory health class in high school taught abstinence only and focused on traditional marriage. "They're excluding gay students in the curriculum," Danny explained. That exclusion triggered activism. He and friends sent letters to the school superintendent and board, and "Sparks attended a board meeting to address members regarding both the absence of comprehensive sex education and what he saw as the shocking lack of responsibility." School authorities' response was that parents wanted the abstinence-only education. Danny then began working with LGBT groups to educate parents. He explained that in his school there is "an ignorance, stigma around sex in general due to abstinence-only. Even if it's just about HIV and condoms, people are really ignorant on the issue." His plan at the time was to continue his LGBT activism and possibly work toward a career in politics.[28]

Examples of other teen activists for comprehensive sex education are members of CREATE, a youth advocacy council sponsored by Colorado Youth Matter. CREATE stands for the group's mission: "to Change, Respond to, Engage, Advocate for, Transform and Empower youth on issues related to sexual health, access to comprehensive sex education and promoting social justice in communities across Colorado."[29] In testimony before the Colorado Health and Human Services

See This Documentary

This Is What Love in Action Looks Like is a 2011 documentary that tells the story of Zach Stark of Memphis, Tennessee. The documentary, directed and filmed by Morgan Jon Fox, was released on DVD in 2012. Zach's experience as a teenage gay person and activism on his behalf became an international news story, which prompted the documentary.

Zach was sixteen years old in 2005 when he told his parents that he was gay. Within days his mother and father, who thought their son was a psychological misfit, arranged for him to attend a fundamentalist Christian program in Memphis called Refuge. The program was part of a larger effort known as Love In Action. The boot camp program, which has since closed, claimed that homosexuality is a sin and that getting close to God was the way to turn gays into straights.

The documentary describes Zach's stay at the "refuge" where he spent eight weeks undergoing therapy and intensive counseling designed to convince him that he was not right with God. Every day during the two-month period, Zach's high school peers and members of the local community stood outside the facility and protested the forced indoctrination. Zach prevailed as the person he really is—a young gay man. After he left Refuge, Zach did not want to be part of any publicity and asked to be left alone.

Filmmaker Fox spent six years producing the documentary; he sought interviews with former residents at the boot camp and also with John Smid, who ran Love In Action while Zach was at Refuge. Smid has since changed his views and has acknowledged that he is gay although he was once married to a woman and said he did not plan to leave her. However, in 2008 the couple divorced and in 2011 Smid married his same-sex partner, Larry McQueen.

Did You Know?

At least forty-eight states allow conversion or reparative therapy programs designed to turn LGBT minors straight. Some lawmakers have tried to ban these therapies, calling them "quackery" and harmful. But such legislation has failed in most cases. Yet California state senator Ted Lieu introduced a bill in 2012 to prohibit conversion counseling. The law passed and Governor Jerry Brown signed it into law. However, supporters of the therapies appealed to the Ninth U.S. Circuit Court of Appeals in 2013, and the federal court ruled in favor of the ban. Supporters then appealed to the U.S. Supreme Court. In 2014, the High Court declined to hear the case, which meant that the California law could be enforced—it had been on hold during the appeals process.

New Jersey also passed a law in 2013 banning counseling to change a minor's sexual orientation. That legislation, signed by Governor Chris Christie, was challenged and appealed to the Third U.S. Circuit Court of Appeals in July 2014. The court of appeals upheld the ban. "Another eight states and the District of Columbia have pending legislation modeled after the California and New Jersey laws," the Associated Press reported on June 30, 2014.[c]

Senate Committee in early March 2013, Scarlett Jimenez, a CREATE member, spoke in support of a bill to expand comprehensive sex education in schools. She explained that it "is a tool of empowerment for young people. It teaches abstinence as well as about condoms and contraceptives, providing youth with ALL of the information that they need to make healthy and responsible decisions. It is inclusive of everyone, and works to fight misconceptions and stigma of people who may not fit the 'norm.'"[30] The bill passed on March 18, 2013. The legislation provides grants for public schools to expand sexual education curriculum and increase access to comprehensive sex education.

CAMPAIGNS AGAINST SEXUAL VIOLENCE AND TRAFFICKING

"Rape is not a laughing matter." "Rape jokes are not jokes."
"Victim blaming is not okay."—slogans on placards carried by teenagers and
shown on HuffingtonPost.com, July 18, 2014[1]

Stories about sexual violence, especially rape, are usually hush-hush. Many victims do not report the attacks, feeling shame or fear of being rejected by family and friends. They also fear recrimination—more violence or even death. Often, victims are seen as guilty parties—she or he asked for it, say the perpetrators. Some media commentators also imply that the victims are somehow responsible because they were in the wrong place or with a disreputable crowd, or if female, they wore provocative clothing and too much lipstick.

Rape

Rape—being forced to have sex without consent—or being attacked sexually is a crime, whether committed by a single individual or by a gang. One of the most underreported assaults is date rape, which is not a legal term but refers to sexual assault by a person (often a male) who has some sort of relationship with the victim (often a female). Since there usually are no witnesses, date rape is difficult to prove. Judges may assume that the sexual act was consensual. However, assaults during or after a date may be against a person who is unconscious or drugged; in such cases the perpetrator may be charged with a crime. The National Teen Dating Abuse Helpline (866-331-9473) of LoveIsRespect.org helps teens (thirteen to eighteen) who have experienced dating abuse.

"Unfortunately, current estimates of dating violence are incomplete and sometimes contradictory," the National Opinion Research Center (NORC) at the University of Chicago noted. NORC conducted a National Survey on Teen Relationships and Intimate Violence between October 2013 and January 2014. A second phase of the study began in October 2014.

The initial survey included a random sampling of "667 youths aged 12–18 who'd been dating within the past year and who completed a self-administered online questionnaire," NORC reported. Eighteen percent of the sample, which included both males and females, reported that they were victims of physical and sexual abuse in dating relationships, while 12 percent were perpetrators of abuse. A much larger percentage—64 percent—reported being victims of psychological abuse, which ranged from name-calling to stalking.[2]

The topic of rape gets widespread attention when the attacks are so vicious that media cover the stories or when some victims have the courage to speak out. Sixteen-year-old Aleesa Perez in Northern California found the courage to speak out about her attack years after it occurred. In April 2014, she told about her attack during Sexual Awareness Month at an event sponsored by the advocacy group SafeQuest Solano. Perez described being sexually assaulted at age thirteen; she was in her own home babysitting her nineteen-month-old brother while her mother was out. Perez fell asleep beside her little brother when an intruder brutally awakened her. She was stabbed forty-seven times and raped. Her brother was stabbed thirteen times. Perez told the group, "Though the healing process hasn't been easy, thanks to countless blessings, miracles and God's healing hand, we are both here today." She added, "It took me months to acknowledge the sexual assault part of the crime. I was so ashamed of what happened, but by being with you today, I refuse to have shame. . . . No matter the intensity of the crime, rape is rape. . . . We can help prevent it by bringing awareness and let people know it's not OK. . . . We can't let fear get the better of us." Her story was reported by Catherine Mijs writing for the *Contra Costa Times*.[3]

Sexual Assault Cover-ups at High Schools

Media seldom focus on sexual assault and rape on high school campuses. At the local level, news sources may hesitate to cover incidents of attacks on high school students—they keep quiet to protect attackers, or victims do not come forward. Victims often are fearful or embarrassed or feel they are to blame. Sometimes victims and their families are harassed when they publicly accuse someone of rape. If a case gets widespread attention it is often because of Internet posts or text messages that spread the story rapidly.

It Happened to Jada

Because of sexual violence, sixteen-year-old Jada's story was in the news and on social networks in the summer of 2014. It began on a June evening when she was invited to "hang out" at a friend's home, where she reportedly was offered some punch to drink. Beyond consuming the drink, she has no recollection of what happened next because she passed out. She believes the punch was spiked with some kind of drug and that she was raped.

Jada told her story to the news media because she only found out what happened to her when friends and classmates sent her text messages, asking whether she was OK. Photos and videos of Jada naked from the waist down and unconscious on the floor were circulating on social media. To make matters worse, many on social media began mocking Jada and blaming her for whatever occurred.

In July 8, 2014, Jada appeared for an interview on a Houston news channel KHOU 11. Although the TV channel does not usually identify rape victims, Jada's mother gave permission to use her daughter's first name only. Both Jada and her mother want the rapists caught. As reported in the *New York Daily News*, Jada told KHOU, "There's no point in hiding. . . . Everybody has already seen my face and my body, but that's not what I am and who I am."[a]

Police investigated Jada's rape claim, and in December 2014 they arrested and charged an adult, nineteen-year-old Clinton Onyeahialam, with sexual assault, and an unnamed sixteen-year-old whom they turned over to Juvenile Probation officials. Meanwhile, Jada continued speaking out, saying how angry she was. She began a Twitter account showing her with an #IAMJADA sign and her fist raised. After that image began circulating, she received many supportive messages. People also expressed outrage over the attack on Twitter posts. These were publicized prominently on the *Ronan Farrow Daily* show on MSNBC.[b]

Consider the case of Daisy Coleman, a fourteen-year-old high school freshman and cheerleader in Maryville, Missouri, who was drugged and raped. Daisy and her mother, Melinda, allowed public interviews in their effort to be activists on their own behalf. As the story goes, in the winter of 2012, Daisy and another teenage girl sneaked out to meet high school football players who were friends

Many young people campaign against those who think sexual assault is a laughing matter—it is not.

of Daisy's brother. One of those boys was Matt Barnett, who raped Daisy and dumped her, unconscious, outside her home in below-freezing weather. Melinda Coleman took Daisy to a hospital where doctors confirmed that she had been sexually assaulted. The Colemans contacted local law enforcement, and although police arrested Barnett, weeks later the prosecutor dropped the charges. Melinda Coleman publicly asserted that the prosecutor's actions were political. Barnett's

Some Facts on Rape

The CDC's National Center for Injury Prevention and Control surveyed high school students in 2011 and found that 11.8 percent of girls and 4.5 percent of boys in grades 9–12 reported that they were forced to have sexual intercourse at some time in their lives. Of the female victims, 42.2 percent were first raped before age eighteen and nearly 30 percent were first raped between the ages of eleven and seventeen. The survey also included younger victims—12.3 percent of girls and 27.8 percent of boys reported they were first raped when they were age ten or younger.

grandfather served four terms as a Missouri state representative; he was also a state trooper for thirty-two years.

When the news became public, it circulated quickly on social media. At the time, very few activists came to the Colemans' defense. Instead, Daisy was harassed on the Internet, was bullied at school, and became so depressed that she attempted suicide. The harassment became so unbearable that Melinda Coleman moved her family to Albany, their original home, about forty miles west of Maryville. Not long afterward, their home in Maryville burned down under mysterious circumstances.

In the fall of 2013, "*The Kansas City Star* published a lengthy account of Daisy's claims, which the newspaper spent seven months investigating. The case and resulting publicity shook the small college town of Maryville." Finally, social media "widely criticized" the town "for turning its back on an alleged sexual assault victim. The outcry led to a protest on Maryville's courthouse square in which a few hundred people showed up to show their support for Daisy and lambaste what they labeled as a 'rape culture' that allowed the girl's assailant to go unpunished," according to the Associated Press.[4]

At the request of the Colemans' lawyer, a special prosecutor reexamined Daisy's case. Barnett was charged in January 2014 with child endangerment, a misdemeanor. Because of the time gap, the felony charge of sexual assault would not hold up in court, lawyers said. Barnett pled guilty, and the judge sentenced him to two years of probation. He was also barred from drinking and having any contact with Daisy and her family.

Another cover-up story involved two high school football players who raped a drunken sixteen-year-old girl at a party in Steubenville, Ohio, in August 2012. The case "got national attention after photos and videos of the incident made their way onto social media," CNN reported. In 2013, the football players, Ma'lik Richmond and Trenton Mays, were arrested, convicted, and "sentenced to a minimum of one year in a juvenile correctional facility. Mays got two years."[5]

That was not the end of the story, however. Investigations regarding the case continued, and in 2014 prosecutors charged superintendent of Steubenville City Schools Michael McVey with tampering with evidence and obstructing justice, which are felonies, and falsification and obstruction of official business, which are misdemeanors. Mark Gillispie of the Associated Press reported,

Three other school employees were also charged. One was a volunteer coach whose house was the scene of a teen drinking party that August evening. He pleaded no contest to two charges and received a sentence of 10 days in jail. Two elementary school principals, one of whom served as the team's strength coach, were charged with failing to report possible child abuse or neglect. Prosecutors agreed to drop those charges if those defendants performed certain requirements, such as community service and certain training.[6]

McVey was suspended from the school district and a grand jury indicted him. He pleaded not guilty and a judge set a trial date for October 14, 2014, but it was delayed until January 12, 2015. However, McVey resigned his position as school superintendent and charges against him were dismissed.

Another sexual assault case involving an unconscious sixteen-year-old girl made national news in 2014. The girl accused three teen boys at Calhoun High School in Georgia of raping her at a party after a school prom. The rape with a "foreign object" was so brutal that the girl had to be hospitalized. "Her injuries were substantial," Sheriff Stacey Nicholson reported. Georgia sheriff's deputies charged Fields Chapman, Avery Johnson, and Andrew Haynes with the crime. In July 2014, a grand jury indicted the three on charges of aggravated sexual battery.[7] In January 2015, the three faced additional felony charges, including public indecency and sodomy, along with sexual assault. The accused pleaded not guilty. As of late June 2015 no trial had been set.

Title IX Protections

Many U.S. school personnel, students, and their families (as well as employees at libraries, museums, and vocational rehabilitation programs) are not aware that Title IX, a federal regulation, protects sexual assault victims. Title IX of the Education Amendments of 1972 states, "No person in the United States shall, on the basis of sex, be excluded from participation in, be denied the benefits of, or be subjected to discrimination under any education program or activity receiving Federal financial assistance." Although the statement does not seem to cover sexual violence, an article in a 2014 issue of the *Nation* explained,

> Many people think Title IX is just about women's sports, but in fact it prohibits all forms of gender discrimination in education, including sexual violence and harassment. As part of their Title IX responsibilities, schools that receive any federal funding must actively combat gender-based

violence and respond when students of any gender are harmed. When they don't, they deny survivors access to the full range of educational opportunities available to their peers: as many survivors can attest, it's impossible to pursue a full range of educational opportunities when you're studying, eating and sleeping on the same campus as your rapist.

If school officials take little or no action regarding sexual assaults, victims can send complaints to the Department of Education's Office of Civil Rights (OCR). As a penalty, the OCR could refuse schools all federal funds. But that could create numerous problems for a great many students who, for example, depend on federal grants or other types of federal government assistance to attend school. So the usual pattern is for the OCR to investigate and then allow schools a second or third opportunity to make changes in how they handle sexual assaults. Since most schools do not make changes, the OCR in early 2014 "published a list of the dozens of colleges and universities currently under investigation for Title IX violations—an unprecedented move on the agency's part and an important first step to hit universities where it hurts: their reputations," the *Nation* reported.[c]

Sexual Assaults on College Campuses

At the college and university level, administrators seldom investigate, let alone report, sexual assaults on college campuses. On July 14, 2014, the Rape, Abuse and Incest National Network (RAINN) noted on its website, "An alarming 41 percent of [U.S.] institutions of higher education have not investigated a single report of sexual violence in the past five years, according to a new national survey of colleges," which was initiated by Senator Claire McCaskill of Missouri, a former sex crimes prosecutor. The survey also found that "22 percent of institutions leave it up to their athletic departments to address claims of sexual violence involving student athletes." RAINN's president noted that he respects coaches and athletic directors, but "sexual-assault investigation is probably not one of their primary skills."[8]

Administrators contend that one reason sexual violence investigations are lax is because of student privacy policies. In addition, they argue that they can best handle such situations on their own. School personnel usually do not alert or call law enforcement unless they determine an attack is very serious and a continuing threat. Even when authorities acknowledge a rape on campus has occurred, they do not like to label anyone a rapist. Instead, they call rape "non-consensual sexual penetration" and refer to sexual assault as "non-consensual sexual contact." Those euphemisms anger many activists who say emphatically that rape is rape and a criminal act that should be publicly reported. If people do not know about a crime, they cannot protect themselves.

The Center for Public Integrity conducted a yearlong investigation of sexual assault on college campuses in 2010, which was updated in 2014, and found that perpetrators

> face little or no consequence for their acts. Yet their victims' lives are frequently turned upside down. For them, the trauma of assault can be compounded by a lack of institutional support, and even disciplinary action. Many times, victims drop out of school, while their alleged attackers graduate. Administrators believe the sanctions commonly issued in the college judicial system provide a thoughtful and effective way to hold culpable students accountable, but victims and advocates say the punishment rarely fits the crime.[9]

An example occurred at Oklahoma State University (OSU) in Stillwater. In 2012, five male students filed "sexual misconduct complaints against fellow student Nathan Cochran, 22. The incidents were said to have happened sometime between November 2011 and August 2012," according to a report in *USA Today*. School administrators suspended Cochran for three years, but did not report the accusations against him to local police. "Formal investigation of Cochran did not begin until the OSU student newspaper, the *Daily O'Collegian*, called the police department seeking information about the allegations. Before a reporter called the station, local authorities knew nothing of the case."[10]

Cochran eventually turned himself in to police and "was charged with three counts of sexual battery." He could have faced a long prison sentence but Associate District Judge Stephen R. Kistler placed him on seven-year probation instead. "As part of the plea agreement, Kistler ordered Cochran to complete a six-month inpatient substance-abuse and behavioral-treatment program in the Tulsa area. Cochran must also register as a sex offender," reported the Oklahoma City news station in September 2013.[11]

In 2014, President Obama's administration created a task force to study the problem. In addition, a bipartisan group of U.S. senators proposed a bill that "would require every university in the United States to conduct anonymous surveys of students about their experience with sexual violence on campus, with the results published online," the *New York Times* reported. The proposed legislation would levy substantial fines on schools that do not comply with the law's requirements.[12]

Washington Post columnist and Fox News contributor George Will highly criticized the government actions. In a June 2014 column he wrote that victims of sexual assaults are given "a coveted status that confers privileges," and therefore victims are "proliferating" at colleges and universities. Will also ridiculed "trigger warnings," such as notices that reading material or videos with graphic depictions of sexual violence might be traumatic for rape victims. Will contended these warnings would lead to more claims of victimization. In his acerbic way, he wrote that warnings "would be placed on assigned readings or announced before lectures. Otherwise, traumas could be triggered in students whose tender sensibilities would be lacerated by unexpected encounters with racism, sexism, violence . . . or any other facet of reality that might violate a student's entitlement to serenity."[13]

Reaction to Will's column from assault survivors was swift. Lisa Reed, for one, wrote on MediaMatters.org,

> I have some words for George Will and others who argue that sexual assault survivors "make victimhood a coveted status": Just stop. We've heard language like yours our whole lives that downplays or discounts our pain, either from ourselves, or close family members and friends that are supposed to love and support us. Your language enforces the prisons that we build for ourselves, locked in a cage of guilt, depression, anxiety and self-loathing. But as more and more survivors come forward because we realize how many other people share their pain and refuse to let it overpower us, we're learning that your voice means nothing against the strength we have amassed after undergoing such horrific experiences. Your refusal to accept or acknowledge the reality of sexual assault doesn't make our experiences any less real.[14]

To call attention to sexual assaults and rape on college and university campuses, some media have started to report attacks and raise questions about how schools handle victims' complaints. For example, the *New York Times* published Jenny Wilkinson's story in April 2015. Wilkinson, who is now a veterinarian and a lecturer in equine science at the University of Vermont, wrote that she was "sexually assaulted in 1997 by a fellow student at the University of Virginia. At a closed hearing, the university's committee on sexual assault found him responsible. His punishment? A letter in his file." Wilkinson continued,

> I went back to class on Monday morning a different person, not only because I had been assaulted, but because I had chosen to speak to the police and deal with the consequences of that. Even surrounded by supportive friends, I felt as if there was a huge flashing arrow over my head. I felt as

if everyone knew what had happened, even though in reality few people knew anything. I felt like a victim.

Over the next year and a half, I told the same story in a criminal court-room and at a university hearing, but also in front of my sorority, in my apartment with my friends, and at home with my family. I became that girl, the one who had been assaulted. Somewhere along the way, in the repeated telling of my story, in listening to other women's stories of sexual assault, I stopped feeling like a victim and started feeling like a survivor.[15]

Wilkinson described her feelings of frustration as she observed the student who assaulted her go on with his life without reprimands. In conclusion, she stated that if the university had expelled her attacker, "[I] would have felt justice had been served and could have continued my college years feeling safe, protected and valued as a member of the community. As it is, I'm left to hope that my story, added to our current national dialogue on sexual assault, will help colleges and universities come up with a better way to deal with a problem that hasn't gone away."[16]

Organizations Working to Prevent Sexual Violence

Along with survivors who speak out, nonprofit activist organizations are also calling attention to sexual violence in U.S. society. For example, OneInFourUSA .org focuses on "the collegiate and military setting." According to its website, the organization has established prevention programs with chapters at colleges and universities nationwide, from Connecticut College to the University of Redlands in California. In these chapters members can take part in the Women's Program or Men's Program. The point for women is that few of them see themselves as possible rape victims, so they learn "how to identify men's potentially high-risk behaviors and how [they] can be effective bystanders with their friends in high-risk situations, particularly those involving alcohol."[17] The Men's Program has three primary goals: "1) To help men understand how to help women recover from rape. 2) To increase the likelihood of bystander intervention in potentially high-risk situations. 3) To challenge men to change their own behaviors and influ-ence the behaviors of others."[18]

Students Active for Ending Rape (SAFER) is another activist group, which organized at Columbia University in 2000. SAFER's website declares the organi-zation "fights sexual violence and rape culture by empowering student-led cam-paigns to reform college sexual assault policies." SAFER helps students organize through workshops, an online resource library, databases on sexual assault poli-cies, and networks of allied students.[19]

Anyone who is a victim of rape or sexual assault can contact RAINN, the nation's largest anti-sexual-violence organization. RAINN operates the National Sexual Assault Hotline at 1-800-656-HOPE (1-800-656-4673) and a web-based hotline (Online.RAINN.org).

Campaigns against Sex Trafficking

Sexual violence also includes the deplorable practice of human trafficking. The U.S. State Department says "trafficking in persons" and "human trafficking" are "umbrella terms for activities involved when one person obtains or holds another person in compelled service."[20] It is a form of slavery. Human trafficking offenders are often part of organized crime; they treat their victims like property to be controlled and exploited (such as being forced into prostitution or involuntary labor).

The Federal Bureau of Investigation (FBI) puts it this way: "It's sad but true: here in this country, people are being bought, sold, and smuggled like modern-day slaves. They are trapped in lives of misery—often beaten, starved, and forced to work as prostitutes or to take grueling jobs as migrant, domestic, restaurant, or factory workers with little or no pay."[21]

In the United States, many people link human trafficking with undocumented immigrants who are brought into the country illegally. Seldom is such activity associated with U.S. citizens. And rarely do people in towns and cities across the country associate sex trafficking with the folks next door. However, according to a teen activist organization called Rights4Girls,

> Today, throughout urban, rural, and tribal regions of the nation, American-born girls are being trafficked and sold. It is estimated that there are approximately 293,000 American children at risk of commercial sexual exploitation today. The majority of them are girls, with the average age of entry into sexual exploitation being between just twelve and fourteen years old. They are generally runaways from troubled homes or foster care placements where they have been abused or thrown away by their families. They are abducted or lured by traffickers and then routinely raped, beaten into submission, and sometimes even tattooed by their captors. Instead of treating these girls as victims in need of services, they are treated as delinquents and routinely put behind bars.[22]

In June 2014, the FBI "rescued 168 child victims of commercial sex trafficking in a nationwide sweep . . . and arrested 281 alleged pimps," *USA Today* reported. The June sweep was part of Operation Cross Country, which "in the past seven years has identified and recovered about 3,400 children who have been sexually exploited. . . . The operation also has led to 1,450 convictions, 14 life prison terms and the seizure of more than $3.1 million in assets."[23]

For the report, FBI director James Comey emphasized, "These are not children living in some faraway place, far from everyday life. . . . These are our children. On our streets. Our truck stops. Our motels. These are America's children."[24]

Beyond investigating and convicting sex trafficking criminals, the FBI has an Office for Victim Assistance (OVA) and victim specialists in their field offices. OVA and service providers from U.S. Attorneys' Offices and nongovernmental agencies "work with human trafficking victims to advise them of their rights and ensure they get the help they need to address their short-term and long-term needs, including medical, mental health, and legal services; immigration relief; housing; employment; education; job training; and child care."[25]

In December 2012, NBCBayArea.com reported a horrific story of sex slavery in the San Jose, California, area. Reporters Stephanie Chuang and Liza Meak conveyed Minh Dang's life story on the network. As a youngster Dang was physically, emotionally, and sexually abused; at the age of ten, Dang's parents "teamed up to sell her for sex." Dang told the reporters, "[My parents] actually recruited people, so my mom placed ads in Vietnamese newspapers and magazines. . . . My dad took me to these businesses, they were cafes, and they were fronts for brothels. He would take me to brothels and leave me there for weeks on end, and brothels sell children for sex so that was my job while I was there."[26]

Dang went to school in Los Altos and Mountain View; she was a "straight A student" and star hockey player. Her teachers and coach knew nothing about her life after school until years later. Dang left San Jose and went to college but was still trafficked by her parents. As Dang explained, "The first two years I was going to college . . . I was still being sold by my parents. . . . Then they paid my final bill for college, and that's when I cut all ties with them, that I would contact the police if they contacted me again, and then that was it." Dang went to work as an activist for DontSellBodies.org to help stop human trafficking and support survivors.[27]

More Campaigns against Sex Trafficking

Along with Don't Sell Bodies, other organizations trying to prevent human trafficking include DoSomething.org and Girls Education and Mentoring Services (GEMS), whose mission is "to empower girls and young women, ages 12–24, who have experienced commercial sexual exploitation and domestic trafficking to exit the commercial sex industry and develop to their full potential."[28]

On school campuses, students may establish university or high school clubs to raise awareness about sex trafficking and encourage their communities to alert local law enforcement of likely offenders and their victims. Or students and others can contact the National Human Trafficking Resource Center hotline (1-888-373-7888) to report suspicious activity or call the National Center for Missing and Exploited Children (1-800-843-5678) to report seeing a missing child.

The FBI, the U.S. Department of State, the Department of Homeland Security, the Department of Health and Human Services, and other federal agencies have programs to raise awareness of human trafficking. One endeavor is the National Slavery and Human Trafficking Prevention Month observed in January each year.

Another major effort was undertaken by a 2013 documentary titled *Tricked*, which depicts the three-billion-dollar-a-year sex trafficking industry. The film includes interviews with the pimps who manipulate and abuse primarily women and girls (and sometimes boys), the police who pursue traffickers and rescue victims, the "johns" who pay for sex, the survivors of sexual exploitation, and their families. Filmmakers Jane Wells and John Keith Wasson spent three years developing the documentary, which began when Wells read an article in 2010 about sex traffickers bringing women to the Super Bowl host city—Miami at that time. "That headline caught my eye so I started investigating the subject and interviewing survivors. I gradually came to realize just how big a story sex trafficking is," Wells explained in a 2014 PBS *NewsHour* interview.

NewsHour's Saskia de Melker asked Wells and Wasson whether there was a difference between sex trafficking and prostitution. Wells pointed out, "Many people believe that legalization [of prostitution] is the answer, and that somehow all of the trends we're seeing of more violence, younger children, and police enforcement problems will disappear with legalization. Nothing I saw led me to believe that's the case, but the public at large seems to have two enormous misapprehensions: One is that it's a victimless crime. And the second is that legalization will magically make all these issues disappear."[29]

Wasson explained further: "Prostitution is, in theory, a girl or guy who is choosing to participate in offering sex for money at their own volition. Then you have sex trafficking, which is any minor who's involved, who's selling sex for money. And whoever is aiding or working with that child to buy or sell sex is committing a crime. And that kid is a victim of sex trafficking. And for anybody who's over 18, it's trafficking if they are tricked into selling sex through force, fraud or coercion."[30]

Tricked was sponsored by 3 Generations, a nonprofit organization founded by Wells. The organization helps victims of sex trafficking and survivors of atrocities by enabling them to tell their stories on film as part of their healing process. In the documentary, Danielle Douglas tells how she escaped abusive pimps and traffickers and has become "a passionate advocate" for other victims. She also wrote a blog post for HuffingtonPost.com in 2013 about her experiences. She hopes that *Tricked* will "reach a wide range of people and possibly transform their beliefs around sex trafficking. The diverse stories and viewpoints depicted throughout the film allow for a fuller understanding of the issue."[31] *Tricked* premiered in 2013 and became available in 2014 on video-on-demand.

Off the Bookshelf

Girls Like Us: Fighting for a World Where Girls Are Not for Sale, an Activist Finds Her Calling and Heals Herself by Rachel Lloyd is a book that activists young and old will find both disheartening and hopeful. Published in 2011, the memoir is full of candid and graphic details of the horrendous, brutal, and sometimes deadly attacks that sex trafficking victims endure. Lloyd explains how she ended up on the streets of London as a teenager; after befriending her, an older man sold her for sex. She was able to escape "the life," as the girls call it, and move to the United States. In New York, she earned a BA in psychology and MA in urban anthropology and in 1998 founded GEMS to provide needed services for sexually exploited and trafficked girls and young women.

The scenes in this book are not designed for readers with a weak stomach or who find some rough language offensive. Readers may also be shocked by the statistics about girls trapped in the sex industry. These are the preteens and teenagers who may be runaways, impoverished, alcohol or substance abusers, or victims of abuse. But, Lloyd writes, they may also be

> children from middle-class backgrounds, children who haven't suffered extreme trauma or abuse, children who have been sheltered and cared for. Commercial sexual exploitation can happen to any young person. . . . The Internet has opened up a whole world of information to children and yet it has also brought the threat of predatory strangers right into our homes. . . . Exploiters are utilizing the Internet more and more to search for vulnerable children and adolescents who can be used for both sexual and commercial purposes.[d]

In addition, Lloyd points out how difficult it is for girls and young women to leave the pimps and other exploiters because of violence and the lack of any other choices. They do not have the skills to get good jobs, have no help from relatives or friends, and are poorly educated or uneducated—sometimes illiterate. And the juvenile and criminal justice systems usually assume that the girls arrested have primarily themselves to blame. The girls' stories are raw and painful, but some are also triumphant for young women who have been helped by understanding and caring activists and nonjudgmental police officers.

Recognizing Victims of Sex Trafficking

The Polaris Project, which fights against human trafficking and modern slavery, points out that anyone can become a victim of trafficking but certain populations are especially vulnerable. These may include undocumented immigrants; runaway and homeless youth; victims of trauma and abuse; refugees and individuals fleeing conflict; and oppressed, marginalized, and/or impoverished groups and individuals. Young people are often targeted by pimps and traffickers who are skilled at manipulating child victims and maintaining control through a combination of deception, lies, feigned affection, threats, and violence. Since sex trafficking is a hidden crime, the victims are not always apparent. But there are some clues. The individuals may

- appear to be under someone else's control;
- be unable to speak for themselves;
- be unable to leave a home or workplace;
- have few personal belongings;
- look malnourished;
- have bruises or burns or seem injured in some way;
- be disoriented.[e]

Anyone who has had contact with a possible victim of sex trafficking should call local law enforcement or an organization such as the National Human Trafficking Resource Center (1-888-373-7888) operated by Polaris.

CRUSADERS FOR THE EARTH

....

"We think we can't make a difference until we graduate college, get a job, and become an adult. We think 'Oh, I'm just a kid.' We have to realize that adults will listen to us. It's necessary that they listen to us because we are the future."—thirteen-year-old Xiuhtezcatl Martinez of Earth Guardians in Boulder, Colorado, April 2014[1]

Many Americans have participated in some type of activism to protect their local, state, or national environment. They take part in recycling efforts, planting trees, cleaning up waterways and shores, picking up litter along roads, composting, conserving energy, and other activities to save our planet from environmental degradation. Teens and young adults are often in the forefront as environmental activists. They are crusaders for Mother Earth.

In 2010, Marisa McNatt wrote in an Earth911.com blog post that the environment was a "top concern" for many teens and they "are finding innovative ways to conserve energy and reduce waste in their schools." As an example, students at her New Vista High School in Boulder, Colorado, "developed and implemented their own composting system" and adhere to a steadfast recycling effort.[2] The environmental programs have continued, and in 2014 students initiated garden projects, practicing skills they learned in academic classes such as how to plant, maintain, and harvest foods.

Charles Orgbon III of Dacula, Georgia, became an environmental activist in 2008, when he was only twelve years old. He organized a group to pick up litter and founded a nonprofit advocacy organization called Greening Forward. The organization has grown and become "one of the largest entirely youth-driven not-for-profit organizations," according to its website.[3] The group helps young people start Earth Savers Clubs and raises money and makes cash grants to the clubs for their environmental projects.

Charles travels to various states to talk to students about the environment. In 2014, during Earth Day week, eighteen-year-old Charles went to Rochester,

New York, under the sponsorship of the Sierra Club, to give presentations at five schools. Charles explained to the Rochester *Democrat & Chronicle* that Greening Forward empowers "young people to take action on the environmental issues they care about." He added, "If the environmental movement hopes to make a meaningful difference in the world, we are going to have to find every reason to be more inclusive. That means recognizing that there are different interests and different needs for the communities we hope to serve. . . . For example, we can't go into communities talking about saving polar bears if we are not ready to talk about what does it mean to reduce crime or to talk about food deserts"—urban areas where there is little access to fresh food. As an African American, Charles stressed that more diversity is needed in the environmental movement. He pointed out, "If communities of color only see white environmentalists, they are going to be frustrated and wonder where they fit in."[4]

Indigenous Environmental Activists

As far as environmental activism is concerned, Native Americans in the United States and First Nations people in Canada may wonder sometimes "where they fit in," but they still manage to be crusaders for the Earth. In fact, that is an obligation for many. Some have been activists for years.

Consider Winona LaDuke, whose father, a member of the Anishinaabeg (Ojibwe) White Earth Tribe, enrolled Winona as a member when she was born. LaDuke spent most of her growing-up years in California and graduated in 1982 from Harvard with a bachelor's degree in Rural Economic Development. She then moved to the White Earth Reservation in northern Minnesota. She has fought against unfair uranium mining practices on reservations, battled for food sustainability in Indian country, and led efforts to stop the Keystone XL Pipeline. If approved, the pipeline would cross eight states to transport tar sands oil, one of the dirtiest fuels, from Alberta, Canada, to refineries on the Gulf Coast of Texas for shipment overseas. Because the pipeline crosses international borders, it must receive a permit from the U.S. government. Native activists like LaDuke have argued for years that the pipeline should not be allowed because it endangers the Ogallala Aquifer, a shallow underground water supply below the Great Plains; the pipeline could pollute ecosystems and jeopardize public health.

Young indigenous people obviously do not have the experiences of their elders, but they are part of "a dynamic environmental activism movement pioneered by highly engaged youth from native communities [which] is spreading across North America," wrote Ben Whitford in an undated article for the *Ecologist*. Whitford is a British print and news-media journalist based in Chicago. In the *Ecologist*, he pointed out that "the new face of indigenous activism [is] propelled by young, highly educated and Web-savvy" youth. They organize online and "stage their protests not on remote reservations but on elite college campuses and in other urban areas."[5]

An example of a young activist is Rose Bear Don't Walk, whose family home is the Flathead Indian Reservation in western Montana. She flies to New Haven, Connecticut, to attend Yale University (Yale class 2016), taking with her a drum that is one of her tools for activism. During her first year at Yale, she and other Native American students staged a protest, "beat out rhythms on their drums, sang, and danced a traditional round dance" to gain attention and pass out flyers to classmates. The flyers described a teach-in about an indigenous movement called Idle No More, which focuses on environmental issues such as conservation and clean water protections and the rights of indigenous people.[6]

Young indigenous activists have joined rallies in Seattle, Washington, to protect the Salish Sea and the ecosystems of Washington State's Puget Sound, the Strait of Juan de Fuca, the San Juan Islands, British Columbia's Gulf Islands, and the Strait of Georgia. The public gatherings in August and September 2014 were protests against the increase of fossil fuel transports in Puget Sound waters and by trains on land carrying coal and oil that would cross the Lummi Nation's sacred burial ground.

Kinder Morgan, an energy producer, applied to the Canadian government to "build a new pipeline to transport additional crude oil from the tar sands of Alberta to Vancouver, B.C., where it will be put on tanker vessels and shipped

Environmental activists often campaign against pollutants in waterways that kill fish and other aquatic life.

to Asia," according to the Coast Salish Sea Tribes and Nations. In an article for *Indian Country*, they wrote, "If approved, the proposal would result in expanded transport of crude oil from approximately 300,000 to 890,000 barrels per day. This is a 200 percent increase in oil tanker traffic through the waters of the Salish Sea. Vessel groundings, accidents, leaks, and oil spills are not only possible, they are inevitable."[7] At the protest rallies, there were prayers, songs, drumming, canoe trips, and symbolic ceremonies to block train crossings in Seattle.

A Post from the Past

Earth Day was U.S. Wisconsin Senator Gaylord Nelson's idea, which occurred to him in the 1960s. Nelson was concerned about the polluted environment and wanted to raise public consciousness about it. He spoke to students at college campuses and began to organize grassroots protests about environmental pollution. In 1969, he attended a conference in Seattle, Washington, and announced that there would be a nationwide grassroots demonstration on behalf of the environment in 1970. He invited everyone to join in. As he recalled,

> The wire services carried the story from coast to coast. The response was electric. It took off like gangbusters. Telegrams, letters, and telephone inquiries poured in from all across the country. The American people finally had a forum to express their concern about what was happening to the land, rivers, lakes, and air—and they did so with spectacular exuberance.[a]

At least twenty million people across the United States were involved in the first Earth Day on April 22, 1970. Ever since, Earth Day has been celebrated each year for one day, a weekend, or for a week in April. Events have included concerts, speeches, and numerous environmental cleanup activities. Following the first Earth Day, the U.S Congress soon passed the Clean Air Act of 1970, the Water Pollution Control Act of 1972 (commonly known as the Clean Water Act), the Endangered Species Act of 1973, and many other environmental laws.

Climate Change Activists

Young activists across the United States are attempting to persuade governments worldwide to do something about a problem that affects planet Earth. It is climate change—also called global warming and once popularly known as the greenhouse effect. In 1896, a Swedish chemist Svante Arrhenius noted the similarity between Earth's atmosphere and a greenhouse and was the first person to use the term *greenhouse effect*. When gases trap heat near Earth, the process is similar to what happens in a greenhouse. The sun's light and heat pass through a greenhouse's glass roof, which also keeps the heat from escaping. So the inside of the greenhouse stays warm. On Earth, the greenhouse effect prevents too much heat from escaping back into space.

Scientists link global warming to Earth's layer of atmospheric gases such as oxygen, nitrogen, hydrogen, carbon dioxide, water vapor, methane, and ozone. Sunlight passing through the gases warms the planet. Some of the gases also trap heat near Earth. Without that process, the world probably would be too cold to sustain life.

For millions of years, the atmosphere basically had the same amount of greenhouse gases, but as the United States and other nations became more industrialized, people began to burn more fossil fuels—coal, oil, and natural gas—which release carbon dioxide (CO_2) into the atmosphere. Increasingly over hundreds of years, extra CO_2 has intensified the greenhouse effect, trapping more heat and creating higher temperatures on Earth in a process now called global warming. Scientists have warned that global warming leads to long-term changes in climate. In other words, as the Earth gets warmer, rainfall patterns change, sea levels rise, and ice in the North and South Poles melts, affecting plants, wildlife, and humans.

According to the Worldwatch Institute, about ten thousand climate change activists, mostly college students, descended on the U.S. capital in 2007 "for the largest-ever [at that time] collective action on climate change in the United States."[8] Since 2007, young activists have increased in numbers as well as in their efforts to challenge governments to initiate programs and policies to decrease global warming.

One such activist is Eamon Umphress of Austin, Texas. He joined a crusade in 2011 to urge legislators to clean up air pollution. At age fifteen, he became "part of a groundbreaking legal effort to protect the atmosphere for future generations, to ensure that we have a planet when we grow up," he wrote in a blog post that appeared on MomsCleanAirForce.org in 2012. He explained,

> I became part of the iMatter/Our Children's Trust legal action along with kids from 49 other states petitioning their state and federal government to protect the atmosphere from damage caused by greenhouse gas emissions.

We used an ancient legal concept called the "public trust doctrine." The doctrine is based on the idea that the government has an obligation to protect things that the community relies on, like water. But it has never been applied to the atmosphere before.[9]

Eamon was one of the petitioners in a lawsuit against his state to persuade a judge to extend the Public Trust Doctrine to atmospheric protection. He was shocked when a judge agreed that the doctrine applied to all natural resources. "The amazing thing is that the legal breakthrough happened in Texas, a state with a reputation for conservative judges and weak environmental laws. It really showed me that if you want something to happen, and you step up and make the effort, it just might," he wrote.[10]

Another young climate change activist is Alec Loorz of Ventura, California, who founded Kids vs. Global Warming when he was only twelve years old and later the iMatter campaign. As a teenager, he demanded that the U.S. government decrease greenhouse gases. "I think a lot of young people realize that this is an urgent time, and that we're not going to solve this problem just by riding our bikes more," Alec declared. In other words, bike riding, walking, and using public transportation are not enough to conserve energy and reduce CO_2. He also noted, "I used to play a lot of video games, and goof off, and get sent to the office at school. . . . But once I realized it was my generation that was going to be the first to really be affected by climate change, I made up my mind to do something about it."[11]

In 2011, when he was in high school, Alec and four other teenagers filed a lawsuit first in California and then in Washington, DC. The suit was based on the public trust doctrine against Lisa Jackson, the administrator of the U.S. Environmental Protection Agency (EPA), and the heads of the U.S. Commerce, Interior, Defense, Energy, and Agriculture departments (*Alec L., et al. vs. Lisa P. Jackson,*

Weather and Climate

There is a difference between weather and climate. Weather is what happens on a particular day, such as sunshine and high temperatures or heavy snow and below freezing on the thermometer. "Weather can change from minute-to-minute, hour-to-hour, day-to-day, and season-to-season," says the National Oceanic and Atmospheric Administration (NOAA). "Climate, however, is the average of weather over time and space. . . . So when we are talking about climate change, we are talking about changes in *long-term* averages of daily weather."[b]

et al.). In their suit, represented pro bono by the law firm of Paul McCloskey, the students demanded that the federal government start reducing national emissions of carbon dioxide by at least 6 percent per year.

However, in May 2012, U.S. District Judge Robert L. Wilkins ruled that the federal courts did not have jurisdiction in the case and dismissed it. The judge said the issues raised were best left to the states and federal agencies and that the U.S. government had no constitutional responsibility to protect the atmosphere on behalf of present and future generations of Americans (which the plaintiffs say is contrary to the public trust doctrine). Alec and the other plaintiffs then filed a motion asking the court to correct its legal errors and reconsider its decision to dismiss the case, but in 2013, the court declined. Nevertheless, the plaintiffs petitioned the Federal Court of Appeals to consider their federal public trust claims. In June 2014, the appeals court affirmed the district courts judgments, reiterating that the public trust doctrine is a matter of state, not federal, law.[12]

Climate Change Deniers and Skeptics

Although the majority of Americans say that climate change is occurring, others deny that the climate is changing due to human activities. Or they express uncertainty. When asked about climate change, some politicians try to evade the issue by saying they aren't scientists so they cannot determine whether there is global warming. Deniers also cite a few studies that show scientific uncertainty about climate change. Some have called global warming a "hoax" or a "fraud." Or they say people who advocate for regulations to control greenhouse gases are "alarmists." Another tactic is to prohibit the use of the term *climate change*. For example, "In Wisconsin, when asked about average temperature increases in the region over time, or the area's susceptibility to drought, wildfires and insects such as gypsy moths, employees of the Commissioners of Public Lands have been prohibited from calling the causes of such phenomena by name," wrote Katy Lederer for the *Tampa Bay Times*. "In Florida, when asked to speak about sea level rise . . . employees of the state's Department of Environmental Protection have been similarly told" not to mention climate change and to evade the issue.[c]

A "Legendary" Trip

Students for Sustainability (SFS), a teen group in Port Townsend, Washington (located in Jefferson County), are dedicated activists working to reduce global warming and related concerns such as acidification of the oceans due to excess carbon dioxide that the seas absorb from the atmosphere. CO_2 is changing the chemistry of seawater and hinders the development of shellfish like oysters and clams. "Climate change is the issue of our generation," teenager Ewan Shortess, president of SFS noted in December 2013. "We want to start a wave, to make an impact and help decision makers find solutions."[13] SFS members are also concerned about hydraulic fracturing, or fracking, the process of drilling large amounts of water and chemicals at high pressure far underground to extract natural gas from shale rock. A fracking well can use up to five million gallons of water plus hundreds of chemicals, some of them carcinogens.

Ewan Shortess cofounded SFS when he was a high school sophomore. As a senior in 2014, he explained in detail about the beginning of SFS. In his words,

> The club got started because of a vacancy on the Jefferson County Climate Action Committee. Laura Tucker, who is one of our advisors, was teaching a climate change curriculum in our sophomore science class. She found out that the local Jefferson County Climate Action Committee (CAC) was looking for a student representative. She asked for volunteers in our class, hoping that maybe she could get one. Instead, there were about 10 hands raised. Laura didn't want to tell one person yes and the rest no. So, she decided that we would form a subcommittee of the CAC. The City of Port Townsend said that would not work for legal reasons, so we formed our own group. That summer, four students (including myself) and our two advisors met and got things kind of rolling. As the school year started, we gradually gained more support.[14]

Ewan had personal reasons for being part of the club, which in 2014 had thirty members. He wrote, "Working with the city/county sounded like fun, and also a lot of responsibility (which I was attracted to). I also wanted to make a difference in my school, community, state, and nation. . . . I knew that the problem of climate change was pressing and action needed to be taken immediately. I also knew that it wouldn't come easily, or happen on its own. I knew that action started with behavior changes in my actions, and everyone else's as well."

Action for eleven members of SFS was a round-trip train ride during spring break to Washington, DC, where they had arranged to meet with U.S. senators and representatives about climate change, fracking, and ocean acidification. The group, accompanied by three adult chaperones, left Port Townsend on March

27 and returned home on April 7, 2014. Their twelve-day cross-country trip by Amtrak, rather than by plane, was an intentional decision. They had planned to use public transportation (ferry, bus, train) as a means of reducing greenhouse gases and to save on expenses.

On the train, they discussed and made notes about their presentations to senators and other government officials. Ewan explained what happened while in DC:

> We were only able to meet with democratic senators/house members. This was somewhat unfortunate, because we ended up "preaching to the choir" some. Both Senators Patty Murray (D-WA) and Maria Cantwell (D-WA) . . . the only two senators we got face-to-face meetings with were both very receptive to our ideas. Both have taken steps to mitigate ocean acidification, a serious climate change effect in the Pacific North West. . . . The offices of Sen. Robert Casey (D-PA) and Sens. Amy Klobuchar and Al Franken (D-MN) were also both receptive. . . .
>
> I think the thing that surprised me the most about government officials is that they are actually willing to listen to us, as a populous. . . . Our elected officials want to hear from us all the time. They want to hear our thoughts on the bills that come up on the floor, or what we thought of their last vote. Many of the senators thanked us for meeting with them, even though we were taking very valuable time out of their day to do it.[15]

In addition to meetings with congressional members, students visited the National Oceanic and Atmospheric Administration office in Silver Spring, Maryland, and met with James Shambaugh, a management and program analyst in NOAA's Climate Program Office. They also met with Clare Sierawski, a senior advisor at the State Department Office on Climate Change, and senior advisors at the Council on Environmental Quality. During their three days in the nation's capital, SFS also "learned about Sen. Casey's FRACK act, which would require fracking companies to disclose the chemicals in fracking, and also be subjective to the Safe Drinking Water Act." In addition, Senator Patty Murray presented SFS with an environmental protection award.

Reflecting on their trip, Ewan noted that Port Townsend and Jefferson County have been very supportive of the club and it has new members who will continue environmental programs at the high school and in the town. "All of the participants who traveled to Washington, DC, will be going to college in the fall," he noted, "but the experience of the trip and the work that we did has inspired many of us to study environmentally related activities or participate in environmental clubs/activities next year. Although another trip likely won't happen [in 2015], it is very likely to happen again. What we did was legendary and I would not give up the experiences for anything."[16]

Climate change activists protest the toxic fumes from smokestacks like these that contribute to global warming.

Cleaning Up Toxic Pollution

For decades, teen and adult activists have been participating in efforts to clean up polluted waterways, wetlands, beaches, roadsides, and parks. They have also called attention to and campaigned for laws to reduce sources of air pollutants and contaminants in underground (aquifer) water supplies. Some of those efforts have paid off.

One dramatic example is the cleanup of the Cuyahoga River that runs through Cleveland, Ohio. In the 1950s and 1960s, meat packers, oil refineries, steel plants, paint companies, and tar distilleries dumped tons of pollutants into the river each day. Concentrations of methane gas and oil slicks caused a series of fires on the river surface. One 1969 blaze burned across several miles through an industrial section of Cleveland. That fire prompted media coverage nationwide and motivated activists to become involved in the clean water movement, which led to the formation of the Environmental Protection Agency and passage of the Clean Water Act of 1972.

During the 1970s another pollution story made headlines and demanded activism: Love Canal, a neighborhood near Niagara Falls, New York. It was built over a toxic waste landfill. From 1947 to 1953, the Hooker Chemical Corporation (a subsidiary of Occidental Petroleum) dumped 21,800 tons of industrial hazardous waste into the canal. The city of Niagara Falls bought land encompassing

See This Documentary—Gasland II

Gasland II is a follow-up to filmmaker Josh Fox's *Gasland* (2010), which was nominated for an Academy Award. The first film shows how rural landowners, primarily farmers, get offers to lease their property to oil and gas companies that drill for natural gas, using a process called hydraulic fracturing or fracking. When Fox received an offer of $100,000 to lease his land along the Delaware River in Pennsylvania, he refused the money and instead toured twenty-four states to learn about the effects of fracking. *Gasland* and *Gasland II* are activist films some would argue—they depict health and environmental dangers of hydraulic fracturing. Industries and some government officials disagree with that assessment, and their views are aired in the film.

Gasland II premiered in 2013 and graphics in the film help explain how the process works. When fracking occurs, methane gas (which contributes to the greenhouse effect) is released and sometimes leaks from wells, contaminating underground water supplies. Sections of the film include interviews with families who have become seriously ill and forced to leave their homes due to chemicals in their water. Some of the most dramatic footage shows a farmer turning on a water supply, igniting it, and sending huge methane gas flames into the air.

The oil and gas industries are highly critical of the films and claim that filmmaker Josh Fox has made false accusations or misleading statements about the dangers of fracking. A public relations and research firm of the Independent Petroleum Association of America has even released an alert to the industry debunking *Gasland II*. In addition, the EPA issued a report in 2015 declaring that the agency found no evidence that fracking had a widespread effect on the quality or quantity of drinking water. However, the EPA noted there was a potential that chemicals used in fracking could contaminate water resources.

Obviously, the documentary is controversial. Yet, by watching the film viewers can certainly learn what some of the issues are regarding natural gas production, which is taking place across the United States and numerous other countries at a rapid rate.

Love Canal and covered the dump, allowing builders to construct homes and a school on top of it.

After Harry and Lois Gibbs and their children moved to the community, their son Michael began having frequent infections and rashes, and their daughter Melissa developed a rare blood disease. In 1978, Lois Gibbs began to question her neighbors about their health. She discovered there was a high rate of miscarriages among the women living in Love Canal, and numerous infants faced significant health issues at birth. With this information, Gibbs organized her neighbors into the Love Canal Homeowners Association (LCHA) representing about one thousand families, and she became a knowledgeable spokesperson for LCHA on toxic waste issues. She learned that chemical waste had seeped into groundwater.

Gibbs led LCHA members on an activist campaign to get the New York Department of Health, the EPA, and eventually U.S. president Jimmy Carter to help Love Canal families. Eventually, Carter signed legislation that provided funds to evacuate families from the toxic waste site and later the U.S. Congress passed the Comprehensive Environmental Response, Compensation and Liability Act of 1980 (commonly called the Superfund Legislation) allocating $1.6 billion to search out and clean up Love Canal and other toxic dumps.

In the 1990s, about 260 homes were refurbished and sold. Although government officials and Occidental Petroleum declared that Love Canal was no longer a problem, new residents in the area were not convinced. Some families have complained about health problems similar to those suffered by former Love Canal residents. At least six families filed lawsuits against Occidental Petroleum in 2013 and others were pending at that time, according to an Associated Press report.[17]

Teen activists also have been involved in toxic waste cleanups. The Kids Against Pollution video *Teen Fights for Toxic Waste Cleanup* tells one story. The relevant film is narrated by teenager Shadia Wood, who lived near a toxic waste site in New York. She became an environmental activist when she learned that the state's superfund was bankrupt. No money existed to clean up the toxic site. Shadia and other students worked with environmental groups to lobby the New York legislature. After eight years, their efforts were rewarded when the state passed a law to refinance the superfund.[18]

A landfill with toxic coal ash was the focus of Cece Durden's activism. The seventeen-year-old from Uniontown, Alabama, learned that a nearby landfill was receiving coal ash from Tennessee. The waste material was from a massive coal ash dump that burst through a dike in 2008 "sending more than a billion gallons of toxic waste across 300 acres of riverfront property, damaging and destroying two dozen nearby homes. The owner of the dump, the Tennessee Valley Authority, has since spent $1.2 billion in cleanup costs, but as of 2010, only a small percentage of the ash had been cleaned up," according to a report on Earthjustice .org.[19] Cece recruited members of the Sierra Student Coalition to support her

Off the Bookshelf

Scat is a YA novel (Knopf, 2009) by Carl Hiaasen, who often writes about the Florida Everglades and the creatures and humans who live in the swamps. Hiaasen is a fervent advocate for saving the Everglades, which is apparent through his descriptions of wildlife and his criticism of those who damage the swamp. As one person in the novel puts it, "I've got a gutful of anger about what's happening to this land and everything that lives out here."[d] Crusaders for the earth will appreciate this eco-mystery with all its twists and turns and outrageous and sometimes laugh-out-loud scenes.

The main characters in this story are two teenage friends, Nick and Marta, and an ill-fated classmate named Duane, better known as Smoke. (The reason for the nickname is part of the story.) They are students at Truman School, a private academy, and are in the same biology class. Their teacher, Mrs. Starch, has a personality that fits her name—stiff and strict. She belittles her students when they fail to do their homework or cannot answer questions correctly. Marta calls her a witch.

Part of the novel takes place during a class field trip to the Big Cypress Preserve near the Everglades. Mrs. Starch requires each of her students to carry notebooks and list every animal, bird, and plant they see. During the field trip, a wildfire erupts and the class rushes to get out of the swamp, but Mrs. Starch disappears. The story zigzags from incidents with mysterious and eccentric characters to comedic situations to dangerous encounters. Nick and Marta get involved in an effort to protect a Florida panther and her newborn baby. They run into a disguised, mysterious swamp man who is tracking the animal's scat (poop) to save the panthers, an endangered species; he is also stealthily following illegal oil drillers to demand that the criminals *scat!*—get out of the swamp.

As the novel progresses toward the culmination, the identity of the swamp man and the outcome for the panthers are revealed. Readers are left guessing about the fate of the teenage adventurers and Mrs. Starch until the final chapters. As for the biology class, what do you think happens?

efforts to clean up the toxic pollution that threatens her community. She also has been working with a community group to fight pollution from a local wastewater facility, which has contaminated a number of waterways.

Another teenager, Hannah Gross, has concentrated on banning toxic chemicals in household products and cosmetics. At the age of fifteen, she was "shocked" to learn that the federal government does not regulate most of the chemicals in beauty products, so she joined Teens Turning Green (TTG). "The main goal [of TTG] is really to change the world, and specifically to help people eliminate chemicals from their community," she told Paldon Dolma of *YCteen* magazine in 2011. "The way to do that is to empower youth to be informed change-makers, and that's through advocacy, through events, through supporting policy changes." Hannah explained, "It's not just cosmetics—it's also the chemicals used in the clothing you buy, the electronics you use, anything in your house like cleaning products." Hannah has made changes in her lifestyle since becoming a TTG activist. Learning "that most of the products I was using at home are probably harmful, both to me personally and to the environment, totally changed my mindset about what environmentalism means," she explained. "I looked up all my products and gradually switched everything. Now, I really think about ingredients and look up companies before I support them. I became more conscious as a consumer."[20]

ADVOCATES FOR ANIMALS

"Young kids and teens have an advantage over everyone else. THEY ARE A VOICE THAT IS RARELY HEARD FROM. Recognize that and use it, but stay authentic and honest. People will see through any lies you might be telling."—advice to activists from twenty-year-old ocean conservation campaigner Elora West in 2014[1]

Countless people believe that humans, who are part of the animal kingdom, have moral obligations to provide for the well-being and humane treatment of other animals. In other words, they are animal welfare supporters or are animal rights advocates. There are differences.

Animal welfare is spelled out in the Animal Welfare Act of 1966 signed at the time by U.S. president Lyndon Johnson. The act is the only federal law that regulates the treatment of animals in research, in exhibition, in transport, and by dealers. There have been numerous amendments to the act, the most recent in 2008, and the U.S. Department of Agriculture (USDA) enforces it. In 2013, the USDA issued the Animal Welfare Act and Animal Welfare Regulations with requirements for operating animal facilities, animal research, transportation of animals, specifications for animal care and use, humane standards, protection of pets, prohibitions on animal fighting, and other rules.

Who Are Animal Activists?

In the United States (and worldwide), activists for animals range from elementary and high school students and young adults to the elderly. Some animal activists are against humans using animals for any purpose. One organization is Last Chance for Animals (LCA), which "opposes the use of animals in food and clothing production, science experimentation, and for entertainment," according to its website.[2] Kids and teens are encouraged to get involved in LCA with the Don't

Be Cruel campaign, along with many other options. LCA focuses on varied campaigns including ethical treatment of animals in entertainment, banning the use of fur for clothing and accessories, animal testing, and factory farming. The LCA website has a downloadable pdf of the national and international companies that perform animal testing; it also has a version with a list of companies that do not test on animals.

Some teen activists belong to organizations such as Kids Against Animal Cruelty (KAAC) founded by Lou Wegner, a teen actor who has been in numerous films and TV shows. His hometown is Columbus, Ohio, but he also lives part time in Burbank, California.

Lou has been an animal activist since visiting an animal shelter when he was a youngster. He explained,

> I arrived at the shelter very excited about volunteering and helping out. I did not expect to see a line of people turning in their animals. There was a window outside for drop-offs. People would literally walk up to the window, answer some questions and drop-off their pets. I was in shock. There were so many people. It was beyond sad. I then discovered that the shelter was crowded and animals in the back had to go to make room for animals coming in. Had to go. . . I was horrified. I had no idea they would be put to sleep.[3]

Lou's reaction was his motivation for founding KAAC in 2010, with a long-term goal of chapters in all fifty states and an expansion of global chapters. He noted,

> The beauty of KAAC is that it is powered by social media. There are no time constraints. I can check in with my Nepal Chapter via my phone if I'm not at home on my computer. I have discovered that technology is animal friendly. Snow leopards to Chihuahuas, I can check on them with a click of the mouse any time of the day or night.

When asked what other teens, or anyone for that matter, could do to bring about an activist culture pertaining to animal welfare, Lou declared,

> My generation is the key to changing the tide of death for shelter animals and for protecting what is left of our wildlife. We have to do a better job at being responsible. It has to be learned at the earliest age possible. I formed KAAC chapters to help kids and teens take the steps towards leadership. They would represent their states and countries and recruit other kids and teens to their cause. The mission is simple. Most kids love animals. They want to take care of them. We educate the importance of pet responsibility and wildlife conservation. We promote kindness.

Lou explained that KAAC uses social media and school programs to promote the organization. For example, he and a friend, actress Emily Capehart, attended a school prom, wearing badges with pictures of shelter dogs to call attention to the need for animal adoption. He told an interviewer for Dogster.com that "the most rewarding part of his work is 'finding forever, happy homes for animals who were abandoned by their families and scheduled to die.'"[4]

Another celebrity activist for animals was Sam Simon, the cocreator of *The Simpsons*, one of America's top-ten, longest-running, prime-time television series. Simon worked as a newspaper cartoonist before venturing into directing, producing, writing, and then focusing full time on charitable endeavors after learning he had terminal cancer. He committed his fortune to saving as many animals as he could before he died. Simon was given only months to live but defied that prognosis for several years. He died on March 9, 2015, at the age of fifty-nine. Besides saving the lives of dogs and other animals through the Sam Simon Foundation, he also launched the Simon Society as part of the Save the Children global campaign. "I get pleasure from it. I love it," he said.[5]

It Happened to Elora West

Elora Malama West was born on November 9, 1993, the daughter of Scott West, director of intelligence and investigations for the Sea Shepherd Conservation Society (SSCS), an international movement to protect the oceans and marine life. "Sea Shepherd is the only marine conservation organization that is actively out in the field and enforcing environmental laws or documenting atrocities committed against ocean wildlife and using the media to expose them, all around the world," Elora wrote in 2014. SSCS investigates, reports, and protests illegal killing of dolphins and whales and other inhumane marine activities such as cutting off shark fins while the animals are still alive and dumping the fish into the ocean where they die a slow death.

Elora began her efforts to save dolphins at the age of sixteen when she made plans to accompany her father to Taiji, Japan, to report on the plight of dolphins. At the suggestion of a friend, Jason Leopold, she started a blog in September 2010. At the time Jason "was the senior editor of *Truthout* news and now writes for Vice news." Elora explained that Jason

had heard about our traveling to Japan and encouraged me to start a blog [*The Girl's Soapbox*]. When I first began writing, I really did not realize the impact the site could have. I was very new to blogging, and I had over 100,000 hits. It was then that I realized the power you can have in getting a message out there if you are authentic and tell stories through a first person narrative. . . . My young age combined with that made for a very effective way of using the media.

Elora turned seventeen while in Taiji, where she observed SSCS's Cove Guardians at work. The guardians are volunteers from around the world, and they document the Japanese fishermen who herd dolphins and small whales into a small, hidden cove in order to kill the animals or capture them for sea parks. Because the guardians have raised awareness of these hunts, many people worldwide have spoken out against the drives. As Elora put it, SSCS has "brought international media attention to the horrors in the cove. The world can no longer ignore what happens in Taiji." SSCC hopes the exposure will help bring an end to hunts. As Elora noted,

> The police teams monitoring Sea Shepherd's Cove Guardians in Taiji have doubled in numbers, costing the taxpayers a lot of money. They have built a smaller "police box," or station, in the parking lot of the Taiji cove. The dolphins' killers are continuing their efforts to block what is happening in the killing cove—including completely blocking off the tsunami escape route that leads to the top of the killing cove. They are no longer using the gutting barge so that the water does not turn red, and there are now painted lines on some of the streets and parking lots separating where Sea Shepherd is allowed to be and where is "off limits." All of this is an indication to me that the pressure put on them due to our constant presence throughout the hunt season is working; why else would they be going to such great lengths to hide what they are doing? It is still an uphill battle.

When she was eighteen, Elora returned to Taiji with SSCS, but the government did not welcome them. "We were stopped at the border and 'interviewed' (interrogated) for a little over three hours. I have not attempted to re-enter since 2012," she reported.

In 2014 at the age of twenty, Elora West was enrolled in Burlington College in Vermont, working toward a degree in media activism. She explained that her goal is

> to tell stories that make people care or pay attention to issues that the mainstream media is not reporting. I want to utilize my writing, photography, and storytelling skills to do this. I know with whatever I go to do, it will be for the environment, for the voiceless, and will need to involve a lot of travel. I am happiest when I have a plane ticket in my hand. I want to show people parts of the world that are still somewhat undisturbed, and remind everyone what an amazing planet we live on and why we need to protect our one and only home.
>
> This is the perfect degree to set that foundation; it recognizes that mainstream media shapes the dominant consciousness. So the program, which is actually now a minor that I am turning into an individualized major, is set up to create independent storytellers for the greater good.[a]

Activists against Factory Farming

For decades, U.S. activists who care about animal welfare have campaigned against giant "factory farms" or "animal factories" that breed, raise, slaughter, and process animals for food. Factory farms are large, industrial operations that raise large numbers of animals. These farms focus on profit and efficiency, rather than animal welfare. More than 99 percent of farm animals nationwide are raised in factory farms, according to the American Society for the Prevention of Cruelty to Animals.[6] Some big corporate farms operate concentrated animal feeding operations (CAFOs) and each year process tens of thousands of animals such as cattle, poultry, and pigs. With their huge operations, CAFOs are able to raise many animals at low cost and to sell pork, chicken, beef, and other meat at low prices.

A typical U.S. hog factory is just one example. It is usually part of a major meat-processing company, which constructs row after row of metal buildings to

A dolphin in captivity at a sea park.

house the hogs. Each building holds eight hundred to one thousand hogs that live in elevated steel pens. Grates underneath their feet allow feces and urine to fall through to a concrete floor below. Workers flush this waste from the buildings, and pipes carry the waste to nearby ponds, called lagoons. These lagoons often overflow, especially during flooding, and contaminate land and water resources.

CAFOs and massive industrial farming are the focus of numerous activists, some of them teenagers who take part in campaigns like Meatless Mondays that supporters say will help stop factory farming. Students urge school cafeterias to observe Meatless Mondays by highlighting or even strictly serving vegetarian meals. Some young people give up eating meat altogether and become vegetarians, which they contend is not only healthy but saves animals in factory farms.

Activists criticize CAFOs for their environmental impact and the mistreatment of animals in confined spaces. One teenager explained in an English class essay that sick and downed animals in factory farms are "sent to the slaughter for human food." In the essay, later published in *Teen Ink*, he noted,

> To me that is wrong and not right to the animals. . . . Sadly, even sick and suffering animals spell profit to many in the meat and leather industry. Profit, not humane considerations, guides industry practice. What is really wrong is the reason there [*sic*] doing this is because downed animals will make a profit for them. That's why if everybody were a vegetarian

For many years activists have campaigned against factory pig farms that jam animals together so tightly in cages that they can hardly move.

these factory farms will not make any profit because no one is buying there meat. My opinion about this is downed animals who have been suffering . . . should be euthanized without pain. . . . They should not be slaughtered for humans to eat and get sick from.[7]

The Humane Society of the United States (HSUS) "works on many fronts to protect farm animals from some of the most egregious abuses on factory farms." As a result of efforts by HSUS and other activists, some reforms have been enacted in the way farm animals are treated. In 2014 alone

- Heinz announced that it would switch 20 percent of its eggs to cage-free throughout its North American operations by the end of 2015.
- Clemens Food Group, a major pork producer, eliminated its gestation crates for sows.
- Cargill announced it would convert all company-owned and contractor-owned sow operations away from gestation crates by the end of 2017.
- DineEquity, owner of restaurant icons IHOP and Applebee's, asked its pork suppliers to produce annual reports regarding their progress toward providing pork produced without the use of gestation crates.
- Denny's said it would ensure its pork supply comes from farmers using group housing instead of gestation stalls.

Many other accomplishments from 2014 and earlier years are listed on HSUS's website.[8]

Along with HSUS, another organization fighting against factory farming abuses is the Society for the Prevention of Cruelty to Animals (SPCA). It is dedicated to eliminating all types of animal cruelty, including abuse of animals in the food production process. The Humane Farming Association (HFA) is also dedicated to protecting farm animals from cruelty and abuse. In addition, HFA campaigns to protect the public from the misuse of antibiotics, hormones, and other chemicals used to enhance growth of farm animals. Overuse of antibiotics and hormones can have a negative effect on human health. "HFA also operates Suwanna Ranch [in Northern California]—the world's largest farm animal rescue and refuge facility."[9]

Mercy for Animals (MFA) uses hidden cameras to conduct undercover investigations to draw attention to animal abuse on farms. One video films a Nestlé facility—a Wisconsin dairy that is a major supplier of cheese to Pizza Hut, Domino's, and Papa John's. It shows workers "viciously kicking, beating, and stabbing cows and dragging 'downed' cows by their fragile legs and necks using chains attached to tractors."[10] In August 2014, an MFA blogger reported that Nestlé "announced it will eliminate many of the cruelest forms of institutionalized animal abuse from its supply chain, including an end to the practices of tail docking and dehorning of dairy cattle, an end to the castration of piglets without painkillers, and the phaseout of growth promoters for poultry. The mega company has also committed to ending the intensive confinement of baby calves in veal crates, pregnant pigs in gestation crates, and egg-laying hens in battery cages."[11]

Animal Rescue Operations

Activists for animals are involved in varied operations that rescue dogs, cats, and other creatures, including wildlife. One example is the Arizona Animal Welfare League (AAWL) and the Society for the Prevention of Cruelty to Animals (SPCA), which work together to maintain the state's "largest and oldest no-kill shelter in Arizona." AAWL and SPCA also sponsor a Teen Tracks program for youth ages thirteen to seventeen. Through the program, teenagers receive "training in animal body language and animal handling skills, assist with daily care of the animals, participate in guest presentations and educational field trips, and help lead other education programs held at the shelter," according to the program's website.[12] In its newsletter *Teen Track Times*, one participant, Samarrah Stephan, wrote,

> Teen Tracks is great program and I have learned so much. . . . My favorite days and experiences are those spent working directly with the animals

and around the shelter. On November 22 [2014], we had a service day at AAWL. I helped by cleaning the cat condos and cat rooms. . . . This was a great opportunity to help the animals and work together with other members of the Teen Tracks. We all regrouped and walked dogs. This gave the dogs exercise and us another opportunity to practice handling animals.[13]

Operation Paws for Homes (OPH) is another example. OPH "rescues dogs of all breeds and ages from high-kill shelters reducing the numbers being euthanized." According to the operation's website, most of its "dogs come from rural shelters in South and North Carolina. With limited resources, the shelters are forced to put down anywhere between 50% and 90% of the animals that come in the front door." The OPH does not house the dogs, but "provides pet adoption services to families located in Virginia, Washington, DC, Maryland, Southern Pennsylvania and neighboring states."[14]

Centers for teenage substance and alcohol abuse may adopt dogs to help in therapy. The dogs improve the temperament among teenagers who live in residential treatment centers. Multiple photos of the dogs appear on https://ophrescue.org/dogs. They include, in no particular order, German shepherds, boxers, Labrador retrievers, pit bulls, Rottweilers, beagles, Chihuahuas, collies, Siberian huskies, Great Danes, Alaskan malamutes, Australian shepherds, and many others.

The Gentle Barn in Santa Clarita, California, is part of a rescue operation whose mission is to teach "people kindness and compassion to animals, each other and our planet." Over 160 different animals reside at the Gentle Barn. It is a safe haven for animals rescued from abusive situations and then rehabilitated, treated with care, given proper medical attention, and loved. Some of the rescued animals include dogs, horses, turkeys, chickens, goats, calves, and young cows. Once rehabilitated, the animals become ambassadors, teaching children as well as adults about unconditional love and nonjudgmental attitudes.

Children naturally identify with animals, and groups working with at-risk youth take them to the Gentle Barn where they have the opportunity to feel safe, learn to have compassion, and help with the animals. One group leader at Pacific Lodge Boys' Home noted,

The instant connection with the animals that is made each and every time we bring our boys there is almost impossible to describe without using words like "extraordinary," and "uplifting." There is more to the connection than just curiosity on both the boys' and animals' parts. There is an understanding of what it means to have a second chance. Whether you happen to walk on 2 feet, 4 hooves, or merely just enjoy the sensation of watching as two completely different creatures, human and animal, learn something that books can't teach.[15]

Other rescue operations such as Operation WildLife (OWL) service injured and orphaned wild animals in northeast Kansas and northwest Missouri. OWL takes in many baby animals—squirrels, rabbits, opossums, raccoons, and song-birds. The operation receives thousands of wild animals each year; after rehabili-tating them, OWL releases an average of 69 percent of them.

"No-Kill" animal shelters also rescue and care for animals. Operation Kind-ness, for example, is a north Texas shelter that takes in homeless or unwanted cats and dogs. The shelter pledges not to euthanize animals and to care for them until they are adopted. Most other states have similar shelters that can be located by browsing on the Internet or checking local phone books.

Protests against Animal Exploitation

A great variety of animals are raised to amuse people visiting such facilities as sea parks, circuses, zoos, road shows, movie theaters, and even pet shops, especially those that sell exotic animals. Activists often argue that breeding, capturing, and using animals purely for entertainment is inhumane—that is one reason an orga-nization called Circus Protest formed.

Founded in 2012, Circus Protest is true to its name. It focuses on circus ani-mal abuse and assists "activists and organizations across the country by providing advice, literature, branding, posters, and online support in order to stage effective and professional anti-circus actions across the country." The organization works to free animals "enslaved by the circus through the implementation of strategic action centered on community-based education and awareness-raising."[16]

Born Free is an animal advocacy organization that "believes that it is outdated and unacceptable to use wild animals in circuses or to market products by making animals perform unnatural behaviours. Such acts misrepresent the true nature of the animals; require the animals to be subjected to an unnatural and often abusive lifestyle; and undermine public respect for the natural world. Born Free challenges the use of wild animals in circuses and performance, raises awareness about the issues, and campaigns for national and international legislation to bring this practice to an end."[17]

Some of the most heated protests regarding the abuse of circus animals focus on elephants, especially babies that are taken from their mothers before they are weaned to be trained as circus performers. In its November–December 2011 is-sue, *Mother Jones* published a major feature "The Cruelest Show on Earth" with the subtitle "Bullhooks. Whippings. Electric Shocks. Three-Day Train Rides without Breaks. Our Yearlong Investigation Rips the Big Top Off How Ringling Bros. Treats Its Elephants."

The magazine's investigation of Ringling Brothers, now owned by Feld En-tertainment, found that "Ringling elephants spend most of their long lives either in chains or on trains, under constant threat of the bullhook, or ankus—the menacing tool used to control elephants." As Deborah Nelson reported for the magazine, the elephants "are lame from balancing their 8,000-pound frames on tiny tubs and from being confined in cramped spaces, sometimes for days at a time. They are afflicted with tuberculosis and herpes, potentially deadly diseases rare in the wild and linked to captivity."

Animal welfare activists have reported severe beatings of elephants, "and local humane authorities have documented wounds and lameness. None of that has moved regulators to action," Nelson wrote. After several baby elephants in the Ringling circus died, the USDA investigated, and owner Kenneth Feld finally "admitted under oath that his trainers routinely 'correct' elephants by hitting them with bullhooks, whipping them, and on occasion using electric prods."[18] Activists and some in the general public continually raised concerns about the welfare of circus elephants, and in March 2015, Feld Entertainment announced that Ringling would phase out elephant circus acts by 2018.

Protesting Cruel Animal Sports

The notorious felony case of Michael Vick and his dog-fighting operation has been widely publicized, but such practices continue clandestinely—dog fighting is

Elephant calves not yet weaned from their mothers are often captured to be trained as circus performers, a cruel practice animal activists insist.

Off the Bookshelf

The Lost Dogs: Michael Vick's Dogs and Their Tale of Rescue and Redemption (Gotham Books/Penguin, 2010) by Jim Gorant is a story that will be difficult to read at times. This nonfiction book (published in paperback in 2011) is about animal cruelty and the well-known case of NFL star quarterback Michael Vick and his team's brutal dog-fighting operation and how it was stopped. Gorant, a senior editor for *Sports Illustrated*, first published an article about Vick's dogs in the magazine and then provided much more detail in his book.

The first part reads like a mystery novel but is a factual account of the discovery of the Bad Newz Kennels in Surry County, Virginia. There men tested dozens of dogs to determine if they were fighters, and shot, hung, drowned, electrocuted, or beat poor-performing dogs to death. Local witnesses and investigators finding evidence of dog fighting had little help from Gerald Poindexter, the attorney representing the Virginia commonwealth. Poindexter implied that he believed the case was being pursued because Vick was a famous African American athlete.

However, the FBI finally became involved and two federal agencies charged Vick and his three associates with a felony—violating the Conspiracy to Travel in Interstate Commerce in Aid of Unlawful Activities and to Sponsor a Dog in an Animal Fighting Venture and hosting dogfight participants from other states at Bad Newz Kennels. In 2007, Vick was arrested, tried, and sentenced to twenty-three months in prison and to a three-year probation period; the judge forbade Vick to own or have any contact with dogs except to support humane organizations.

Part 2 of *Lost Dogs* is more uplifting than the previous section. After the rescue of dozens of dogs, a team of animal rehabilitation experts tested their fitness. Gorant explained that they placed the dogs in five categories:

> Foster/Observation, Law Enforcement, Sanctuary 1, Sanctuary 2, and Euthanasia. Foster dogs were the best of the lot. These dogs seemed to be well adjusted and capable of living as a family pet. . . . The law enforcement category was for healthy, high-energy dogs who showed the drive and motivation to get through the rigorous training that was required of dogs

that did police or other investigative and patrol work. The Sanctuary 1 label went to dogs that had long-term potential but needed help. . . . The Sanctuary 2 dogs were good, healthy dogs but . . . could probably not live outside managed care. . . . The final category Euthanasia needed no explanation.[b]

The final part of the book describes the lives of some of the rescued dogs and the people who care for them. As many activists for animals already know, it is not easy to help dogs or other creatures rescued from abuse. That point is well taken in this informative book, which also emphasizes the joys of being able to rehabilitate seriously injured dogs so that they become a person's "best friend."

---

illegal in all fifty states. Promoters of this type of "entertainment" are motivated by the money earned from gambling on their dogs and a kind of blood lust, such as spectators displayed when gladiators fought in ancient Rome's Coliseum.

Activists try to call attention to cruel animal sports through organizations like the Animal Legal Defense Fund, Anti-Dogfighting Campaign, HSUS's Knock Out Dog Fighting, the United Kingdom's League Against Cruel Sports, and others. These groups also oppose cockfighting, another illegal and merciless "sport" that nationwide involves thousands of roosters and sometimes chickens. These birds fight among themselves on occasion to defend their territory or food sources. But breeders of fighting roosters raise their birds to fight until they die, cutting off the birds' natural spurs and attaching curved steel blades to their legs. The American Society for the Prevention of Cruelty to Animals (ASPCA) reported that it "has observed that cockfights in New York City are often a family-run business passed down through generations. Fights may be held in an abandoned factory, a backyard or even a basement. To avoid suspicion, organizers regularly move the events to new locations."[19]

The Humane Society explains what this type of "amusement" is all about:

In a cockfight, two roosters fight each other to the death while people place bets. Cockfighters let the birds suffer untreated injuries or throw the birds away like trash afterwards. Besides being cruel, cockfighting often goes hand in hand with gambling, drug dealing, illegal gun sales and murder.

Left to themselves, roosters rarely hurt each other badly. In cockfights, on the other hand, the birds often wear razor-sharp blades on their legs and incur injuries like punctured lungs, broken bones and pierced eyes—when they even survive.[20]

In addition to fitting their birds with blades, owners feed roosters stimulants and drugs to make them fight longer: steroids, caffeine, strychnine, epinephrine, amphetamines, and methamphetamines. This blood sport, as it is called, is banned in all fifty states and is a felony in thirty-three states. Being a spectator at animal fighting events became a federal offense in February 2014 when the Animal Fighting Spectator Prohibition Act passed as part of the federal Agricultural Act, legislation that is renewed every five years. The spectator prohibition makes it a federal crime to knowingly attend an organized animal fight such as a cockfight, or to take a child to that kind of event.

Watch This Documentary

Blackfish, a CNN documentary, released as a DVD in 2013, tells the story of orcas—huge mammals sometimes called killer whales and also known as blackfish. Footage from the actual lives of these astounding creatures in the wild and those caught and kept in sea parks are the background for the film. The movie presents the story of Tilikum, a 12,500-pound bull whale living in SeaWorld at Orlando, Florida, to demonstrate the dangers for both humans and whales kept in captivity.

Tilikum was two years old when hunters captured him off the coast of Iceland, transferring him to Sealand of the Pacific near British Columbia, Canada. His home there was a small pool only thirty-five feet deep, which he was forced to share with two female orcas. The film explains that in the wild, female orcas are dominant and aggressive toward males.

Sealand trainers made Tilikum perform every hour that the facility was open. When he did not perform correctly, trainers would not feed him or the other orcas. The females would then attack Tilikum. In February 1991, one of the trainers, Keltie Byrne, fell into the pool and all three of the whales pounced on her and tossed Byrne around until she drowned. Shortly afterward, Sealand shut down and sold Tilikum to SeaWorld.

Another tragedy occurred at the Orlando SeaWorld park. In 1999, Daniel P. Dukes was in the park after it had closed for the night. He evaded security guards and jumped into the pool. The next morning, trainers found him dead.

In 2010, SeaWorld trainer Dawn Brancheau was killed. She had a good relationship with Tilikum and was rewarding him for his performance. While the park audience watched, Tilikum pulled Brancheau into the water and thrashed her around until she drowned. SeaWorld argued that Brancheau was partly to blame for her own death because Tilikum grabbed her long ponytail. Witnesses said that story was not true, and SeaWorld later rescinded it.

Much of the documentary includes interviews with former trainers who argue that orcas should not be living in marine parks where they do not have enough room to swim freely. As a result they become frustrated and aggressive. When in the wild, orcas are constantly moving, traveling up to one hundred miles each day. Critics also find fault with trainers forcing orcas to do tricks. As one former trainer, Samantha Berg, put it, "It's time to stop the shows. It's time to stop forcing the animals to perform in basically a circus environment, and they should release the animals that are young enough and healthy enough to be released."

After *Blackfish* appeared, SeaWorld Entertainment officials argued that the film is dishonest and misleading. A SeaWorld website titled "Truth about Blackfish" presents a list of examples, such as the following:

> The film relies on former SeaWorld employees, most of whom have little experience with killer whales, and others who haven't worked at SeaWorld in nearly 20 years: These individuals, who speak with apparent authority, have little or no firsthand knowledge of the incidents they describe. Most of them had no experience with Tilikum, and several never even performed with killer whales in the water. The film's "cast" is completely unfamiliar with current conditions and techniques at SeaWorld, and are certainly in no position to critique a trainer of Dawn Brancheau's caliber or her last interaction with Tilikum.
>
> The film also relies on animal rights activists masquerading as scientists: The film relies heavily on the dubious reflections of scientists who have aggressively campaigned against marine mammal display for decades, and have no expertise with killer whale behavior in captivity.

Additional arguments can be seen on SeaWorld's website.[c]

Some media critics have also questioned the film's authenticity. Nevertheless, activists for animals continue to emphasize a basic *Blackfish* message: Orcas from the wild should not be held in captivity and forcefully trained to perform for people.

Still, cockfighting persists. Law enforcement officers in states ranging from Florida to Washington, from New York to California, have uncovered and arrested people involved in illegal cockfighting. In Rochester, Washington, for example, police raided a compound in April 2014 "whereby officials seized 240 roosters and 60 hens. Those birds had been pumped full of steroids which made the birds aggressive. Officials deemed the birds could not be rehabilitated and as a result, they were euthanized," reported Steve Williams for Care2.com. After the owner of the compound, Victor Hugo Gallegos Chavez, was arrested, he admitted that he was raising the birds for cockfights. He planned to send some birds to Mexico where cockfighting is legal and to states where enforcement of laws against animal fighting is lax.[21]

Activists who suspect that illegal cockfighting or dogfighting is occurring should not try to intervene on their own, say police and animal control officials. Operators of these events could be armed and dangerous. The better option for activists is to alert law enforcement of suspicious behavior.

RELIGIOUS ACTIVISM: PRO AND CON ISSUES

···

"The free exercise of religion includes religion and non-religion. So this country is fundamentally secular. . . . We shouldn't bring in one specific . . . version of Christianity . . . in the public schools."—nineteen-year-old activist Zack Kopplin, speaking about evolution and creationism during a 2013 Bill Moyers show[1]

Some of the most controversial social issues in the United States attract diverse youth activists who have strong religious and/or political beliefs about abortion, birth control, euthanasia, prayer in public schools, evolution, creationism, homosexuality, and other matters. Some activists are likely to base their actions on their personal religious convictions, or lack thereof, and attempt to influence public policy on these social issues. Religious activists certainly have a right to share their views, but in the United States, people expect federal, state, and local governments to recognize that no religion (or belief) should dictate public policy.

Unlike nations in which governments support a state (national) religion (such as Roman Catholicism or Islam), the First Amendment to the U.S. Constitution says the federal government cannot establish a religion—that is, promote, endorse, or identify itself with any particular faith. Thomas Jefferson, author of the Declaration of Independence and later U.S. president (1801–1809), wrote that the First Amendment created a "wall of separation between church and state." That statement was in Jefferson's 1802 letter to Connecticut Baptists who were upset about their state's official support of the Congregationalist Church.

Jefferson could not interfere in state affairs, but explained that "separation" on the federal level applied to the free exercise of religion, which is guaranteed by the First Amendment. Individuals have the right to practice, or not practice, a particular faith.

Portrait of President Thomas Jefferson (1801–1809).

Religious Proselytizing in the Public Square

Religious proselytizing is an effort to recruit or try to convert someone to a new faith or belief. Americans have the constitutional right to preach their religion in the public square. Individuals young and old, for instance, can stand on street corners and sermonize or bellow their evangelical beliefs through loudspeakers. Billboards or signs in public places may tout religious beliefs. People may also go from one home to another to deliver their religious messages, as is the practice of such denominations as Jehovah's Witnesses and the Church of Jesus Christ of Latter-day Saints.

The American Civil Liberties Union (ACLU) points out as well, "The Constitution properly protects the right of religious figures to preach their messages over the public airwaves. Religious books, magazines, and newspapers are freely published and delivered through the U.S. Postal System. No other industrialized democracy has as much religion in the public square as does the United States."[2]

Even though religious rights in the public square are assured, some religious proselytizers take advantage of these liberties or defy other's rights, as was the

A Post from the Past

In the decades before the 1940s, some states required public school children to take part in ceremonies pledging allegiance to the U.S. flag. Students who did not participate could be expelled from school and in a few states their parents could be charged with a criminal offense. Some religious groups such as Jehovah's Witnesses, some Mennonites, and others protested participating in the pledge, arguing that doing so went against biblical laws.

In 1940, a member of the Jehovah's Witnesses challenged the mandatory flag salute and pledge, but the U.S. Supreme Court upheld the law, ruling that the ceremony supported unity and national security. The High Court's decision prompted attacks against Witnesses. Some Americans called the religious group disloyal and unpatriotic and physically assaulted them or destroyed their property. At the same time, Americans who believed that a compulsory flag salute violated First Amendment rights began to object. Three years later, another Witness case reached the Supreme Court. In *West Virginia State Board of Education v. Barnette* (1943), the Court reversed its earlier ruling. Justice Robert Jackson, who delivered the Court's opinion, wrote, "If there is any fixed star in our constitutional constellation, it is that no official, high or petty, can prescribe what shall be orthodox in politics, nationalism, religion, or other matters of opinion or force citizens to confess by word or act their faith therein. If there are any circumstances which permit an exception, they do not now occur to us."[a]

case in the Chesterfield County School District in South Carolina. The ACLU won a lawsuit in 2012 on behalf of nonbelievers Jonathan Anderson and his son, a student at New Heights Middle School, who was subjected to repeated proselytizing. According to the ACLU,

Religious iconography, including a copy of the Ten Commandments, adorned school walls; and teachers incorporated Biblical scripture into lessons. Mr. Anderson's son was even ordered to copy religious essays as punishment for minor rules infractions, such as forgetting his belt and gym

What Is the "Public Square"?

In political discussions, religious activists, whatever their persuasion, often speak out in the public square. How do you define the *public square*? For some Americans, it is any location that is open to all citizens. For others, the public square has a broader meaning—a local event or national celebration that brings people together. Increasingly, the public square is also the Internet where diverse religious activists present their views on social media, forums, videos, and personal or organizational websites. That means people of diverse religious groups—Buddhists, Christians, Hindus, humanists, Jains, Jews, Muslims, pagans, Sikhs, Wiccans, and others—are entitled to a voice in political discussions and no one religion should dominate public policy.

When religious activists promote their beliefs in the public square, they are free to do so, even if their views are offensive to others and even when they express hatred for others' beliefs. But there are limitations. In various cases, the U.S. Supreme Court has held that freedom of speech does not include the right to incite actions that would harm others; to make or distribute obscene materials; to burn draft cards as an antiwar protest; or to permit students to print articles in a school newspaper over the objections of the school administration, to make an obscene speech, or to advocate illegal drug use at a school-sponsored event.

clothes. When Mr. Anderson objected to these activities, he was informed by the school principal that he needed to "get right with God."[3]

In another instance at the school, an assembly "featured a Christian rapper who calls himself B-SHOC. The assembly also included a sermon delivered by an evangelical youth minister, and students were asked to sign cards pledging themselves to Jesus. Students who did not want to attend the assembly were told that they could instead spend the afternoon in in-school suspension." A federal judge ordered the school district to end the unconstitutional practices "and restore the Establishment Clause rights of the Andersons and all families throughout Chesterfield County schools. . . . At the same time . . . students who wish to pray or express their faith are still free to exercise those rights consistent with the protections offered by the Free Exercise Clause and Free Speech Clause of the First Amendment."[4]

Some religious proselytizers such as the Westboro Baptist Church of Kansas deliver messages outside military funerals, churches, schools, graduation ceremonies, and concerts. They carry signs such as "God Hates Fags" (also the title of their website) and hand out flyers deriding their opponents as "phony-salt-of-the-earth-small-town-pseudo-patriot-pretend Christians."[5]

In June 2014, the Westboro group picketed Wilson High School in Washington, DC, because the principal had announced that he was gay. Their signs declared "You're Going to Hell," and "Christians Caused Gay Marriage," and "No Peace for the Wicked." An estimated one thousand students plus other supporters of the school principal met the Westboro group waving rainbow flags and carrying such signs as this one by a student: "I Have 2 Moms and Life Is Good."[6]

A type of tit-for-tat case unfolded in Orange County, Florida, in 2014. A religious group known as the Satanic Temple created a public outcry when members announced they would distribute their materials in public schools, such as *The Satanic Children's Big Book of Activities*. They also provided pamphlets on Satanist philosophy plus information about children's legal rights to practice Satanism if they choose to do so. That kind of proselytizing, Satanists declared, was due to the fact that earlier the school district had permitted evangelical Christians (The World Changers of Florida) to hand out Bibles and other religious reading materials in the schools.

The Freedom from Religion Foundation brought a lawsuit (*Freedom from Religion Foundation, Inc. et al. v. Orange County School Board*) in July 2013 against the school system. In July 2014, a judge dismissed the case, "without prejudice for lack of subject matter jurisdiction." Nevertheless, the Orange County school district decided in September 2014 "to let any religious and atheist materials be provided in schools," according to a news report. "The Temple said that although it does not agree with the school board's decision to allow religious materials in schools, it will continue 'to ensure that pluralism is respected whenever the Church/State division is breached.'"[7]

In short, "Public spaces ought to be secular," wrote Robyn Pennacchia in an online magazine article. "You just have to believe that schoolrooms and other publicly funded spaces are not the appropriate place for religious proselytizing."[8]

Religious Issues in the Public Schools

Public schools in the United States are supported by taxpayer funds and are required by law to be neutral on religious matters. Yet religion enters into debates on such issues as prayer and Bible reading in public schools. In colonial times, schools conducted prayers in classrooms and read biblical verses or taught religious beliefs (usually Protestant Christian). In fact, the main purpose of schooling was religious instruction.

After the Revolutionary War, founding father Thomas Jefferson advocated for public schools free of church control. Jefferson opposed the use of tax funds for religious groups, including church-sponsored schools. By the early nineteenth century, state legislatures began to pass laws establishing public schools. Since that time, activists have presented both pro and con arguments regarding religious activities in tax-supported schools.

During the 1960s, the U.S. Supreme Court entered the debate. In 1962, for instance, the New York Board of Regents, the state's governing body for public schools, recommended that each morning students recite a "neutral" prayer, acknowledging dependence on God. Parents of ten students charged in a lawsuit that the practice was unconstitutional. When the case *Engel v. Vitale* (1962) went to the High Court, eight out of nine justices agreed, ruling that school-initiated prayer in the public school system violated the First Amendment.

In spite of the Court ruling, prayers and Bible readings continued. In 1963, the Edward Schempp family in Germantown, Pennsylvania, sued its state for mandating that ten verses of the Bible be read daily in public school classrooms. This case also went to the U.S. Supreme Court, which ruled that Bible reading in public schools was unconstitutional—it promoted one religious belief.

Still, the debate has gone on for decades, with many religious activists incensed over the banning of prayers and reading biblical verses in public schools. On the opposing side, activists point out that students have diverse religious affiliations and should not be subjected to only Christian supplications. In addition, students are not banned from praying on a voluntary basis as long as it does not interfere with the rights of other students or disrupt school functions. "Students can pray in school buses, at the flag-pole, in student religious clubs, in the hallways, cafeteria, etc. If the school has as few as one extra-curricular student-led and student-organized group, then students have a legal right to organize a Bible or other religious club to meet outside of classroom time," explains ReligiousTolerance.org.[9]

Activism in the Abortion Debate

If ever there were religious activism in the public square, it is with the issue of abortion. Aborting an embryo (from conception to nine weeks in a pregnancy) or a fetus (the developing human in the womb) has been legal nationally since 1973. That year the U.S. Supreme Court struck down severely restrictive state abortion laws in the now-famous *Roe v. Wade* case. The High Court ruled that the state laws were unconstitutional because they did not protect a woman's right to privacy. In the *Roe v. Wade* decision, the Court held that (1) during the first trimester (three months) of pregnancy, a woman had the right to an abortion for any reason; (2) during the second trimester, states may pass laws regulating abortion to protect a woman's health; (3) during the last three months of a pregnancy, when the fetus can live outside the womb, states may pass laws to protect the fetus by prohibiting abortion except to preserve the health or life of the pregnant woman.

The Guttmacher Institute, which promotes sexual and reproductive health and rights, reported that "from 1973 through 2011, nearly 53 million legal abortions occurred." In 2011, 1.06 million abortions were performed compared to 1.21 million in 2008, a decrease of 13 percent. Some antiabortionists claimed that the decline is due to various legislation they supported, but the law's true intentions were to close abortion clinics, prevent doctors from performing abortions, or require women to undergo ultrasounds or other procedures. Many of these rulings have been or are being challenged, and some have been overturned. In *Perspectives on Sexual and Reproductive Health, 2014*, the Institute noted, "The national abortion rate has resumed its decline, and no evidence was found that the overall drop in abortion incidence was related to the decrease in providers or to restrictions implemented between 2008 and 2011."[10]

Nevertheless, abortion debates continue. People who support the right of women to choose to abort a fetus refer to themselves as pro-choice. Those opposed to abortion call themselves pro-life. The two sides—including teenagers and adults, male and female—frequently face off in public protests. They also publicly advocate for or against proposed laws regarding abortions.

In Illinois, for example, teens were part of a 2014 protest in Springfield, the state capital, against the Parental Notice of Abortion Act of 1995. The law requires that youth must notify parents or obtain their consent before obtaining abortion services. However, the act had not been implemented because the ACLU challenged it as unconstitutional. In 2013, the Illinois Supreme Court determined the law constitutional.

In April 2014, about fifty Illinois teenagers joined the ACLU of Illinois, the Chicago Abortion Fund, and the Illinois Caucus for Adolescent Health for a day of protest against parental notification at the state capitol. According to a ProgressIllinois.com report, several teens spoke against the enforced law. Seventeen-year-old Torrance Johnson from Calumet City noted,

> You may know someone who will want to have an abortion. Everybody does not live in an ideal situation and some parents want to put their children out [on the street if they become pregnant]. Everyone doesn't have a fortunate situation for their parents to understand and to listen, or even to just have a conversation . . . it's very common in my community for individuals to have unplanned pregnancies and unprotected sex, and

it's saddening that a lot of the rights we have are taken away as youth and individuals. Sometimes it's forgotten that adults were once us before.[11]

Another teenager, Nichole Glass, pointed out that she was fortunate to "have supportive parents, and they wouldn't really judge me on my choice." She noted that her parents would help her out if she wanted an abortion. "They wouldn't be against me, but there are [teens] who don't have those choices and supporting parents like that."[12]

Groups also rally to call attention to their pro-choice or pro-life positions. Pro-life teens, for example, may gather outside Planned Parenthood offices, former abortion clinics, schools, churches, government buildings, or other facilities to demonstrate their convictions. Pro-choice activists do the same.

In December 2013, pro-life teens gathered for a Catholic School Life Rally in Wichita, Kansas. The location was a clinic where George Tiller, MD, performed late-term abortions; he was shot to death in the foyer of his church in 2009. Before Tiller's murder, antiabortion activists killed other abortion doctors and clinic workers.

In 2013, Tiller's clinic (renamed South Wind Women's Center) reopened. At a school rally there that December, one of the young people, Kellan Niewald, reportedly said, "The reason why I am standing up against abortion is because it is killing a living child that can't even take its first breath. We as a school are trying to show the world that a big journey, like peacefully protesting against abortion, is a step towards making it illegal." Another classmate, seventeen-year-old Katie, spoke out, saying in part,

> I believe every human life is precious . . . whether they are the mom seeking the abortion, the baby growing inside the womb, a clinic worker inside the abortion clinic or an abortion doctor. I believe that no matter if you are black, white, green or purple, Mexican or Chinese, God finds so much value in your life and so do we. . . . I believe that every human being has value and is loved by God. Every single human being is loved by God, I know this for a fact.[13]

A pro-choice group also attended the rally to protest the antiabortion gathering. Those who support a woman's right to abort a fetus have been a presence in Wichita since before and after Dr. Tiller's murder. According to a Reuters report, abortions at the reopened clinic are performed "through the 14th week of pregnancy, even though abortions are legal through about 20 weeks under Kansas law." That is what the doctors at the clinic prefer, a spokesperson noted.[14]

Only a small number believe that the "abortion war," as *Newsweek* called it, will end soon. A feature by Allison Yarrow in August 2014 concludes, "America is

Antiabortion Extremists

● Some activists against abortion take extreme measures to advance their cause. According to Jill Filipovic writing for *Cosmopolitan* in May 2013,

Since the late 1970s, anti-abortion extremists have committed eight murders, 17 attempted murders, 42 bombings, 181 arsons, 99 attempted bombings or arsons, 1,495 acts of vandalism, 100 butyric acid attacks, 663 anthrax or bioterrorism threats, 198 acts of assault and battery, 428 death threats, four kidnappings, 183 burglaries, and 550 acts of stalking. The number of hate mail and harassing calls totals more than 15,000. In just under four decades, there have been more than 33,000 arrests—a point of pride for many of the arrestees.[b]

as deeply divided as ever on abortion. Half of Americans believe abortion should be legal 'only under certain circumstances,' views that haven't changed much in four decades. . . . More Americans identify as pro-choice than pro-life, as of May [2014] but by only one percentage point."[15]

Atheists and Activism

Nonbelievers, atheists (who do not believe there is a deity), and agnostics (who are unsure God exists) seldom publicly acknowledge their nonreligious status. Atheists often remain silent because they are usually subjected to discrimination or harassment. In some cases, believers want to "save" them or convert them to their religion. If known, atheists are likely to be barred from some public offices, jobs, charity functions, and school events.

An example is Jessica Ahlquist, a sixteen-year-old student at Cranston High School in Rhode Island, who lost friends and gained enemies when she openly identified herself as an atheist and objected to a prayer banner in her school. Jessica went to several school subcommittee meetings of the School Committee of the City of Cranston to complain about an eight-foot-tall prayer mural titled "A School Prayer." It begins with "Our Heavenly Father" and ends with "Amen." She joined parents who wanted the banner removed from the school auditorium. School officials insisted that it was not a prayer, but simply a historical document that the class of 1963 presented to the school.

At the last meeting of the full committee, members voted to keep the prayer. Afterward, Jessica became a plaintiff in a lawsuit filed by her father Mark Ahlquist on her behalf and with the assistance of the ACLU. The suit demanded that the prayer be removed. "In school the next day, I went into homeroom and people were already talking about it," Jessica reported. "They were saying that I was 'mad, stupid' and things like that, so when we all rose to say the pledge, which I don't say because 'under God' doesn't belong there, people at the appropriate time turned and yelled 'under God!' at me. That was probably the first time that I realized the magnitude of what was happening. People who had never talked to me before were judging me and calling me names, and it was really hurtful, I was really bothered by it. I went home crying that day."[16]

Continued harassment and even physical threats forced Jessica to leave the school, but she continued with the lawsuit. Her attorneys argued in *Ahlquist v. Cranston* (2012) that the prayer banner was a violation of the Constitution. U.S. District Judge Ronald Lagueux agreed, ruling in January 2012 that "the banner should be removed immediately. He also upbraided school officials for holding community meetings about the mural that 'at times resembled a religious revival.' At one meeting, several school officials read from the Bible or declared their faith," according to the *Huffington Post*.[17]

In another case, fifteen-year-old Kalei Wilson also endured harassment as an open atheist. In October 2013 her older brother Ben asked permission to start a chapter of Secular Student Alliance, a national organization of college and high school students, at Pisgah High School in Canton, North Carolina. After Ben left the school, Kalei made repeated requests to permit the club, but the school ignored her—until the Secular Student Alliance, the Freedom from Religion Foundation, and the ACLU of North Carolina reminded school officials that they could be violating the Equal Access Act of 1984. The federal law states that if a public secondary school offers any group activities not related to the curriculum, then that school must allow equal access to other group functions without discrimination in regard to religious, political, or philosophical beliefs.

The school granted Kalei permission to launch the secular club in late February 2014. However, soon afterward she gave up her plan, citing harassment and threats. She received messages from a Christian girl who called her "Satan" and a "dumb c&^t b★&^h!" Kalei's family then posted this message:

> It saddens us to report that due to the numerous threats and the verbal attacks on Kalei along with the vindictive witch-hunt to hurt the reputations of affiliated local groups and our own family, Kalei will not be continuing with the group. . . . We never expected our family and friends to be sought out and demonized. Please know that we recognize the importance of the

club but we can not justify our involvement with the risk of our families safety and well being.[18]

Hemant Mehta at Friendly Atheist's website had this to say about the threats and attacks on Kalei:

> No one—atheists, Christians, anyone—should have to deal with this sort of retaliation from other people because of who they are or what they believe.
> The whole episode is a sad and painful reminder of the formal and informal persecution, intimidation and harassment that atheists, agnostics and other freethinkers often must face.
> It is also a stinging indictment of the hypocrisy, the arrogance, and the cruelty of the Christian community at large. One can only wonder, where were the so-called good Christians while this teen was being threatened and harassed?[19]

Creationism versus Evolution

Creationism versus evolution has a long history in public school controversies. Religious activism is involved in arguments over whether creationism should be taught in public schools along with or instead of evolution. *Evolution* is a basic term for scientific evidence showing how plants and animals—including humans—have evolved over hundreds of thousands of years. It is the basis for the study of biology. Creationism, in general, is a religious belief that humankind and the universe were created by God in six days approximately six thousand years ago, as described in the biblical book of Genesis.

The debates over creationism and evolution are not new. The story of John T. Scopes, a young biology teacher in Tennessee during the 1920s, is probably familiar. Scopes taught his class Charles Darwin's theory of evolution. At the time, Tennessee law banned any teaching that denied divine creation of the world. The state sued Scopes for violating the law. Although Scopes was convicted, the famous attorney Clarence Darrow representing Scopes threatened to take the case to the U.S. Supreme Court. Eventually, the Tennessee Supreme Court reversed the decision of the trial court.

Not all creationists have the same beliefs. Some contend that each of the biblical six days could represent a period of thousands or millions of years. Some creationists believe in scientific creationism or "intelligent design." They argue that creation of the world is so complex that a divine being had to be involved in its origin. But no one identifies who the intelligent designer is.

No matter what the differences are in creationist beliefs, activists try through political action to have their views taught in public schools. In some parts of the United States, creationists have succeeded in getting laws passed in their favor. The Louisiana Science Education Act (LSEA) is one example; it became law in 2008.

The act allows public schools to use supplemental education materials that oppose evolution and other scientific subjects in order to "foster an environment within public elementary and secondary schools that promotes critical thinking skills, logical analysis, and open and objective discussion of scientific theories being studied including, but not limited to, evolution, the origins of life, global warming, and human cloning."[20] In other words, the "origins of life," critics argue, can be construed as teaching creationism in some form by allowing teachers to discuss the subject without being subjected to legal retaliation. The U.S. Supreme Court banned the teaching of creationism in public schools in *Edwards v. Aguillard* (1987).

Zack Kopplin, a college student and political activist, has been speaking out against LSEA ever since 2008 when he was fourteen years old. At the time, he wrote a research paper on the act and criticized the teaching of creationism. "Creationism is not science, and shouldn't be in a public school science class—it's that simple," he told a reporter. "Creationism confuses students about the nature of science." Kopplin is not against discussing creationism in religion classes, but he noted in an interview, "if students don't understand the scientific method, and are taught that creationism is science, they will not be prepared to do work in genuine fields, especially not the biological sciences. We are hurting the chances of our students having jobs in science, and making discoveries that will change the world."[21]

On the Bill Moyers PBS show in March 2013, Kopplin, who at the time was a Rice University history major, explained that he has gone beyond the fight against LSEA to combat school vouchers. He found in his research that creationism is taught in private schools that receive government-funded vouchers paid for with tax money. Kopplin noted that he would

> look up a school and look up its website. And I'd go find a school that said, "Scientists are sinful men." . . . And they rejected . . . theories like the age of the earth and anything else . . . that goes against God's word is an error. . . . I found a school that put in their student handbook that students had to defend creationism against traditional scientific theory. And so these are schools receiving millions in public money (through vouchers).[22]

Kopplin said he has identified "over 300 schools in voucher programs in nine states and Washington, DC, [that] are teaching creationism. We have schools that

In biology classes, students like this teenager study plants and animals.

See This Documentary

Judgment Day: Intelligent Design on Trial is a PBS two-hour documentary that aired on NOVA in 2007 and was released on DVD in 2008. The film describes and depicts how teaching evolution in public schools bitterly divided the community of Dover, Pennsylvania. The turmoil began in 2004 when a Dover High School student painted a mural showing the evolution of humans from ape-like ancestors. Some parents were incensed and complained to school board members. The mural was taken down and destroyed. Board members then set a policy requiring science teachers to read a statement to biology students saying there was another theory of life's origin called intelligent design and that copies of a textbook titled *Of Pandas and People* on intelligent design were available. Science teachers refused to read the statement. As one teacher in the documentary notes, "Saying that you don't believe in evolution is almost saying, for us, well, 'We don't believe that the Civil War ever took place in the United States.'"

A group of eleven parents who were opposed to intelligent design claimed that presenting the theory in a science class was a roundabout way to insert a religious belief—that is, creationism into the classroom. The parents filed a lawsuit in federal court accusing the school board of violating the constitutional separation of church and state. The federal case *Kitzmiller v. Dover School District* (2005) was the first to determine whether intelligent design should be included in science curriculum. The film is based on news clips and interviews with some of the participants and Judge Jones's decision in the case. NOVA sums it up this way:

> During the trial, lawyers for the plaintiffs showed that evolution is one of the best-tested and most thoroughly confirmed theories in the history of science, and that its unresolved questions are normal research problems— the type that arise in any flourishing scientific field.
>
> U.S. District Court Judge John E. Jones III ultimately decided for the plaintiffs, writing in his decision that intelligent design "cannot uncouple itself from its creationist, and thus religious, antecedents." As part of his decision, Judge Jones ordered the Dover school board to pay legal fees and damages, which were eventually set at $1 million.
>
> A verbatim transcript of the documentary is on NOVA's website.[c]

---

call evolution the way of the heathen. And so it's become pretty clear if you create a voucher program, you're just going to be funding creationism through the back door."[23]

Moyer noted that a critic defended creationist teaching and wrote that Kopplin in his activism "is prohibiting others from learning what he doesn't like." To that criticism, Kopplin responded,

> We have a separation of church and state in this country. And creationism is fundamentally religious. And evolution is just science and is not reli-

It Happened to Liesl Darger

In 2013, Liesl won a Youth Activist Scholarship from the ACLU of Utah for her religious freedom advocacy. As a Southern Utah University freshman, Liesl wrote an essay about growing up in an Independent Fundamentalist Mormon polygamous family that included "three moms, one dad and twenty-three brothers and sisters." She explained, "In Utah polygamy is a third degree felony and is an unconventional way of living." While she was growing up, she "had problems . . . outside of the family; being in elementary school having a rock thrown at my head and being called a 'polygamist!' It was so demeaning the way people used it. Even being in high school I had girls writing on social media sites about 'polygamist bitches having sex with their dads.'"

The harassment was discouraging, but she wrote, "I realize that I am who I am and that is never going to change and that I love who I am and my family. I found that those who matter don't mind, and those who mind don't matter. My family and home is a place of love and understanding."

Her parents wrote a book *Love Times Three: Our True Story of a Polygamous Marriage* (2011), published by HarperOne, "so people could look at our life through a different eye," Liesl explained. The publicity following the publication provided an opportunity for Liesl to appear on many TV programs and take part in media interviews to advocate for decriminalizing polygamy for consenting adults. "I have a newfound confidence in who I am and I realize the power I have and the use I can put it to. The voice I have that others do not have." She has been able to initiate conversations "about tolerance and acceptance not only towards polygamy but other misjudged cultures." Her plan as described in the essay is to continue her activism and "find ways to speak out and give a voice to all those who do not fit the mainstream."[d]

gious. The free exercise of religion includes religion and non-religion. So this country is fundamentally secular. And . . . we shouldn't bring in one specific . . . version of Christianity . . . in the public schools and teach it instead of established science.[24]

8

PEACE EFFORTS

....

"This is our cry, this is our prayer, peace in the world."—a plaque on a memorial to
Sadako Sasaki (1943–1955) of Hiroshima, Japan, who died of leukemia brought on
by radiation from the atomic bomb; she was responsible for making the origami
paper crane a peace symbol that many U.S. students create to advocate for peace[1]

Young people involved in peace efforts may be members of historic peace
churches such as the Brethren, Mennonites, and Quakers. Others may join
organizations such as CODEPINK and the Campaign for Nuclear Disarmament
that are part of the antiwar protests or peace movements in the United States. Antiwar and peace activists usually protest specific wars, whereas pacifists advocate
for worldwide peace no matter what the armed conflict. Among such activists are
young people opposed to military recruitment and the possibility of reinstating
conscription—that is, a draft of young men into the military.

Although conscription in the United States ended in 1973, male citizens and
immigrants between the ages of eighteen and twenty-six must register for the
draft in case they are needed for a war. If the draft is reinstated, the registrants
may be called for training and service until the age of thirty-five. So who currently serves in the U.S. military? Volunteers make up all branches—Air Force,
Army, Marine Corps, Navy, and Coast Guard. In spite of a volunteer military,
many Americans say they are tired of war.

Many Wars

Throughout U.S. history, there has been one war after another. Colonists fought
the Revolutionary War (1775–1783) to gain independence from Britain. In 1812,
another war with Great Britain followed. The Civil War (1861–1865) nearly destroyed the country. During the 1800s, other wars were fought to obtain territory
from indigenous people and from Mexico. The United States took part in two
world wars—in World War I from 1917 to 1918 and World War II from 1941 to

1945. From the 1950s onward, Americans also have engaged in wars to establish democracies in various parts of the world such as Korea, Vietnam, Iraq, and Afghanistan.

After the terrorist attack on the World Trade Center in New York City and the Pentagon in Washington, DC, on September 11, 2001, war was on most Americans' minds. Just before the tenth anniversary of that day in 2011, Janet Penn, executive director of Youth LEAD, interviewed some young people involved in the organization's program that inspires youth leaders to act together to address local and global challenges. Here is what Divya, a young Hindu at Mt. Holyoke College in South Hadley, Massachusetts, had to say: "Nine/eleven shattered early on my assumption that the world was always a happy place. I suddenly realized that hatred and violence exist on a grand scale, and that people do die or get hurt as a result of it."[2]

Another Hindu, Aashna at Sharon High School in Massachusetts, declared, "The term 'terrorist' is skewed in our minds because of the media and our upbringing. No matter how much we know and however many dialogues we have with others, they still seem to associate terrorism with Islam."[3]

A Muslim at Mt. Holyoke, Rabya, noted that the anniversary of September 11

represents the change in discourse about the perception of my religion in a negative way. I believe extremists of all religions need to be seen in the same light because they all cause the same pain, terror, and damage to humanity. . . . All terrorists, whether they are right-wing Christian fundamentalists or Muslim extremists, are convinced they are right and that innocent blood spilled for their beliefs is acceptable. We need to differentiate between terrorism and religion and realize that any religion in itself is not to blame, rather the warped sense of ideology that these terrorists have is what needs to be countered by the rest of us.[4]

In 2013, young Muslim women in New York City held a news conference to point out how anti-Muslim sentiment has continued and has affected them. Some carried signs "Youth against Islamophobia." Namia Sulaiman told how she has been searched twice by police at the subway because she was carrying a large backpack. "This made me feel angry, because I am not accepted in a country I call my own. I'm standing here today to make people aware that the issue of Islamophobia is real, and it needs to stop before it destroys us as a community."[5]

Fifteen-year-old Ahlam Almoflihi explained, "People basically look at me different because I wear a scarf. . . It's not fair, it's not right for a whole group of people to be targeted. . . . But it's kind of made me stronger because I know that we have to speak up about it."[6]

Other groups of young people also are speaking out, sometimes on the Internet. "There is no future in war," wrote members of CODEPINK on the Common Dreams website in September 2014. "We, the youth of America, have grown up in war, war, war. War has become the new norm for our generation. But these conflicts—declared by older people but fought and paid for by young people—are robbing us of our future and we're tired of it. We, the youth of America, are taking a stand against war and reclaiming our future." That was the beginning of a manifesto, which states in part,

> We, the youth of the United States of America, oppose war.
> We oppose war not because we don't care about the rest of the world; we oppose war precisely because we do.
> We oppose war not because we don't care about our security; we oppose war precisely because we do.
> We oppose war not because we don't care about our troops; we oppose war precisely because we do.
> We oppose war not because we aren't concerned with our future; we oppose war precisely because we do.[7]

Nevertheless, after the barbaric attacks in the Middle East by the Islamic State of Iraq and Syria (ISIS) in the summer of 2014, U.S. and other nations' planes began bombing ISIS targets. But that was not enough for some U.S. citizens and politicians; they began calling for the United States to send forces to fight the terrorists on the ground. Many Americans believe ISIS is a major threat to the United States, and in late 2014 a majority opposed sending U.S. combat troops to Iraq and Syria. Some protested. A sampling from late 2014:

- On September 16, 2014, antiwar activists with the organization CODEPINK interrupted hearings to protest the U.S. military strategy against ISIS. One woman held up a sign "More War = More Extremism."
- Antiwar protestors blocking an entrance to the White House on September 23, 2014, were arrested as they rallied against U.S. airstrikes on Syria.
- On September 27, 2014, fifty antiwar activists stood along a busy highway in Tampa, Florida, protesting U.S. bombings on Syria. They chanted, "Hands off Syria!" and "No more war!"
- In Denver, Colorado, antiwar activists held a rally on October 1, 2014, at the state capitol; they stretched a huge banner "We Don't Want Another War with Iraq and Syria."
- Twenty antiwar protesters in Manchester, New Hampshire, stood along a major street on October 4, 2014, with signs such as "No U.S. War in Iraq, Syria."

Military men and women who make the ultimate sacrifice in war may be buried in Arlington National Cemetery in Virginia. Since the 1860s more than four hundred thousand people from the United States and eleven other countries have been buried in this cemetery.

- On October 10, 2014, President Barack Obama gave a speech at a Democratic fundraiser in San Francisco, California, where demonstrators protested U.S. air strikes and other war moves, aggression, and military action in Syria and Iraq.

However, the Brookings Institution noted in January 2015, "The reluctance to engage in a ground war against ISIS is predominately felt among Democrats and Independents. . . . 53 percent of Republicans would turn to U.S. troops if air strikes fail."[8] But as weeks passed, a majority of Americans in polls seemed to favor going to war. A CBS News poll in February 2015 found that 57 percent of Americans supported sending U.S. ground troops to fight ISIS.

Civil Disobedience as Protest against War

Acts of civil disobedience have a long history worldwide as well as in the United States, beginning with those who took part in the American Revolution. The term itself was used much later by Henry David Thoreau (1817–1862) of Massachusetts. In one of his many protests against slavery, Thoreau refused to pay poll taxes (levied for the right to vote). When the United States declared war against

Mexico in 1846, Thoreau publicly condemned the U.S. invasion of Mexico as a plot to occupy the territory and expand slavery in the Southwest. That act of defiance inflamed the tax collector, who had a sheriff arrest Thoreau. However, he was released the next day—without his permission, an unknown person had paid his taxes. Later, Thoreau gave a lecture titled "Resistance to Civil Government," which he revised and published in 1849 as "Civil Disobedience."

Since Thoreau's time, activists for many diverse causes such as civil rights, environmental protection, prison reform, suffrage, and world peace have practiced civil disobedience—nonviolent, passive resistance—to call attention to a policy or law considered unjust. Activists declare that the demands of their conscience take precedence over the law. Practitioners often risk being harassed, physically attacked, or jailed for their actions.

One example involved three antiwar activists who have been members of Transform Now Plowshares, a pacifist group. In July 2012, Boertje-Obed, fifty-eight; Walli, sixty-five; and Sister Megan Rice, eighty-four, stealthily cut four fences and entered a Y-12 Nuclear Weapons Complex in Oak Ridge, Tennessee, which includes a warehouse of weapons-grade uranium. According to a news report from Nukewatch, the trio "poured blood on the walls and spray painted 'Woe to an Empire of Blood' and 'The Fruit of Justice Is Peace.' They also chipped a corner of the concrete wall with a small hammer, a symbolic act reflecting the Old Testament prophecy of Isaiah who said, 'They shall beat their swords into plowshares.'" The three were arrested and charged with depredation of property and sabotage. In their court appearance, they pointed out that the United States was violating "the 1970 Nuclear Nonproliferation Treaty (NPT) at the Y-12 plant in Oak Ridge, Tennessee. In testimony at hearings before trial, former U.S. Attorney General Ramsey Clark called the production of nuclear weapons components at Y-12 'unlawful'—and the work there 'a criminal enterprise'—because the NPT obliges the U.S. government to pursue good faith negotiations for the complete elimination of nuclear weapons."[9]

The antinuclear activists were convicted, and in February 2014 Federal District Judge Amul R. Thapar sentenced Boertje-Obed and Walli to five years and two months in prison "plus three years of heavily supervised probation. Sr. Megan Rice . . . was sentenced to 35 months in prison plus three years of probation," according to GlobalResearch.ca.[10] In August 2014, counsel for the defendants appealed their case, claiming government errors and lack of evidence that the three peace activists intended to interfere or obstruct national defense. In March 2015, attorneys for the activists filed a brief with the Sixth U.S. Circuit Court of Appeals in Cincinnati, Ohio. Lawyers argued that "the sabotage charge was government overreach that should not have been applied for the activists' symbolic, nonviolent actions," according to an Associated Press news story. "Trespassing and vandalism do not amount to sabotage," the brief stated.[11] As of May 2015, there was no decision on the appeal.

Some young American peace activists practiced civil disobedience in July 2014 to protest Israel's continued attacks on Gaza. "The activists . . . are putting their bodies on the line in an attempt to draw attention to how the U.S. is implicated in the conflict in the Gaza Strip," wrote Alex Kane in Mondoweiss.net. According to his report, "Actions began on July 16th, when five people were arrested inside the lobby of Boeing's office in Chicago; they were protesting the fact that Boeing has supplied weapons to the Israeli Defense Force. The demonstration, which included members of Jewish Voice for Peace and Chicago Divests, was meant to call attention to the corporation's sale of fighter jets and other equipment to the Israeli army, which the state buys with American taxpayer dollars. They wore white shirts splattered with red—a symbolic image conveying Gaza's mounting death toll."[12]

A similar civil disobedience action took place in Seattle, Washington, by the city's Jewish Voice for Peace. On July 28, 2014, nine activists blocked the entrance to a Boeing office by lying down in a crosswalk and stopping traffic. Forty other protesters joined in a symbolic "die-in" on a nearby sidewalk.

On the same day, July 28, 2014, in New York City, "over 70 American Jews, most of them young, gathered in front of the Conference of Presidents of Major American Jewish Organizations to protest the key Jewish establishment group's support for Israel's attack," Kane reported. "The young protesters . . . [came]

under the banner of If Not Now, When? . . . formed to press Jewish groups into voicing opposition to the Israeli assault." They had requested a meeting with the president of the organization, Malcolm Hoenlein, who refused to see them. Nine members of the group would not leave the lobby of the office and police arrested them.[13]

Other peace activists have practiced civil disobedience to

- protest wars in Afghanistan, Iraq, Syria, and some African countries;
- stop underwater nuclear testing;
- call attention to and protest the use of drones that can cause civilian deaths in war; and
- reveal and publicize secret government documents regarding military actions.

No doubt, as long as there are wars, there will be activists against armed conflict. Some will use civil disobedience tactics to peacefully resist regardless of likely arrest, imprisonment, and possibly death.

Activists Who Refuse to Fight

Peace activists may go beyond protesting the military and totally refuse to take up arms. They apply for conscientious objector (CO) status, a legal exemption from the armed forces because of religious or moral beliefs. Even though currently there is no draft in the United States, COs reject the requirement that males (females are exempt) eighteen to twenty-five must register for the military. Applicants for CO status must object to war in general, not one war in particular.

Throughout U.S. history, COs have been members of historical peace churches such as Brethren, Quakers, some Mennonites, Moravians, and Shakers. Religious objectors also have included people of Catholic, Jewish, and Muslim faiths. In addition, atheists and humanists may claim CO status. Obviously, atheists and humanists do not claim a religious objection; rather they apply because of strong moral objections to war.

In 2007, the U.S. Department of Defense issued a revision of its 1997 directive on CO exemptions to the military, defining religious training/belief as

> belief in an external power or "being" or deeply held moral or ethical belief, to which all else is subordinate or upon which all else is ultimately dependent, and which has the power or force to affect moral well-being. The external power or "being" need not be one that has found expression in either religious or societal traditions. However, it should sincerely occupy

a place of equal or greater value in the life of its possessor. Deeply held moral or ethical beliefs should be valued with the strength and devotion of traditional religious conviction. The term "religious training and/or belief" may include solely moral or ethical beliefs even though the applicant may not characterize these beliefs as "religious" in the traditional sense, or may expressly characterize them as not religious. The term "religious training and/or belief" does not include a belief that rests solely upon considerations of policy, pragmatism, expediency, or political views.[14]

To obtain CO status, an applicant must provide written statements on how he arrived at his beliefs and how his beliefs have influenced his life. He might also ask people to appear before the local draft board to testify on his behalf. The board decides whether to grant or deny a CO classification. According to the Selective Service System,

> Two types of service are available to conscientious objectors, and the type assigned is determined by the individual's specific beliefs. The person who is opposed to any form of military service will be assigned to Alternative Service. . . . The person whose beliefs allow him to serve in the military but in a noncombatant capacity will serve in the Armed Forces but will not be assigned training or duties that include using weapons.

Alternative service can be jobs in conservation, care for the very young or elderly, education, or medical services. Jobs must make a meaningful contribution to the maintenance of the national health, safety, and interest.[15]

Peace Builders

Countless U.S. teenagers and young adults participate in national and international peace efforts sponsored by such organizations as the American Friends Service Committee (AFSC). AFSC youth programs "seek to influence young people and be influenced by them, especially regarding their thinking about key issues of peace and justice. The programs develop youth leadership in order to enhance movements for justice, peace and the empowerment of oppressed peoples as well as build bridges of understanding and active alliances among young people from diverse backgrounds and perspectives," says AFSC's website.[16]

Hands of Peace (HoP) is especially designed for Israeli, Palestinian, and American teens who get together for eighteen-day summer programs in the Chicago area and in San Diego. HoP was founded in 2002 by three Chicago-area moms—one Christian, one Jew, and one Muslim. Christian and Muslim Palestinians and Jewish and Arab Israelis stay in local homes and, along with American teens, they take part in dialogue sessions held each day. According to the United Church of Christ in Glenview, Illinois, which hosted teens from Palestine and Israel in 2008, the young people take part in "team-building exercises and cultural activities. During the rest of the year, Middle East teens and U.S. participants gather for follow-up meetings and projects."[17]

"Hands of Peace changed me," reported Itamar, a Jewish student from Israel. "I feel like it showed me that it isn't 'we' versus 'them.' They are humans on the other side, and we should want peace."[18]

"At times it was hard to hear about how both sides are struggling and suffering, but by the end of our two weeks together we made a lot of progress and lifelong friendships," said Diane, a Christian participant. "I learned so much, not only about the conflict and these two groups, but also about myself."[19]

Yaseen, a West Bank Palestinian, described an important part of the program: "Hands of Peace allowed me to meet new people from a different nation, and to explain to them how we struggle in the situation that we live in. In addition to that, I made such wonderful friends there in Chicago. That is why it was the best experience I had in my life that I will never forget."[20]

Hands of Peace has continued its summer camp in the Chicago suburban area, and according to the *Chicago Tribune*, "North Shore teenagers with Arab, Jewish and Christian backgrounds" have taken part as "councilors of sorts." Nour Abbelmonem is "a Northbrook teenager who has been involved in the Hands of Peace program since 2010." When interviewed in 2014 about the upcoming summer program, Nour said, "The first couple of days are usually the roughest because everybody is disagreeing because they're not that comfortable with each other. . . . One of the most valuable parts of the dialogue is to disagree, to hear and listen to the other side."[21]

Other international organizations with youth programs include Global Peace Youth Corps, which educates young people between the ages of eighteen and thirty-five to become future leaders who are activists for worldwide peace.[22] Peace Jam is a program in which Nobel Peace Prize laureates work personally with youth to inspire a new generation of leaders and to complete a *Global Call to Action* project that addresses peace and service issues in their communities.[23] Seeds of Peace helps young people develop skills to advance peace in diverse nations worldwide.[24]

Seeds of Peace holds a three-week summer camp in Maine each year for teenagers from conflict areas around the world. In 2014, about 180 teens arrived "from the United States, Egypt, Jordan, Afghanistan, Pakistan and India." They also came "from warring neighbors Israel and Palestine," the *Bangor Daily News* reported. Seventeen-year-old Ophir (for security reasons no last names were given) from Israel said, "Sometimes you're yelled at. . . . It's not really comfortable or fun.

But they [facilitators] work on how to separate the person from his or her point of view. . . . I want to emphasize that this is a really long process."[25]

Another teen, Kahatib, decided to participate in the camp because he "wanted to meet that enemy that I always run away from. . . . I wanted to tell him about my suffering. I consider myself as on the weak side as a Palestinian. I became the strong side; my voice was heard."[26]

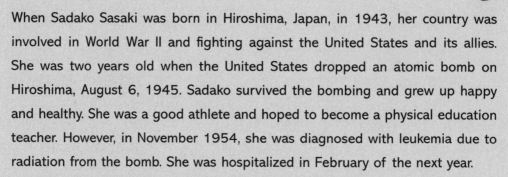

A Post from the Past

A Peace Symbol

When Sadako Sasaki was born in Hiroshima, Japan, in 1943, her country was involved in World War II and fighting against the United States and its allies. She was two years old when the United States dropped an atomic bomb on Hiroshima, August 6, 1945. Sadako survived the bombing and grew up happy and healthy. She was a good athlete and hoped to become a physical education teacher. However, in November 1954, she was diagnosed with leukemia due to radiation from the bomb. She was hospitalized in February of the next year.

While in the hospital, a friend brought Sadako an origami paper crane. Origami is a Japanese paper folding art—*ori* (to fold) and *kami* (paper) combined is origami. Origami designs include animals, fish, birds, and toys. The crane is a sign of good health, and Sadako hoped that by folding paper cranes she would get well again. Her goal was to fold one thousand cranes, but she died October 25, 1955, before she could reach that number. Her classmates helped make more cranes and one thousand were buried with her. In addition, children in her school collected funds for a memorial to Sadako, which was erected in Hiroshima Peace Park in 1958. It is a tall structure and on top is a replica of Sadako with arms outstretched and holding a giant crane. A plaque at the bottom, created by school children, says, "This is our cry, this is our prayer, peace in the world." Since then the origami paper crane has become a symbol representing peace. Many U.S. students make the paper cranes to give as gifts and to advocate for a peaceful world. Instructions for folding are on several websites.

A white dove, often holding an olive branch, has long been a symbol of peace for many people in diverse cultures from early Egyptians to present-day Americans. Another well-known peace symbol is the V-sign as shown by the teenage boy on the right.

A Way of Peace

Her name at birth was Mildred Norman (1908–1981), but she called herself, and others knew her as Peace Pilgrim. In 1952, she decided to make a twenty-five-thousand-mile walk across the United States in a pilgrimage for peace. She began on January 1, 1953, in Pasadena, California, at the Tournament of Roses Parade. At the start of this walk she vowed to be a wanderer until people learned the way of peace. She carried her message, which simply said, "This is the way of peace—overcome evil with good, and falsehood with truth, and hatred with love."[a] Her only possessions were the clothes on her back and the few items she carried in the pockets of her blue tunic: a comb, a folding toothbrush, a ballpoint pen. Her tunic read "PEACE PILGRIM" on the front and "Walking Coast to Coast for Peace" on the back. She had no organizational backing and carried no money. She did not ask for food or shelter, but accepted it when offered. When no one took her in, she slept in wheat fields, haystacks, cemeteries, and drainage ditches; under bridges; and by roadsides. Although many people thought she subjected herself to dangerous situations, she believed they were tests of her faith and her way of peace. She was arrested twice for vagrancy, but behind bars she found a receptive audience for her philosophy and songs.

Peace Pilgrim reached her twenty-five-thousand-mile goal in 1964. After that, she crossed the United States again—seven times. Although she continued to walk daily, she was often asked to speak to various groups. As her speaking schedule increased, Peace Pilgrim began to accept rides to get from one engagement to the next. And so it was—in a somewhat ironic twist of fate—that on July 7, 1981, while traveling near Knox, Indiana, Peace Pilgrim was killed in an auto accident. Friends of Peace Pilgrim compiled a collection of her writings and recorded words in *Peace Pilgrim: Her Life and Work in Her Own Words*, published by Ocean Tree Books in 1982; it can be accessed on the website PeacePilgrim.org.

It Happened to Rachel Corrie (1979–2003)

Rachel Corrie was born in Olympia, Washington, the youngest child of Craig, an insurance executive, and Cindy, an accomplished flutist. She had an older brother and younger sister. When Rachel was seven years old, an exchange student from Japan lived with the Corries; later when Rachel was at Capital High School, exchange students from other countries shared their home. After a visit from a Russian student, Rachel went to Russia in 1995 as an exchange student herself.

Rachel graduated from high school in 1997 and attended Evergreen State College in Olympia. She left college for a year to be a volunteer in the Washington State Conservation Corps and a volunteer for a crisis center and a mental health program. In 2001, she joined the Olympia Movement for Justice and

Peace (OMJP), which formed after terrorists' planes crashed into the World Trade Center in New York City and the Pentagon on September 11, 2001. OMJP hoped to avoid violent U.S. retaliation and to seek peace and justice.

In addition, Rachel was active in other peace groups and was known as a behind-the-scenes organizer. But she had "misgivings" about spending time in these activities when, as she put it, "people were offering themselves as human shields in Palestine."[b]

As a member of various peace groups in Olympia, Rachel began to focus on the conflict between Israel and Palestine in the Middle East. She learned about the International Solidarity Movement (ISM), founded in 2001 by Palestinian and Israeli activists who use nonviolent, direct-action methods to resist military occupation of Palestine. Rachel Corrie left the United States to join ISM volunteers in January 2003 and learned how to be a nonviolent protester in Gaza.

On March 16, 2003, Rachel Corrie was standing as a human shield in front of the home of her friends Samir Nasrallah, his brother Khaled Nasrallah, and their wives and children. Rachel was nonviolently trying to prevent bulldozers from destroying the Nasrallah home, which was occupied by the family. A large bulldozer with two soldiers in the cab came toward the home in the late afternoon. Rachel was wearing an orange fluorescent jacket as she tried to ward off the bulldozer. According to multiple reports, she tried to climb up on the pile of dirt to get the soldiers' attention, but she fell and the bulldozer drove over her and then backed up. Her friends ran to help her, but by the time an ambulance arrived, Rachel was dead.

The Israeli military claimed that Rachel's death was an accident and that she fell and hit her head. The bulldozer operators insist they did not see her. Eyewitnesses to the incident said otherwise.

Reaction to Rachel's death was widespread and diverse. Rachel's parents sent her email letters from Gaza to the *Olympian* and other U.S. newspapers and the British newspaper the *Guardian*. The emails were the basis for a one-person play titled *My Name Is Rachel Corrie* (2005) and also appeared in book form as *Let Me Stand Alone* (2008).

The play and book have been criticized by numerous members of the Jewish community as well as by the organization StandWithUs, which advocates for Israel. For example, Roberta Seid, education director of StandWithUs, was highly critical of Rachel Corrie's journal in an article she wrote for *Commentary* magazine:

> There is not a word in the journals about the terrorist campaign unleashed on Israel in September 2000, not a word that reveals that Gaza, especially Rafah (where Corrie stayed) was a hotbed of terrorism and arms smuggling. She apparently never watched the videos of suicide bombers' last statements, or questioned the increasing radicalization of Palestinian society. Rachel never mentions the Palestinian Authority or Yasser Arafat, and gives no inkling of Gaza as a clan-based society with competing clans vying for power. There is no sense that she tried to understand or was even aware of the society in which she now lived.[c]

Other critics have called Rachel an accomplice of terrorists and charge that her published journal and the play based on the journal entries are anti-Israeli propaganda that promotes hatred for Israel. Critics argue that Rachel was misguided and, as one journalist claimed, she "was in Gaza with a group of anarchists to lend aid to Hamas terrorists in the region and to interfere with the Israeli military."[d] Jonathan S. Tobin wrote in a 2012 issue of *Commentary*,

> The structures that she [Corrie] was attempting to protect . . . were fronts for tunnels along the border between Egypt and Gaza through which munitions and explosives intended to kill innocent Israelis were being smuggled. Even more to the point, the idea that Corrie was in Gaza to promote peace is a myth. The purpose of the International Solidarity Movement's activities in Gaza was to shield Hamas and Fatah terrorists and to prevent the Israel Defense Forces from carrying out measures intended to stop the flow of arms and terrorist activity.[e]

Even as Rachel's critics and supporters debate, her parents and activists have established the Rachel Corrie Foundation for Peace and Justice in Olympia,

Washington. The foundation supports grassroots efforts for peace and justice. Craig and Cindy Corrie also filed a civil lawsuit in Israel against the Israel Ministry of Defense. The court found in 2012 that Rachel Corrie's death was a regrettable accident but that she had deliberately put herself in harm's way to protect terrorists, and the state of Israel was not responsible. The court rejected the lawsuit. Rachel's parents appealed and the Israeli Supreme Court heard the case in May 2014. In February 2015, the Supreme Court of Israel dismissed the appeal.

"Seeds provides hope for the rest of the world when there is absolutely no hope," teenager Valerie of Chicago declared. "If you say that's just how it is, it's going to become a reality. The only way to make it not a reality is to not accept that."[27]

NBC News also reported on the Seeds of Peace summer camp in Maine. One camper, Salma from Gaza, told Andrea Mitchell, "It's so complicated for me and confusing, because I'm here having fun, laughing, while the children in Gaza are dying." Seventeen-year-old Yoran said, "People think it's not the right time to talk about peace. We say the opposite, this is exactly the right time."[28]

HATE GROUPS AND ANTI-HATE ACTIONS

"Do we want to stagnate our community with hate and build a foundation on hate or do we want to build one on love?"—anti-hate protestor in Kansas City, Missouri, commenting in 2013 about white supremacist demonstrations[1]

Every week, the American news media publish or broadcast hundreds of stories about people who demonstrate their dislike, intolerance, and hate for others whose views, cultures, or skin color differ from theirs. Sometimes counter stories appear about activists attempting to combat intolerance and hate. Like other types of activist events, anti-hate campaigns are varied. Actions depend on the situation and whether a hate crime has been committed. The United States Department of Justice says a hate crime

> is the violence of intolerance and bigotry, intended to hurt and intimidate someone because of their race, ethnicity, national origin, religious, sexual orientation, or disability. The purveyors of hate use explosives, arson, weapons, vandalism, physical violence, and verbal threats of violence to instill fear in their victims, leaving them vulnerable to more attacks and feeling alienated, helpless, suspicious and fearful.[2]

According to a U.S. Bureau of Justice Statistics (BJS) report issued in 2013, between 2007 and 2011, an average of 259,700 hate crimes against people aged twelve or older occurred each year in the United States. The BJS noted,

> The majority of hate crime victimizations were motivated by racial or ethnic bias. However, the percentage of hate crime motivated by racial bias dropped slightly, from 63 percent in 2003–06 to 54 percent in 2007–11. The percentage of hate crimes motivated by religious bias more than doubled across the two periods, from 10 percent to 21 percent. About 92

> ### Hate Groups
>
> ● On its website and in its publications, the Southern Poverty Law Center (SPLC) describes how it monitors hate groups in the United States and informs law enforcement agencies, the media, and the public about hate activities. In 2014 SPLC counted 784 active hate groups in the United States. Its list of hate groups was broken down by state with California leading the pack with fifty-seven, Florida with fifty, and Georgia with twenty-eight. Names of the groups included neo-Nazis, Klansmen, white nationalists, neo-Confederates, racist skinheads, black separatists, border vigilantes, and others. Added to the number were so-called patriot groups, including armed militias, who are extremely antigovernment and believe that the U.S. government is taking away individual rights and conspiring to establish a one-world socialist regime.[a]

percent of all hate crimes in 2007–11 were violent victimizations, up from 84 percent from 2003–06. Violent hate crimes accounted for a higher percentage of all nonfatal violent crimes in the U.S. in 2007–11 (4 percent) than in 2003–06 (3 percent).[3]

Protesting Hate

Counteracting hate takes many forms—protests, marches, sit-ins, forums, Internet, and other media messages. In some cases, a few activists can inspire others such as student groups that hosted a Speak Up Against Hate forum in September 2013 on the University of Michigan campus in Ann Arbor. The Sikh Student Association along with the Muslim Student Association, Hindu Student Council, and the South Asian American Network hosted the event, in part to remember the attack on a Sikh temple in Oak Creek, Wisconsin, on August 5, 2012. On that day neo-Nazi Wade Michael Page gunned down worshipers, leaving six people dead and five wounded. Afterward, people of all faiths joined the Sikh community for vigils to remember those who died.

The 2013 forum was set up "to allow students to share their experiences and propose solutions to hate crimes." Nine student speakers described how they had dealt with discrimination and hate. Angubeen Khan, a junior at the university, explained that "one of the great things about these events [is] that we get to meet people who are going through similar experiences."[4]

This woman is an example of someone aggressively pointing out the target of her hatred.

In November 2013, protestors in Kansas City, Missouri, also gathered to face off against white supremacists. The protestors and supremacists were lined up along opposite sides of a downtown street, with police in between. The two groups "spent hours expressing their thoughts and beliefs in many different ways, and each side's message was loud and clear," Melissa Stern reported for Fox News. A white supremacist expressed his view: "If you don't drive them [nonwhites] out of our nation, they will turn our children against our God. . . . I think everyone should go back to their homeland."[5]

One anti-hate protestor asked rhetorically, "Do we want to stagnate our community with hate and build a foundation on hate or do we want to build one on love?" When the groups dispersed, none of the supremacists had changed their minds, but as one of the anti-hate protestors commented, "We're here to say that we don't tolerate hate in our city."[6]

In June 2014, a group of African American students and civil-rights activists staged protests against the United Klans of America (UKA). Members were distributing white-power flyers in Anniston and Calhoun County, Alabama. One section of the flyer stated that the UKA wanted to "help secure future for white children, and that the beauty of the white Arian woman must not perish from this earth." Ed Moore III, a senior at Jacksonville State University, declared that the UKA was not welcome in Anniston and Calhoun County. On ABC News, Moore further made it clear to the UKA, "There are plenty of garbage cans throughout the county for you to dispose of your trash, and it does not belong on the yards of citizens. Your power, whatever little that you have remaining, is quickly fading away. Your missions are hateful, insensitive, and divisive, and in the year 2014 the best way to describe you is sad." According to ABC News, the city council of Anniston, which is the Calhoun County seat, "passed a resolution calling on those who distributed the flyers to cease and desist."[7]

At Emory University in Atlanta, Georgia, about two hundred students, faculty, and staff gathered in October 2014 outside the administration building for a Teach-In Against Hate. The event was a "response to vandalism at Emory's Alpha Epsilon Pi (AEPi) fraternity. . . . Images of swastikas [were] spray painted onto the exterior walls of the historically Jewish fraternity's house," the university newspaper reported. After the gathering, the president of AEPi, Jack Kuhr, pointed out that Emory's president publicly condemned the vandalism and that numerous groups expressed their concern and support for the fraternity. Kuhr noted that he was "grateful it's now given our community a platform to address previously ignored acts of hate and to embark on a new path of a more tolerant Emory." As Andra Gillespie, associate professor of political science, put it, "I'm African American and very, very, very Christian. . . . I was not directly impacted by the swastikas on the AEPi house—or so you think. And that's the reason why I'm here—a hate crime doesn't have to affect me personally for it to affect me. You don't have to be Jewish to recognize that what was done to the AEPi house and to its members was wrong, [you] don't have to be directly impacted by hate to speak out against it."[8]

In 2015, another fraternity gained attention for hateful actions. This time fraternity members of a Sigma Alpha Epsilon (SAE) chapter at the University of Oklahoma were filmed on a bus as they joined in an ugly racist chant; the words included a liberal use of the "N-word" and an assurance that a black man would be lynched if he tried to join the fraternity. The film was posted on social media and quickly created demonstrations of disgust across the nation. As a result, the national office of SAE shut down the chapter and the university's president evicted SAE members from its fraternity house. The university also expelled two fraternity members who were shown leading the racist chant.

Even before the Oklahoma debacle, other universities also have disciplined SAE chapter members for taking part in the same SAE chant or other racist incidents. According to an article by Jamelle Bowie in *Slate* magazine,

In 2013, officials at Washington University in St. Louis suspended a chapter after pledges sang racial slurs at black students as part of a rush event, and last November [2014], the University of Arizona suspended its chapter after members attacked Alpha Epsilon Pi, a Jewish fraternity. . . . [In December 2014], a chapter at Clemson University in South Carolina suspended its activities after members hosted a "Cripmas" party where they dressed in gang costumes and mimicked black stereotypes.

In fairness, these acts aren't unique to Sigma Alpha Epsilon or schools in the South. "This behavior is endemic throughout the country," says Nolan Cabrera, an assistant professor of higher education at the University of Arizona, in an interview with the *Chronicle of Higher Education.* "This is something that occurs on a very, very regular basis. They just happened to have the bad foresight to have it recorded and then uploaded on the Internet."[9]

When Teens Take Action

Each year the Maltz Museum of Jewish Heritage in Beachwood, Ohio, conducts a Stop the Hate: Youth Speak Out essay and scholarship contest for students from grades six to twelve in northeast Ohio. Students submit five-hundred-word essays about discriminatory acts they have personally experienced or witnessed and creative ways they can help end discrimination and indifference in their communities. Winning essays for the 2013–2014 school year were published in March 2014. One of the finalists who received an honorable mention award of five hundred dollars was Madison Jackson of Salon High School. In part, she wrote,

> I was in 2nd grade, at a public school assembly, when my classmate said he hated me because I was Jewish. That was the first time I experienced the harsh realities of discrimination, and realized life was not an easy game of chutes and ladders. At that moment, I felt the pain that anti-Semitism inflicts on people and the fear of being left out because of my religion. . . .
>
> Being only 7, I was too young to take action. However, my mom wrote an editorial in the newspaper, expressing her sadness and taking a stance against discrimination. As I grew older, I wanted to teach others what it meant to be tolerant. I realized the boy in my 2nd grade class hated Jews because this is what his parents taught him. Perhaps they taught him this because they knew little about Jews. It was time for me to take action, educate others, and stop the hate.[10]

Madison became a mentor for Create a Safe School, teaching fifth graders about bullying and discrimination and how "students can prevent similar situations like the one I experienced in 2nd grade. If parents can't teach their kids, maybe kids can teach their parents." She concluded, "I'm not forgetting what that boy in 2nd grade said to me. I'll always remember it—not to hold a grudge, but to motivate me to take action and to get involved like I've done already, in order to stop the hate."[11]

Teenager Treshawn Abram of Omaha, Nebraska, has taken another type of action. He has been beaten and harassed because of the color of his skin. In February 2014, he told a reporter for KMTV news that one day as he was leaving school, "I was jumped by a group of gentlemen." He added that he does not use terms like *thugs*, but instead calls "everyone a gentleman or lady because no matter how you come off, you can always change." In addition to being a victim of hate violence, two of his uncles were killed, and it was common to hear gunfire outside his home. He could have resorted to some type of hateful revenge, but he decided to take a different path. He wrote a letter to the Omaha police, who posted it on the Facebook page of the Omaha Police Officers Association. In part, the letter stated,

> As a 16-year-old "black teen" and the youth director at New Covenant Church of God in Christ . . . sometimes I am embarrassed to go places because of my race.
>
> I believe that the good citizens—like me—should have more programs and activities available in which black people could come and enjoy themselves while not being afraid of violence or dying. . . .
>
> If some black people hate being talked about, in my opinion, they should put the guns and drama away and not give others something to talk about.
>
> Our police chief is busy trying to get the crime rate down.
>
> He should focus on the poverty stricken areas and the neighborhoods where police only come to when they are called. . . .
>
> If we get no help from our city officials, then we will have nothing.
>
> If anything, the police or other citizens could just go door to door, talking to residents to share safety tips or just simply reach out to ensure they have a presence!
>
> I'm tired of having fear while simply walking outside my own door step.
>
> I shouldn't have to carry tasers, batons or mace for my own personal protection!
>
> I'm sick of it!
>
> It's time for a change.[12]

Whether any change in Omaha will happen in the future is uncertain. But at least Treshawn expressed his opinion even though he was at risk of being harassed or attacked again.

Fighting Hate through National Organizations

Along with school and civic groups, numerous national organizations sponsor youth programs to diminish hate. Some examples:

- American-Arab Anti-Discrimination Committee—at its regional office in Michigan, a "Youth for Civil Rights campaign enlightens Arab-American youth about civil rights and inspires them to be valuable advocates of tolerance, coexistence, and peace."[13] The organization has created the Cyber Civil Rights Monitor. The program supports victims of online harassment . . . [and] provides guidance, education, and advocacy for all victims of cyberbullying, regardless of age, ethnicity or religion.[14]
- American Civil Liberties Union has numerous offices. The New York Civil Liberties Union fights in court to defend people who have been bullied or are the victims of hate mail or other cyber harassment. It also campaigns to protect students from overly aggressive school policing and military recruitment practices as well as programs that "transform youth into activists and advocates for their own rights and liberties."[15]
- Asian American Legal Defense and Education Fund helps Asian Americans of all ages who have experienced discrimination or who are victims of hate crimes.
- Anti-Defamation League sends "student leaders to Washington, DC, to attend the annual National Youth Leadership Mission. Beginning at the United States Holocaust Memorial Museum, the delegates spend three-and-a-half days studying the consequences of hatred and discrimination. They return to their regions committed to making a difference in their schools, neighborhoods and homes."[16]
- Beyond Differences sponsors a No One Eats Alone program for middle and high school students to encourage inclusiveness, kindness, and spreading love not hate.
- Campus Pride is a national organization for student leaders and campus groups who work to prevent hate attacks against LGBT students and create a safer college environment.
- National Conference for Community and Justice has numerous projects for students who work to prevent actions prompted by hate, such as Bridges, an antibullying and "prejudice reduction program for middle and high

The Hate Crimes Prevention Project

In New York City, high school students take part in a citywide Hate Crimes Prevention Project, which holds an annual art competition. It is a multicultural project and competition whose goals are to spread awareness and use art to advocate for hate crimes prevention. In 2014, the project was sponsored by the Organization of Chinese Americans, Chinatown Youth Initiatives, and Global Kids. Teenagers not only participate as contestants but also are part of the project staff. Together they emphasize racial harmony, share diverse beliefs, raise awareness of hate crimes, and advocate for constructive social change.

school students," and the Youth Action Coalition, which is "run by, and made up of, young people under the age of 24 to increase knowledge and develop action around social justice issues."[17]

- Partners Against Hate has a Youth Against Hate program that focuses on reducing prejudice, harassment, and violence in schools.
- Sikh Coalition sponsors a Junior Sikh Coalition that trains youth leaders to work for equality and justice and to reduce hate.
- Southern Poverty Law Center is dedicated to fighting bigotry and hate through a variety of programs and publications.

Protecting the Homeless from Hate

For about a decade, activists against hate have advocated for laws to prevent attacks against homeless people in the United States. The National Coalition for the Homeless (NCH) reported in 2013 that between 1999 and 2013, there were "1,437 acts of violence against homeless individuals. . . . These crimes are believed to have been motivated by the perpetrators' biases against homeless individuals or by their ability to target homeless people with relative ease."[18]

The NCH "identified 109 people without homes who were directly involved in attacks [in 2013] because of their housing status. Of the 109 victims, 91 suffered non-fatal injuries, while 18 lost their lives." The NCH also reported that "attacks committed against individuals experiencing homelessness in 2013 occurred across 26 states and Puerto Rico. An astonishing 30 percent of the attacks took place in California and another 12 percent of the incidences were in Florida. These two states have consistently seen high rates of violence and abuse towards their homeless populations."[19]

From 1999 to 2013, NCH "recorded over 500 attacks collectively across these two states, where homeless people tend to be more visible." The NCH explained, "Only attacks perpetrated by housed individuals against un-housed individuals were evaluated. Crimes committed by homeless people against other homeless persons were excluded from this report."[20]

"Housed" teenagers and adolescents have been responsible for some deaths. A few examples: In January 2006, teenagers in Fort Lauderdale, Florida, beat a homeless man to death, and in July 2014, a twelve-year-old shot and killed a homeless man in Jacksonville, Florida. That same month three teenagers in Albuquerque, New Mexico, beat two homeless Navajo men so badly that their dead bodies were unrecognizable. "Police and prosecutors said one of the boys told investigators the trio had been targeting homeless people around Albuquerque for about a year," according to an Associated Press report on HuffingtonPost.com.[21]

Young activists may be involved in programs to help the homeless who have been victims of hate crimes.

What Do You Think?

According to the National Coalition for the Homeless, as of late 2014, thirty-three cities had passed laws making it illegal to feed homeless people on public property. In Fort Lauderdale, Florida, for example, a ninety-year-old man was arrested twice for giving food to homeless individuals on the street. A Fort Lauderdale ordinance forbids public meal-sharing because of health and safety risks. Proponents of the law say it is a way to discourage activists from feeding people living in public places. Other cities such as Dallas, Texas; Los Angeles, California; and Phoenix, Arizona, have similar restrictions. Supporters contend that the laws motivate homeless people to use facilities established for feeding and housing them. In addition, proponents argue that feeding people in parks and similar public spaces creates litter as well as unsanitary food operations. What do you think about such laws?

As a result of such horrific examples, seven states—Alaska, California, Florida, Maine, Maryland, Rhode Island, and Washington—have passed "homeless hate laws" as of late 2014. The laws state that attacks against the homeless are hate crimes and are felonies.

Kicking Hate out of Town

Not in Our Town (NIOT) is a slogan and a movement that began in 1995. That year, the Public Broadcasting Service (PBS) aired a special that depicted a project called Not in Our Town in Billings, Montana. The project was a response to racist and anti-Semitic graffiti that were sprayed on hilltop rocks above the city in 1993. City workers painted over the hate messages, but that did not deter the hatemongers. Graffiti appeared again and again and so did racist leaflets.

As the hate messages escalated, the community began to organize to prevent violence and to help victims of attacks. In one instance, someone threw a cement block through the window of a Jewish home where a menorah was displayed. The local newspaper published a picture of the damage and throughout the town, Jews and non-Jews cut out the picture of a menorah and pasted it on their windows. Other hateful actions brought similar responses from citizens—they demonstrated their unity against hate.

After the PBS documentary highlighted Billings's efforts, other cities began unifying against hate, creating a movement across the United States. NIOT has generated Not in Our Schools and Not in Our Halls projects to free schools of hate and intolerance. In some cases, students may wear T-shirts with a slogan on the back "Turn Your Back on Hate" or some other reference to eliminating racism, bigotry, intolerance, and bullying. On college campuses, the effort is called Not on Our Campus.

Threats and Hate Messages Are Not Jokes

Some mischievous teenagers sometimes think it is fun to threaten to bomb a school. It was a way to skip a day of classes. Or they think a fun event is to use social media to pass on crude, menacing, or hateful comments about classmates, fellow employees, or politicians. But in the advent of school shootings and the deaths of numerous students and injuries to government officials in the past few years, it is obvious that threats and hate messages can lead to tragic incidents.

After the Boston Marathon bombing in 2013 when three people were killed and at least 260 injured, "law enforcement agencies [have been] tightening their focus on the social media behavior of U.S. teenagers," wrote Mark Guarino in the *Christian Science Monitor*. The focus is "not just because young people often fit the profile of those who are vulnerable to radicalization, but also because the public appears to be more accepting of monitoring and surveillance aimed at preventing attacks, even at the risk of government overreach."[22] Guarino's May 2013 feature pointed out instances of teenagers arrested for their threats to kill or to physically harm others.

Cameron Dambrosio of Methuen, Massachusetts, was one of the teens. Police arrested Dambrosio in April 2013 after he posted "online videos that show him rapping an original song that police say contained 'disturbing verbiage' and reportedly mentioned the White House and the Boston Marathon bombing. He is charged with communicating terrorist threats, a state felony, and faces a potential 20 years in prison. Bail is set at $1 million."[23]

Other teenagers mentioned in Guarino's article include "Jessica Winslow and Ti'jeanae Harris, two high school girls in Rapids Parish, Louisiana" who were arrested in February 2013 "and charged with 10 counts of terrorism each after they allegedly e-mailed threats to students and faculty 'to see if they could get away with it.'" In January 2013, high school student Alex David Rosario of Armada Village, Michigan, "was charged with domestic terrorism after he allegedly threatened to shoot fellow employees at the Subway shop where he worked. He told police it was a joke."[24] Clearly, his and the others' threats were not viewed as jests.

> ### ❗ Internet Hate
>
> ● People with a hate agenda often use the Internet to spread messages denigrating specific individuals or groups. Internet hate speech can originate from sources around the globe, and governments can do little to stop it, short of banning access to the Internet totally. In the United States, the Supreme Court has ruled that free speech rights guaranteed by the First Amendment to the U.S. Constitution apply to the Internet just as they do to print and broadcast media, or the public square.

In spite of arrests to prevent threatening or hateful messages, many legal issues arise. As is well known, the First Amendment of the U.S. Constitution protects speech, unless it is a threat to intimidate, injure, or kill someone. For example, when the Westboro Baptist Church members spew their anti-LGBT messages, police do not arrest them. As repugnant as their signs, banners, and website are, they do not necessarily constitute a crime, because they are protected by the right to free speech in the public square.

Joining and Leaving Hate Groups

Hate groups regularly seek new members, and they frequently look for teenagers, especially those who appear easy to impress and recruit. Prime targets are school dropouts, the unemployed, and those who fear change. These teens may be angry and want to blame someone for whatever is making their lives miserable. Lonely youth are also vulnerable for recruitment; being part of a group eases loneliness and isolation.

Recruiters suggest to potential members that they will be part of a social club or political action group. In some cases they may entice young people with music, videos, invitations on social media, or offers of T-shirts and badges. To keep members involved, hate groups conduct training camps and hold frequent rallies to maintain their racist and bigoted beliefs. Members succumb to hate propaganda, believing it to be true and worthy of support. Some never leave a group; others become disillusioned and decide that they have nothing to fear from people different from themselves.

Arno Michaels, a former racist skinhead and leader of a "hate metal" band called Centurion, explained to the *Wisconsin Gazette* why he could no longer be part of a hate group. In a 2010 interview Michaels recalled,

In 1994 another comrade was murdered in a street fight. The thought hit me that death or prison could take me from my daughter. After seven years of involvement I started to distance myself from the movement. Without constant reinforcement, the hate began to fade. The more I allowed myself contact with people of forbidden cultures, the better it felt to let go. As I discovered how much more fun life was, I actually felt like a hedonist! Being partial to extremes, I wallowed in the polar shift from hate to love. I was embraced by an incredibly diverse group of loving and forgiving friends.[25]

Michaels also admitted that he had "hurt many innocent people" with his "brutal music designed to incite atrocity." He noted that his band's music on more than twenty thousand CDs infects people with hate and is "still popular with hate groups today."[26]

Another former skinhead is Frank Meeink. His *Autobiography of a Recovering Skinhead: The Frank Meeink Story as Told to Jody M. Roy* was published in paperback by Hawthorne Books in 2010. When Meeink was a teenager, he "was one of the most well-known skinhead gang members in the country. He had his own public access talk show called *The Reich*, he appeared on *Nightline* and other media outlets as a spokesman for neo-Nazi topics, and he regularly recruited members of his South Philadelphia neighborhood to join his skinhead gang," according to a broadcast and interview with Dave Davies on National Public Radio (NPR).[27]

In Meeink's neighborhood, people were "very proud of being Irish. Proud of being working class. And it was a tough neighborhood," Meeink said. "A lot of drugs and alcohol were really bad in our neighborhood." He explained how he became a skinhead during a summer that he spent with his cousin in Lancaster, Pennsylvania:

My cousin . . . was very into punk rock, very into skateboarding. And I couldn't wait to get up there that summer and live there all summer. . . . So I get up there, and he's not a skateboarder anymore. He's not a punk rocker anymore. He's a skinhead. And in his room, there's a swastika flag and stories about Adolf Hitler and stories about skinheads. . . . And I knew of skinheads, but I didn't know of their beliefs or anything yet. And he kind of introduces me to it. He says, "You know, this is what it is." And now every night, all these other skinheads would come over his house and come drinking and listening to music. And they'd always give me a couple beers. I was the young kid to the group. You know, they're all 15-, 16-, 17-year-old guys who are cool to me. And they gave me a beer, and they start talking "multiracial society will never work."[28]

Off the Bookshelf

Jennifer Brown's 2009 novel *Hate List* (Little, Brown) seems to have an eerie connection to mass murders and school shootings such as at Colorado's Columbine High School in 1999. That year, two teenagers killed twelve students and one teacher, and wounded more than twenty others. Tragically, other school shootings have taken place since then. But this story is not about a real event. It is fiction. And it is about the way the term *hate* can be used loosely such as "I hate broccoli" or "I hate school" and then becomes a catalyst for a horrific crime.

As the title indicates, the book focuses in part on a list of things and people that the main character hates. She is Valerie (Val) Leftman, who appears to be a typical teenager and attends Garvin High School, as does her boyfriend, Nick Levil. Nick is from a broken home and has a neglectful mom; he does not fit in well at the school and is a target of bullies. He is an avid reader and especially favors Shakespeare's tragedies.

Both Val and Nick are quiet, smart, introspective, and contemptuous of fellow students whom they think are "assholes" or "bullies" or whatever other negative label they want to assign. These students become part of a list that Val began as a means of expressing her frustration with her parents' marriage problems. Over and over she wrote in her notebook that she hated their fights and possible breakup. When Nick asks her what the notebook is about, Val in a joking manner calls it her hate list. Nick helps her expand the list to things and people they both hate.

As the list grows and the school year comes to a close, Val does not expect any serious consequences from the list in her notebook. It is just a tool for venting her feelings. But Nick acts out his contempt. The first pages of this novel are a newspaper account of Nick shooting and killing or injuring Garvin High School students who are on the Hate List and killing a beloved teacher who attempts to intervene. Val is shot in the thigh as she saves the life of one girl while trying to stop Nick, who kills himself.

This is a long, tragic story and has few light moments, which may turn off some readers. After the school year ends, Val has to face the aftermath of Nick's actions. Because of her list, her guilt feelings are pervasive. All summer and into her senior year, she has multiple visits with a psychiatrist and a school counselor. She slowly heals from her injury and tries to deal with the loss of her boyfriend and what she loved about him. In addition she faces the anger and hatred of former friends. Perhaps the most difficult task: she has to convince her parents to trust her. Val's mom provides off-and-on support, while her dad constantly blames her for her part in the tragedy.

By the end of the book, there is a somewhat implausible about-face for most of the characters. Val heals emotionally and physically, but the reader is left unsure what her future will be.

That was the beginning of Meeink's indoctrination. He became a skinhead like his cousin and teenage friends and convinced other teens to become neo-Nazis. In his autobiography, he explains, "I didn't need to bother recruiting racists. All I did was befriend kids who were pissed off about being picked on day in and day out. I trusted them to pay me back with loyalty. I trusted that I could turn their humiliation into hate. All I had to do was redirect their rage until it came thundering back as racism."[29]

When he was eighteen Meeink was imprisoned "for kidnapping one man and beating another man senseless for several hours. While in prison . . . he was exposed to people from a variety of ethnic and racial backgrounds and started reevaluating his own racist beliefs." Apparently, Meeink began a radical transformation after seeing photos of the 1995 bombing of the federal building in Oklahoma City, which killed 168 people, including twenty children. One of the photos showed a firefighter carrying a dying one-year-old girl away from the rubble. During the NPR interview, Meeink reported,

I felt so evil. Throughout my life, even when I was tattooed up and wanting to be a skinhead, I felt like maybe I was bad on the outside. But I felt good on the inside. . . . And that day it switched. I felt OK on the outside, but I felt so evil inside. I had no one to talk to. . . . So I went to the FBI and . . . I told them my story. I said, "I don't have any information on anybody, but I just need to let you know what it's like." And of course they wanted to listen, because the Oklahoma City bombing had happened.[30]

After hearing Meeink's confession, "the FBI recommended that Meeink contact the Anti-Defamation League (ADL)—which he did." As a result Meeink began working with the ADL, going to schools to talk to students about racial diversity and acceptance, as well as volunteering with an anti-hate program called Harmony through Hockey.[31]

GUN CONTROL VERSUS GUN RIGHTS ACTIVISTS

···

"American people will not let you take away their firearms but if we make it harder to obtain one maybe we cut down on gun violence."—eighteen-year-old Jason Bergman in an essay for StageofLife.com, 2013[1]

For decades a battle—literally and verbally—has been going on between gun control advocates, who campaign for more restrictions on private gun ownership, and gun rights activists, who argue no further laws are needed. Frequently arguments focus on the meaning of the Second Amendment to the U.S. Constitution, which declares, "A well regulated Militia, being necessary to the security of a Free State, the right of the people to keep and bear Arms, shall not be infringed." Gun control advocates say that the Second Amendment only protects the right of a "well regulated militia to possess firearms," while gun rights activists say the clause "keep and bear arms" applies to all adult U.S. citizens.

One Maryland teenager who has been a strong advocate for gun rights is Sarah Merkle. She is a sports shooter and in 2013 was secretary of the Maryland Rifle Club. She appeared before the state legislature to argue against a proposed gun control law. According to a report in the *Huffington Post*, she said, "'Ever since I first learned how to shoot, the issue with gun violence around the nation became clear—guns are not the problem, people are,' Merkle told the lawmakers. 'Purging our society of violence and murder cannot be done by gun control legislation.'" She also said, "Guns are not needed for mass murder, and robbing American citizens over rights to own them won't solve anything."[2]

The teenager's message was widely publicized on social media and by gun rights advocates, but did little to change the minds of Maryland's lawmakers. The legislature enacted the Firearm Safety Act of 2013. A year later ABC News on its affiliated television station WMDT reported the act was "one of the toughest gun control laws in the country." Vincent DeMarco, president of Marylanders to Prevent Gun Violence, said the law "deters people from getting guns who shouldn't get them—it deters people from buying guns for criminals from criminals lying about their name to get a gun—it's a life-saving measure."[3]

Gun control is also the message of teenager KelseyAN, who wrote an essay in 2013 for a StageofLife.com contest:

> We've all heard from Wayne LaPierre, NRA [National Rifle Association] Executive Vice President, that "the only thing that stops a bad guy with a gun is a good guy with a gun." But, the world isn't divided into good people and bad people. We all have good and bad within us. We don't want to have guns present when someone snaps. In a world with guns readily

Sports shooters and hunters often are advocates for gun rights.

available, a person who snaps is able to act on that bad impulse. The gun is the enabler. Take away the catalyst, you take away the result.

Owning a gun is a constitutional right and must be treated with due seriousness. . . . The Second Amendment is a deterrent to a military overthrow of the government; a check on the armed forces. If [we] arm authority everywhere, we enhance government power and undermine the very purpose of the amendment. The Framers intent was to not have a police state.[4]

Gun Violence

Besides Second Amendment arguments, countless discussions occur about gun violence in U.S. society. *Protect Children Not Guns 2013*, a publication of the Children's Defense Fund (CDF), presents numerous statistics—some from 2010, the most recent year for available data—about gun violence in the United States. Here are selected examples from CDF's publication:

- Guns end the lives of seven children and teens every day in America.
- Children and teens in America are seventeen times more likely to die from gun violence than their peers in other high-income countries.
- 2,694 children and teens died from guns in the United States in 2010.
- More than half of youth who committed suicide with a gun obtained the gun from their home, usually a parent's gun.
- Between 1963 and 2010, an estimated 166,500 children and teens died from guns on American soil, while 52,183 U.S. soldiers were killed in action in the Vietnam, Afghanistan, and Iraq wars combined during that same time period.
- Black, Hispanic, American Indian, and Alaska Native children and teens are disproportionately more likely to die or be injured by guns.
- Total gun deaths and injuries in 2010 cost the U.S. $174.1 billion, or 1.15 percent of our gross domestic product.[5]

The nonprofit Gun Violence Archive (GVA) provides "accurate information about gun-related violence in the United States," according to its website. GVA is not an activist group but collects data for researchers, journalists, legislators, and others interested in gun safety. In 2014, GVA said that the number of deaths from guns totaled almost 12.5 million. Of that number, 2,353 teenagers (age twelve to seventeen) were victims of gun deaths or injuries.[6] Over the next year, 2015, the website showed data for each month, including the cities and states where incidents took place.

The National Rifle Association

Anyone with Internet access can find millions of sites for or against the National Rifle Association (NRA). The organization has been around since 1871 when it was founded by two Civil War veterans who were distressed because so many Union soldiers were poor marksmen. In 1872, the NRA bought a parcel of land in Long Island, New York, to develop a rifle range for practice shooting. The range opened in 1873, and closed in 1892, because of "political opposition to the promotion of marksmanship in New York," the NRA's website reports.[a] The rifle range moved to New Jersey in 1892 and since then the NRA has provided services for planning and constructing other facilities for practice shooting in numerous states. The organization also provides marksmanship training, shooting competitions, firearm training, gun safety education, and similar efforts.

NRA's programs include its political campaigns to defend gun rights according to its interpretation of the Second Amendment to the U.S. Constitution. And many people are familiar with the NRA slogan "Guns don't kill people, people kill people." The NRA has spent millions of dollars on ads and lobbyists who have successfully convinced legislators in Congress and voters to oppose gun control laws. As the Center for Public Integrity put it,

> The power of the gun lobby is rooted in multiple factors, among them the pure passion and single-mindedness of many gun owners, the NRA's demonstrated ability to motivate its most fervent members to swarm their elected representatives, and the lobby's ability to get out the vote on election day. But there's little doubt that money, the political power it represents, and the fear of that power and money, which the NRA deftly exploits, have a lot to do with the group's ability to repeatedly control the national debate about guns.[b]

Besides GVA and the CDF, many other national organizations (some with state affiliates) are concerned about gun violence. They include (in no particular order) Mayors Against Illegal Guns, the Brady Campaign to Prevent Gun Violence, the Coalition to Stop Gun Violence, the Law Center to Prevent Gun Violence, Faiths United to Prevent Gun Violence, African American Church Gun Control Coalition, Moms Demand Action for Gun Sense in America, and the Law Center to Prevent Gun Violence.

Gun Laws

Federal, state, and local laws place varied restrictions on gun ownership. The federal Gun Control Act of 1968, for example, prohibits certain groups of people from possessing firearms or ammunition. These include people convicted of felonies and domestic violence, illegal immigrants, illegal drug abusers, and people committed to mental institutions.

The Brady Handgun Violence Prevention Act, which became effective in 1994, was named after James Brady, who was shot in 1981 while protecting President Ronald Reagan from an attempted assassination. The law requires background checks for people buying guns from licensed dealers. A person must be eighteen or older to buy a rifle or shotgun and twenty-one or older to legally buy a handgun. Individuals can get around these laws by buying guns from private sellers who rarely keep records and do not run background checks. Frequently such transactions take place on the Internet or at unregulated gun shows (temporary markets for firearm sales).

The federal Public Safety and Recreational Firearms Use Protection Act, or simply the Assault Weapons Ban, became law in 1994. It prohibits the manufacture and sale of semiautomatic assault weapons with two or more military features and high-capacity ammunition magazines. These firearms are designed to kill people quickly and efficiently. With assault weapons, shooters are able to spray large amounts of ammunition quickly. But the Assault Weapons Ban expired in 2004, and as of early 2015, Congress had not voted to restore it. As a result, assault weapons are legal unless local or state authorities ban them.

There have been numerous attempts to strengthen gun controls at the federal level, but they have failed. In fact, in 2014 the Law Center to Prevent Gun Violence published a list of what federal laws do not do:

- Require background checks on all gun purchasers
- Regulate ammunition sellers or buyers
- Require firearm owners to be licensed or firearms to be registered

- Ban military-style assault weapons or large capacity ammunition magazines
- Require firearm owners to report to law enforcement if their firearms are lost or stolen
- Limit the number of firearms that may be purchased at any one time
- Impose a waiting period before the purchase of a firearm

Because of the lax federal laws, some states have strengthened their gun controls. The state laws include "universal background checks, as well as bans on military style assault weapons and large capacity ammunition magazines, licensing requirements for gun owners, safe storage requirements, ammunition regulations, and laws to prevent access to guns by domestic abusers and the dangerously mentally ill," reports the Law Center.[7]

Speaking Out on Guns and Mass Shootings

In the United States, public demands for more gun controls have occurred numerous times, especially after mass shootings, such as at Colorado's Columbine High School. On April 20, 1999, seventeen-year-old Dylan Klebold and eighteen-year-old Eric Harris killed twelve students and one teacher and wounded more than twenty others at the school. The killers had planned their shooting spree for a year and "dreamed much bigger. The school served as means to a grander end, to terrorize the entire nation by attacking a symbol of American life. Their slaughter was aimed at students and teachers, but it was not motivated by resentment of them in particular. . . . Their vision was to create a nightmare so devastating and apocalyptic that the entire world would shudder at their power," wrote Dave Cullen in *Slate*.[8]

Appeals for more controls accelerated after mass shootings in 2011 and 2012. On January 8, 2011, in a supermarket parking lot in suburban Tucson, Arizona, a man with a handgun equipped with a 33-round magazine shot and killed six people and injured thirteen others. One of the critically injured was U.S. Representative Gabrielle Giffords, who was shot in the head. Bystanders tackled and held the man, identified as Jared Lee Loughner, until police arrived. Federal officials charged Loughner with killing federal government employees and attempting to assassinate a member of Congress.

Giffords underwent emergency surgery and a long rehabilitation process. She resigned from Congress in 2012. Although her right arm is paralyzed and she has some problems with her speech and eyesight, she and her husband, retired U.S. Navy captain Mark Kelly, were able to launch Americans for Responsible Solutions (ARS) in 2013. ARS is a bipartisan group that backs measures for more gun restrictions and increased programs to prevent gun violence.

In Newtown, Connecticut, on December 14, 2012, a massacre of twenty children and six adults at the Sandy Hook Elementary School created a huge public outcry and continues to prompt actions by gun control supporters. Some government officials and many individuals across the United States want teachers or other school personnel to be armed. As teenager EmiliaCristy wrote in a 2013 essay contest for StageofLife.com,

> Many people are flocking to gun shops to purchase "protection" for them- selves. Fighting fire with fire? When has that ever resulted in peace, when has that ever helped a single human-being? The answer to this tragedy is inexistent [*sic*]. . . . How can anyone begin to comprehend the malevolent, sadistic thoughts of a person who willingly inflicts pain, suffering, and death to innocent children and their families. It is incomprehensible. If the country arms itself and allows teachers to have guns in their classrooms, what effect will that encouragement of violence have on the young people of the United States. I have been taught since elementary not to answer violence with violence; it is common curriculum these days.[9]

In another essay for StageofLife.com, gslangner wrote, "It is the government's job to pass stricter gun laws and help the mentally ill so they do not resort to vio- lence. Many gun rights advocates complain that gun control infringes upon their second amendment rights. However, the second amendment says the need for a well regulated militia and does not mention self-defense."[10]

Eighteen-year-old Jason Bergman's Stage of Life essay noted, "Americans are a country full of people with free speech and they are not afraid to use it. Ameri- can people will not let you take away their firearms but if we make it harder to obtain one maybe we cut down on gun violence. We must enforce the process of background checks."[11]

A nineteen-year-old rifle owner who calls herself winwinhh wrote in her es- say, "My upbringing as a female in a peaceful city leads me to despise the destruc- tive tools that have mercilessly robbed families of loved ones. Yet, the marksman in me loves the rifle that has allowed her to engage in an exhilarating experience. Nevertheless, I believe that accessibility of arms imposes more responsibility on society than some individuals can and should wield. Although weapons can serve as protection, too often they have been effortlessly employed as a means to devas- tate whole families, communities, and countries."[12]

Dozens of other Stage of Life essays echoed similar concerns. However, some declared guns were not the problem. They asserted, "People are evil, not guns," or "Guns are good, people are crazy," or "Guns do not fire without a person behind it."[13] In short, the views communicated in these essays were as varied as opinions expressed by the general public.

Student Opinions about Guns

Along with its essay contest in 2013, StageofLife.com conducted a national survey of U.S. students regarding their feelings about guns. Before submitting essays, 656 students responded to a poll. Some of the results include responses on whether people have a Second Amendment right to own any firearm they choose. Fifty percent answered yes and 50 percent responded no. Asked about teachers carrying concealed weapons, 70.6 percent of respondents were against it. Regarding America's laws on guns, here is what teens said in the poll:

- 10.1% of teens feel gun laws should be eased so that it's easier for law abiding citizens to own and carry guns both at home and in public
- 13.4% of teens feel we should keep current gun laws 'as is'
- 56.4% of teens feel we should keep the 2nd Amendment to the U.S. Constitution intact, but add new federal gun control laws to restrict the access to high-capacity ammunition clips or certain semiautomatic assault weapons, closing gun show loopholes, etc.
- 18% of teens feel guns should be allowed only by the military and police—regular citizens should not have access to them
- 2.1% of teens feel guns in all forms should be completely banned in our society.[c]

More Shootings and Reactions

Still, the shootings have continued. On May 23, 2014, a mentally unbalanced twenty-two-year-old man, Elliot Rodger, went on a rampage at the University of California, Santa Barbara (UCSB), killing two women on campus and three UCSB students in a nearby apartment where Rodger lived, plus a man at a nearby convenience store. After he wounded thirteen others, Rodger killed himself.

Before Rodger ran amok, he had posted a video on YouTube about a "day of retribution" because of his long-held feelings of rejection. Although the video

Guns in schools? Kids sneak them in and usually officials confiscate the weapons. However, a huge debate centers on state laws that allow teachers, administrators, and other personnel to carry concealed weapons in schools. The laws are vigorously opposed by activists against gun violence.

was taken down, the *Los Angeles Times* printed a transcript; Rodger declared in part, "On the day of retribution, I am going to enter the hottest sorority house at UCSB and I will slaughter every single spoiled, stuck-up, blond slut I see inside there. All those girls I've desired so much. They have all rejected me and looked down on me as an inferior man if I ever made a sexual advance toward them, while they throw themselves at these obnoxious brutes. . . . I take great pleasure in slaughtering all of you. You will finally see that I am, in truth, the superior one, the true alpha male."[14]

In Seattle, Washington, on June 5, 2014, a mentally ill gunman "carried out a Columbine-style school massacre. He was armed with a legally obtained Browning shotgun and had about 50 rounds stuffed into his pockets. Three students were shot. One, a nineteen-year-old freshman named Paul Lee, never recovered," the *Washington Post* reported. By August 2014, activists on competing sides were supporting two different gun control laws for the state of Washington. According to the *Post*,

> One of the initiatives, 594, proposes universal background checks. Prospective buyers already have to pass background checks to purchase from licensed firearm dealers under federal law. But 594 would also apply to firearms exchanged at gun shows, through Internet sales and between individuals.[15]

The other initiative, 591, would prevent background checks from being applied without a uniform national standard. Federally mandated background checks would still be allowed—just not individual variations on the state level. It also has a provision emphasizing that the government cannot confiscate firearms without due process.[16]

A majority—almost 60 percent—of Washington State voters approved the 594 measure in the November 4, 2014, election. The law requires background checks on all gun sales except for antiques and guns given to family members.

On November 20, 2014, about 12:30 a.m., a gunman shot and injured three students at Florida State University (FSU) in Tallahassee. The students were in or near a packed library that was open twenty-four hours and many were there studying for final exams. Campus police responded quickly, ordering the gunman to drop his weapon. When he opened fire instead, an officer shot and killed the gunman, who was later identified as thirty-one-year-old Myron May, an FSU alumnus. He graduated cum laude and received a law degree from Texas Tech University. May was an associate trial attorney in Las Cruces, New Mexico, but he moved back to Florida where he had once been a public defender. News sources reported that in the months before the shooting, May appeared to be showing symptoms of a "severe mental disorder" and thought people were watching him through hidden cameras in his apartment; he also heard voices coming through his walls.[17]

On the morning of the shooting and during the day, students gathered to express their feelings. For some, the shooting seemed unreal, and they just wanted to get away from the university for a while. Some wanted to be around friends and other students. A large group formed a prayer circle on the library lawn, the *Miami Herald* reported. "I pray, God, that you will make the students on this campus brave," Tori Reiman implored aloud. The *Herald* also reported the reaction of Samantha Markey, a senior at FSU and a psychology major. She said, "I want to know why it happened and how we can prevent it."[18]

Countless individuals, law enforcement officials, activists groups, journalists, psychologists, and others want to know the same thing about mass shootings.

Over and over again, the questions are raised: Why does it happen and what can be done to prevent it?

The "why" was addressed by Ari N. Schulman in a *Wall Street Journal* article. Schulman explained that "criminologists and psychologists who study mass killings . . . look at qualitative traits like the psychology of the perpetrator, his relationship to the victims and how he carries out the crime." Researchers have classified major types of mass murders, which "include serial, cult, gang, family and spree killings. But it is another kind that dominates the headlines: the massacre or rampage shooting" that occurs "as a single, typically very public event." The article continues,

> Mass shooters aim to tell a story through their actions. They create a narrative about how the world has forced them to act, and then must persuade themselves to believe it. The final step is crafting the story for others and telling it through spoken warnings beforehand, taunting words to victims or manifestos created for public airing.
>
> What these findings suggest is that mass shootings are a kind of theater. Their purpose is essentially terrorism—minus, in most cases, a political agenda. The public spectacle, the mass slaughter of mostly random victims, is meant to be seen as an attack against society itself. The typical consummation of the act in suicide denies the course of justice, giving the shooter ultimate and final control.[19]

This explanation provides some understanding of what motivates a mass shooter, but how can a potential killer be stopped? One suggestion is for the media and law enforcement to refrain from publicizing a mass killing in order to prevent someone from becoming a copycat. Countless news stories about mass killings have influenced others. Since the Columbine slaughter in 1999, potential shooters have seen the carnage as a "template" or an example of how to act. "They study it, and they try to top it in terms of either body count or showmanship. From suicidal ideation grows the delusion of grandeur; from the desire to kill yourself grows the desire to kill as many people as possible, with immortality on the line," writes Tom Junod in *Esquire*.[20]

Cops and Gun Control Issues

Following the mass shooting at Sandy Hook Elementary School in 2012, several states passed or proposed new laws restricting gun ownership. In addition, President Barack Obama called for a federal ban on the manufacture and sale of ammunition magazines that hold more than ten rounds and semiautomatic rifles known as assault weapons. The response from law enforcement has been divided with no uniform stance for or against these laws.

In January 2013, for instance, New York passed and Governor Andrew Cuomo signed the New York Secure Ammunition and Firearms Enforcement Act commonly known as the SAFE Act. But before and after the law went into effect, "political opposition . . . has grown, especially in upstate counties where gun ownership is popular. A growing number of law enforcement officials, especially county sheriffs, now say they're deeply troubled by the law, which bans assault rifles and large ammunition clips. Some officers say they won't actively enforce the SAFE Act," according to Brian Mann, reporting on North Country Public Radio. In upstate New York, many law enforcement officials say the SAFE Act violates the Second Amendment, and gun rights activists agree. However, "the District Attorneys Association of New York issued a statement saying the law would give police 'stronger tools to protect our communities from gun violence,'" and a group called New Yorkers Against Gun Violence supports the law.[21]

PoliceOne.com, an online website for professionals in law enforcement, surveyed more than 15,000 officers in March 2013 regarding gun laws. In response, 10,397, or 71 percent, of those surveyed said "the federal ban on the manufacture and sale of some semiautomatics would have no effect on reducing violent crime. . . . More than 20 percent say any ban would actually have a negative effect on reducing violent crime. Just over 7 percent took the opposite stance, saying they believe a ban would have a moderate to significant effect." The survey also asked, "If you were sheriff or chief, how would you respond to more restrictive gun laws?" Nearly 45 percent said they would not enforce the laws or would publicly oppose them.

When queried about mass shootings, an "overwhelming majority (almost 90 percent) of officers" said they "believe that casualties would be decreased if armed citizens were present at the onset of an active-shooter incident. More than 80 percent of respondents support arming school teachers and administrators who willingly volunteer to train with firearms and carry one in the course of the job."[22]

The pervasiveness of citizens and cops with firearms in the United States dumbfounds many in the United Kingdom. In the British magazine *Economist*, blogger D.K. put it this way: "The shooting of Michael Brown, an 18-year-old African-American, by a police officer in Ferguson, Missouri, is a reminder that civilians—innocent or guilty—are far more likely to be shot by police in America than in any other rich country."[23]

Michael Brown was unarmed when on August 9, 2014, a white police officer Darren Wilson shot the teen multiple times, killing him. Protests and controversy over Brown's death erupted across the United States. Many protesters argue that Brown was shot while walking away from Wilson with his hands up—marching with hands up has become a symbol for demonstrators. Others contend, and Wilson maintained, that Brown struggled with him and was a threat. A county grand jury found no evidence to indict Wilson for any crime, and he later resigned from the police force out of concerns for his own security. The British blogger called America "Trigger Happy" in the title for his article, noting: "In 2012, according to data compiled by the FBI, 410 Americans were 'justifiably' killed by police—409 with guns." In contrast, "British police officers actually fired their weapons three times" in 2013. The number of people fatally shot was zero. In 2012 the figure was just one." D.K. maintains that "guns are rare" in Britain. "Only specialist firearms officers carry them; and criminals rarely have access to them."[24]

The death of Michael Brown was not the only killing that created angry protests. In November 2014, a black twelve-year-old, Tamir Rice, of Cleveland, Ohio, who was playing with a toy gun, was shot at close range by a police officer. The next month, in December 2014, a police officer used a choke hold against an unarmed black man, Eric Garner, in Staten Island, New York, killing him. Also in December, a deranged man assassinated NYPD officers Wenjian Liu and Rafael Ramos. According to numerous news reports, the shooter thought his ambush would avenge the deaths of Michael Brown and Eric Garner.

In 2015, a white deputy sheriff in Tulsa, Oklahoma, shot and killed unarmed Eric Harris, a black man, who was fleeing from the deputy; a white police officer in North Charleston, South Carolina, shot unarmed Walter Scott in the back eight times, killing him. And in Baltimore, Maryland, police arrested unarmed Freddie Gray, handcuffed him, and put him in leg irons before placing him in a police van; Gray died from a severed spinal cord, and an investigation as of May 2015 had not determined how or when he suffered the injury.

The circumstances around these deaths have renewed an issue in America that is decades old: assertions that blacks and other people of color are unfairly treated by law enforcement and that white cops routinely use excessive and deadly force against them. "Police unions and some law-and-order conservatives insist that shootings by officers are rare" and for the most part are justified. "Civil rights groups and some on the left have just as quickly prescribed racial motives to the shootings, declaring that black and brown men are being 'executed' by officers," wrote Wesley Lowery in the *Washington Post*.[25]

When the subject of police killings is raised, few people think, let alone speak out, about the deaths of Native Americans. The Center for Juvenile and Criminal Justice (CJCJ) claims that "the racial group most likely to be killed by law enforcement is Native Americans, followed by African Americans, Latinos, Whites, and Asian Americans." A CJCJ graph on its website shows that 6.6 percent of Native Americans in the age group twenty-five to thirty-four are likely to be killed by police, compared to 5.6 percent of African Americans in the same age group who are likely to be shot dead by law enforcement. Another part of the graph shows that 7.1 percent of African Americans twenty to twenty-four years of age and 4.6 percent of Native Americans in the same age group are in the likely to be killed by police group.[26] There is no explanation regarding the disparity.

Simon Moya-Smith of the Oglala Lakota Nation repeated the assertions in a blog for CNN.com, and pointed out, "When Native Americans are shot and killed by law enforcement, there's rarely much news coverage of those incidents. There are no outcries from any community other than our own," he writes. "There are no white or black faces rallying around us, marching with us, protesting with us over this injustice. Why? Because we are a forgotten people." Moya-Smith, an editor for *Indian Country Today*, cites examples of young Native Americans shot dead by law enforcement. One was Mah-hi-vist Goodblanket. He was an eighteen-year-old Cheyenne and Arapaho youth. Two Oklahoma sheriff's deputies shot him seven times. Goodblanket died on December 21, 2013. According to a CNN report,

> Goodblanket threw a knife at the deputies and then attacked with another knife. They tried a Taser on him, which had no effect. But Goodblanket's girlfriend, Naomi Barron, who was present when he was killed, said in a

The FBI Director Speaks

On February 12, 2015, Federal Bureau of Investigation director James B. Comey was a guest speaker at Georgetown University, where he delivered remarks on the relationship between law enforcement and the diverse communities they serve. There is not space here to include his entire speech of more than 3,400 words, but his focus was on "a disconnect between police agencies and many citizens—predominantly in communities of color." He said in part,

> I worry that this incredibly important and incredibly difficult conversation about race and policing has become focused entirely on the nature and character of law enforcement officers, when it should also be about something much harder to discuss. . . .
>
> First, all of us in law enforcement must be honest enough to acknowledge that much of our history is not pretty. At many points in

American history, law enforcement enforced the status quo, a status quo that was often brutally unfair to disfavored groups. . . .

Much research points to the widespread existence of unconscious bias. Many people in our white-majority culture have unconscious racial biases and react differently to a white face than a black face. In fact, we all, white and black, carry various biases around with us. . . .

But racial bias isn't epidemic in law enforcement any more than it is epidemic in academia or the arts. In fact, I believe law enforcement over-whelmingly attracts people who want to do good for a living—people who risk their lives because they want to help other people. They don't sign up to be cops in New York or Chicago or L.A. to help white people or black people or Hispanic people or Asian people. They sign up be-cause they want to help all people. And they do some of the hardest, most dangerous policing to protect people of color. . . .

[Yet] something happens to people in law enforcement. Many of us develop different flavors of cynicism that we work hard to resist because they can be lazy mental shortcuts. . . .

A mental shortcut becomes almost irresistible and maybe even ratio-nal by some lights. The two young black men on one side of the street look like so many others the officer has locked up. Two white men on the other side of the street—even in the same clothes—do not. The officer does not make the same association about the two white guys, whether that officer is white or black. And that drives different behavior. The of-ficer turns toward one side of the street and not the other. We need to come to grips with the fact that this behavior complicates the relation-ship between police and the communities they serve. . . .

Relationships are hard. Relationships require work. So let's begin that work. It is time to start seeing one another for who and what we really are. Peace, security, and understanding are worth the effort.

Director Comey's speech is on the Internet and quotes from his remarks have been printed in various news media.[d]

statement that Goodblanket had no weapons when the two white deputies opened fire. "He [had] his arms up and his hands were free . . . he had no weapons," she said.[27]

Unfortunately, the U.S. Justice Department does not have a "comprehensive database or record of police shootings, instead allowing the nation's more than 17,000 law enforcement agencies to self-report officer-involved shootings," Lowery explained in his *Washington Post* article. "That number—which only includes self-reported information from about 750 law enforcement agencies—hovers around 400 'justifiable homicides' by police officers each year. . . . Several independent trackers, primarily journalists and academics who study criminal justice, insist the accurate number of people shot and killed by police officers each year is consistently upwards of 1,000 each year."[28] Perhaps that underscores why the British blogger D.K. calls Americans "trigger happy."

IMMIGRATION REFORM ACTIVISTS AND CRITICS

"We were basically raised here, then thrown into another country that they say is your country but it doesn't feel like home. . . . This [United States] is my home, whether I'm here legally or not."—Jesus Ruiz Diego, twenty-six, of San Jose, California, a U.S. resident since age four, speaking in 2012 after being released from a detention center[1]

Presidents, political campaigners, civic officials, activists, and many others have uttered some form of these words: "We are a nation of immigrants" or "Americans are all immigrants" or "Even the first Americans were immigrants." The statements seem all inclusive, but throughout much of U.S. history, some groups of immigrants have faced discrimination and persecution while other groups have been welcomed. In addition, millions of Africans were forced immigrants, brought to the United States as slaves.

Over many decades, federal laws have restricted who is officially allowed to immigrate, and activists have campaigned for or against these restrictions. In 1790, the Naturalization Act, for example, required immigrants to be "free white persons" of "good moral character" and live in the United States for two years before becoming citizens. The residency requirement increased to fourteen years in 1798. The act was revised again in 1892, and immigrants could become citizens after five years of residency.

Currently some activists want laws passed to allow immigrants without legal permits to become citizens through what is called a pathway to citizenship. They advocate for comprehensive immigration reform. But conflicts have been ongoing between those who support immigration reform and those who oppose a pathway to citizenship.

Continuing Debates on Immigration

In Washington, DC, on November 13, 2013, two teenagers—Jennifer Martinez, sixteen, and Carmen Lima, thirteen—confronted U.S. House Speaker John Boehner, who was at a diner waiting for his breakfast order. The teens, members of the Fair Immigration Reform Movement (FIRM), pressed Boehner to bring the immigration reform bill to a vote in the House of Representatives. FIRM is a national coalition of organizations fighting for immigrant rights at the local, state, and federal level. The bill had passed the Senate by a vote of 68–32 and allowed millions of undocumented residents to have a chance at citizenship. The congressman said he would try to convince House members, but later his inaction helped block the bill. Lima told MSNBC's Chris Hayes that she felt "betrayed. . . . I feel like he lied to me."[2]

In 2014, a group with FIRM stood outside the U.S. Capitol to advocate for immigration reform, which, if passed, could prevent deportation of noncitizens like their parents. The group included ten young people ranging in age from eleven to twenty-one; they came from Alabama, Arizona, California, Colorado, Nevada, New Mexico, and Washington State. Family members and FIRM leaders accompanied the youths.

Teenager Brian Sanchez of Arizona was there because of concerns about his mother. As Brian, who is a citizen, explained to reporter Ricardo Ramirez, "I go back to Mexico every year to see my sisters but because of my mom's status, she cannot and she has not seen my sisters in 10 years. . . . It is terrifying to think that my mom could be deported at any time and I would be all alone."[3]

Another teen citizen, Kolby Bautista Lopez of Colorado, feared that both of his parents would be deported. He said, "I'm scared, but I never cry, especially in front of my three younger brothers. Immigration reform would help my parents and many other immigrants stay in this country without having to worry about being deported."[4]

According to Ramirez, "The youths were arrested by Metropolitan Police Department officers, but were not charged and were released to their parents or guardians shortly after the action. The adults were arrested by Capitol Police and released after posting a $50 citation fee for trespassing."[5]

Other immigration organizations have been campaigning for reform in various cities. They include Fast for Families, Coalition on Immigration Reform, Keeping Families Together, and more. One group of clergy made up of Christian, Jewish, and Muslim leaders in Los Angeles has held vigils, emphasizing that comprehensive immigration reform is a moral issue and transcends all creeds, races, and languages.

On the other hand, some Americans have been holding protests, demanding that all illegal immigrants—often called aliens or unauthorized immigrants or simply illegals—be stopped from entering the United States. Hundreds of protesters gathered in cities across the nation during the summer and fall of 2014. In the small southern California town of Murrieta, angry crowds tried to stop three buses carrying undocumented immigrants from Central America to a processing center in the town. Some in the crowd shouted "Deport! Deport!" or "Go back home!" Forced to evade the protesters, the buses took the immigrants to other U.S. processing centers at least eighty miles away in the San Diego and El Centro areas. Protesters insisted they are not against the immigrants themselves, but want people to enter the United States the "right way."

Whether in Murrieta or Boston, people against illegal immigration carry signs demanding "Close the Border Now!" or "Deport Illegals." Their talking points are similar to those of the past. Critics contend that illegals are taking American jobs; they do not pay taxes but receive taxpayer benefits; they are living on welfare; they don't learn English; they are criminals.

However, those statements do not reflect the facts. Immigrants, whether holding legal papers or not, work at jobs that Americans do not want, as many agricultural fieldworkers and farmers can attest. According to TeachingTolerance.org, "The Social Security Administration estimates that half to three-quarters of undocumented immigrants pay federal, state and local taxes, including $6 billion to $7 billion in Social Security taxes for benefits they will never get. They can receive schooling and emergency medical care, but not welfare or food stamps [the Supplemental Nutrition Program]."[6] Most immigrants want to obtain official documents so they can work at well-paying jobs and become U.S. citizens, which usually means they must learn English and have not engaged in criminal activities. Entering the United States illegally is a civil, not a criminal, offense. "Despite the anti-immigrant rhetoric, 'criminal alien' is not a legal term and undocumented immigrants are not 'criminal aliens' under federal law. The term . . . is not defined anywhere in the federal Immigration and Nationality Act," according to the ACLU.[7]

A Post from the Past

Over many decades, numerous federal laws have been passed to regulate who can enter and/or become legal citizens of the United States. Some laws have controlled immigration of national groups, such as the Chinese and other Asians. The 1882 Chinese Exclusion Act, for one, banned Chinese laborers from coming to the United States, primarily because the Chinese worked for lower wages than Americans. U.S. workers blamed Chinese for job losses and declines in their pay. Congress did not repeal the act until 1943.

The Anarchist Exclusion Act of 1903, reenacted in 1906, banned anarchists, people "opposed to all organized government," or those who were members or affiliates of "any organization entertaining or teaching such disbelief in or opposition to all organized government."[a] Congress passed the law after the assassination of President William McKinley, who was gunned down by anarchist Leon Czolgosz in 1901. The law included a provision to not only exclude but also deport those who violently opposed government.

In 1907, Congress expanded the groups excluded from immigration. Section 2 of the Immigration Act of 1907 banned additional categories of immigrants: "All idiots, imbeciles, feebleminded persons, epileptics, insane persons, and persons who have been insane within five years previous . . . professional beggars; persons afflicted with tuberculosis or with a loathsome or dangerous contagious disease . . . persons who have been convicted of or admit having committed a felony or other crime or misdemeanor involving moral turpitude; polygamists, or persons who admit their belief in the practice of polygamy."[b]

During the 1920s, several federal laws limited the number of people allowed to immigrate each year and placed quotas on various nations—such as 3 percent and later 2 percent of a national population. These laws were a response to the influx of immigrants from eastern and southern Europe, primarily Italians and eastern European Jews. Some Americans considered these immigrants unskilled, ignorant, and not easily assimilated into American culture. Nationality quotas were repealed in 1965.

However, Congress continued to pass more immigration laws through the next five to six decades. One that is often in the forefront of current debates about immigration reform is the 1986 Immigration Control and Reform Act passed during the administration of President Ronald Reagan. The law allowed undocumented immigrants to obtain citizenship if they had been in the United States continuously since 1982. It also legalized some agricultural workers and penalized employers who knowingly hired undocumented workers. These same issues are part of the current controversy over comprehensive immigration reform.

What Is Comprehensive Immigration Reform?

The answer depends on whom you ask. "Religion, race, political affiliation and media source are all indicators of the immigration policy that one chooses to support," according to a 2014 survey by the Public Religion Research Institute and the Brookings Institution. A majority of Americans (62 percent) "favor providing a way for immigrants who are currently living in the United States illegally to become citizens provided they meet certain requirements," and 19 percent "favor a policy that would identify and deport all immigrants living in the United States illegally." The survey also found "majorities of all religious groups, with the exception of white evangelical Protestants, support a path to citizenship, including roughly 6-in-10 white mainline Protestants (58%), minority Protestants (62%) and Catholics (63%), and more than two-thirds (68%) of religiously unaffiliated Americans."[8]

The survey also found that people likely to support a path to citizenship are under thirty years old and identify as Hispanic. College graduates, females, and people aligned with the Democratic Party are also likely supporters. In addition, those who say that MSNBC is "an accurate news source are also significant predictors of support for immigration reform." Furthermore, Americans "favor allowing immigrants living in the country illegally who were brought to the U.S. as children to gain legal resident status if they join the military or go to college, a policy which comprises the basic elements of the DREAM Act."[9]

The DREAM Act (Development, Relief and Education for Alien Minors Act) was a bill introduced in Congress in 2001 but did not pass; it has been reintroduced several times since. In 2012, President Barack Obama announced that his administration "would accept requests for Deferred Action for Childhood Arrivals (DACA), an initiative designed to temporarily suspend the deportation of young people residing unlawfully in the U.S. who were brought to the United States as children, meet certain education requirements and generally match the criteria established under legislative proposals like the DREAM Act." According to the American Immigration Council,

> There are roughly 1.8 million immigrants in the United States who might be, or might become, eligible for the Obama Administration's "deferred action" initiative for unauthorized youth brought to this country as children. This initiative . . . offers a two-year, renewable reprieve from deportation to unauthorized immigrants who are under the age of 31; entered the United States before age 16; have lived continuously in the country for at least five years; have not been convicted of a felony, a "significant" misdemeanor, or three other misdemeanors; and are currently in school, graduated from high school, earned a GED, or served in the military.[10]

In November 2014 President Obama announced executive action that he was taking in regard to immigration. He said,

> First, we'll build on our progress at the border with additional resources for our law enforcement personnel so that they can stem the flow of illegal crossings, and speed the return of those who do cross over.
>
> Second, I'll make it easier and faster for high-skilled immigrants, graduates, and entrepreneurs to stay and contribute to our economy, as so many business leaders have proposed.
>
> Third, we'll take steps to deal responsibly with the millions of undocumented immigrants who already live in our country.[11]

The president also noted,

> We expect people who live in this country to play by the rules. We expect that those who cut the line will not be unfairly rewarded. So we're going to offer the following deal: If you've been in America for more than five years; if you have children who are American citizens or legal residents; if you register, pass a criminal background check, and you're willing to pay your fair share of taxes—you'll be able to apply to stay in this country temporarily without fear of deportation. You can come out of the shadows and get right with the law. That's what this deal is.

He added, "To those members of Congress who question my authority to make our immigration system work better, or question the wisdom of me acting where Congress has failed, I have one answer: Pass a bill." In January 2015, the House of Representatives voted to block all funding for the U.S. Department of Homeland Security as retaliation for Obama's executive actions on immigration. The Republican majority also voted to stop funding the DACA program, which if upheld would mean the deportation of children whose parents brought them illegally to the United States. However, in March 2015, Congress passed legislation that will fund the Department of Homeland Security until September 2015. The "clean" bill, however, did not change President Obama's immigration actions.

Immigrant Farmworkers

Fieldworkers—farmworkers who plant and/or harvest much of the produce that Americans eat—are part of the debate over immigration reform. Many of the farmworkers are undocumented immigrants, primarily from Mexico and Central America, who "make up about half of the nation's 1 million to 1.2 million

Activists for immigration reform include young people who were youngsters when they came to the United States with their parents to work in agriculture.

farm-labor force," writes Daniel González of the *Arizona Republic*. The Senate bill, which did not pass, included an agricultural-jobs (called Ag-Jobs) provision that "offers legal status to undocumented farm workers and creates a temporary-worker program to meet the labor demands of farmers."[12]

Those demands are urgent since U.S. citizens are reluctant or refuse to take the jobs. As one undocumented worker from Mexico, Odilia Chavez (who agreed to use her name), put it, "In the 14 years I've been here, I've never seen an American working in the fields."[13] She explained to *Modern Farmer*, a quarterly publication and website, that most fieldworkers are Mexicans while Salvadoran and Guatemalan immigrants usually work in factories and construction.

When Chavez first came to the United States, she paid a coyote (a smuggler) $1,800 to help her illegally cross the Mexico–U.S. border in 1999. (Coyotes now charge much more.) She went to work in Madera, California, and since then has continued fieldwork. She explained,

In a typical year, I prune grapevines starting in April, and pick cherries around Madera in May. I travel to Oregon in June to pick strawberries, blueberries and blackberries on a farm owned by Russians. I take my 14-year-old daughter and 8-year-old son with me while they're on their summer break. They play with the other kids, and bring me water and food in the field. We'll live in a boarding house with 25 rooms for some 100 people, and everyone lines up to use the bathrooms. My kids and I share a room for $270 a month. . . .

The work is hard—but many jobs are hard. The thing that bothers me more is the low pay. With cherries, you earn $7 for each box, and I'll fill 30 boxes in a day—about $210 a day. For blueberries, I'll do 25 containers for up to $5 each one—$125 a day. With grapes, you make 30 cents for each carton, and I can do 400 cartons a day—$120 a day. Tomatoes are the worst paid: I'll pick 100 for 62 cents a bucket, or about $62 a day. I don't do tomatoes much anymore. It's heavy work, you have to bend over, run to turn in your baskets, and your back hurts. I say I like tomatoes—in a salad. Ha. With a lot of the crops, the bosses keep track of your haul by giving you a card, and punching it every time you turn in a basket.[14]

It Happened to Mario

Mario Orellano from Chicaman, Guatemala, was eighteen years old when he posted his story on HuffingtonPost.com in September 2013. At the time, he was a junior at Middle College High School at LaGuardia Community College in Queens, New York. He began his story, telling how he "grew up watching my mother being beat by the man who I called father." His father was a lawyer with a good income but an alcoholic who abused his family. "I grew up seeing things, bad things, horrible things, wanting to do something about it! But I was young, too young. Many suns and moons passed, and my life continued without change. I worked carrying bricks, mixing rocks with concrete, selling gum at the capital, and sometimes selling pupusas [stuffed corn tortillas] my mother had made. I was only six years old." At that time, Mario's mother left for the United States, promising to send money so he could join her. He wrote,

> I was left to live with my aunt, and grandmother, and her two other children. My mother sent money from the United States, but like always,

I ended up getting nothing. And they never told me when she sent money or how much, but I always knew when. Every time I watched my aunt's kids going to the stores, and buying sodas, chips, candies, and sometimes toys, while I only sat and witnessed. I had a deep hatred for everyone, especially my father, a coward of a man, but I had the curse of being his son, the son of an alcoholic man, who beat women and abused his son. Until this day, I remember the voices who made fun of me, "Tu padre te odia! Y tu madre tambien por eso se fue!" [Your father hates you! And also why your mother is gone!]

In 2005, Mario's mother paid a coyote to bring her son to Queens. He was the "only kid in the group" of ten people who journeyed from Guatemala to Mexico and then across the border to the United States. The group traveled on one bus after another, or in vans, and stayed "in hotels and houses not more than a day, or half of it. I brought a little book with me, a book I stole from my cousins. I didn't go to school while in Guatemala, but every time there was no one home, I would search for my cousins' school books and learn words—how to read and write."

In Mexico, the group had to cross the desert, "and the coyote told everyone, 'Si tienes monedas o algo que haga sonido al caminar, tirenlas ahora!' [If you have coins or something that makes a sound while walking, drop them now]." Everyone complied. After walking in intense heat during the day and frigid cold at night, the group finally reached the United States where a van was waiting for them. The coyotes took them to a "small house, somewhere in the south" where they stayed for a while. Then Mario was driven to Jamaica, Queens, where his mother was staying. When he saw his mother, Mario didn't recognize her at first. Then, in his words, "I broke into tears, tears that became my struggles escaping my body. I hugged her tightly, saying, 'Madre ya vine, madre te encontre, madre aqui estoy!' [Mother I came, I found you, mother, mother I'm here!] All the struggles, the pain, the hits, the bruises, the humiliations were worth it. I had found once again my shield, my mother."[c] Mario did not explain what happened to him after being reunited with his mother.

> ## Now You Know
>
> ● As of 2014, the Department of Homeland Security estimated that 11.5 million undocumented immigrants were in the United States. Approximately 1.4 million Asian and Pacific Islanders are among the total. The U.S. Customs and Border Protection (CBP) apprehended 468,651 illegal immigrants nationwide in 2014. Of that number, 468,407 were from Mexico, El Salvador, Guatemala, and Honduras, and nearly all apprehensions were along the southwest border. According to the CBP, they "apprehended 66,638 nationals from El Salvador, 81,116 nationals from Guatemala, 91,475 nationals from Honduras, and 229,178 nationals from Mexico."[d]

Chavez has not worried about an immigration raid on the farms where she works. "Agriculture is dependent on undocumented workers. We need the money from the farmers, and the farmers need our hands," she declared.[15]

Old and New Sanctuary Movements

Providing sanctuary for oppressed people is an ancient tradition and has a long history in the United States. During slavery, runaways found refuge in U.S. churches and homes. Draftees who refused to fight in Vietnam took shelter in varied American locations. Beginning in the 1980s, a sanctuary movement began to help Central American immigrants seeking asylum as refugees.

The movement began with Jim Corbett (1933–2001), although people often credit a Presbyterian pastor John Fife as the originator. Corbett, however, helped initiate and establish sanctuary for Central American refugees. Statistics show that during the 1970s and 1980s, more than two hundred thousand Central Americans were killed in civil wars while countless others tried to escape to nearby countries or to the United States. Many believed they would be able to find safety in the United States because of the 1980 Refugee Act, which allowed asylum for refugees who faced persecution in their countries. The act banned so-called economic migrants—people looking for jobs. Since at the time the United States supported the Central American governments' war efforts, U.S. immigration officials declared that Salvadorans, Guatemalans, and Nicaraguans were not escaping maltreatment but instead wanted to take advantage of economic opportunities. Thus, thousands of people who tried to immigrate into the United States were turned away, which usually meant certain death.

Corbett earned a master's degree in philosophy at Harvard and was prepared to teach. Instead, he decided that he wanted to do something notable. He became a member of the Religious Society of Friends (Quakers), who believe in living their moral convictions and bringing about political change through acts of conscience. He had that opportunity when he learned in 1981 about El Salvadoran refugees who had been caught by the U.S. Border Patrol and were being returned to their homeland. Corbett rescued some refugees and provided safe haven for them in his home. Soon there were more people than Corbett could handle, so he requested help from other Quakers, who established a nationwide support network. In Tucson, Arizona, John Fife, the pastor of Southside Presbyterian Church, mobilized Presbyterians across the county to provide sanctuary.

Over the next few years, Corbett and Reverend Fife, whose church was declared a sanctuary in March 1982, sheltered hundreds of refugees. The sanctuary movement spread, and by the end of 1984, large numbers of Americans endorsed the movement, and hundreds of Protestant, Jewish, and Catholic congregations supported sanctuaries. They provided bail money and legal aid for refugees plus food, medical care, and jobs.

The modern day's new sanctuary movement (NSM), as it is called, is responding to current undocumented immigrants who face deportation unless the federal government reforms the nation's broken immigration system. Dozens of faith groups across the United States are involved, including the Southside Presbyterian Church in Tucson. Churches in Phoenix, Arizona; Chicago, Illinois; and Portland, Oregon, have also offered sanctuary. In addition, support for the movement comes from communities in Boston, Chicago, Denver, Kansas City, New York, Oakland, Philadelphia, Phoenix, Portland, Seattle, and others.

Those who establish a sanctuary say they are following biblical customs as noted in the Gospel of Matthew: "I was hungry and you gave me food; I was thirsty and you gave me drink; I was a stranger and you welcomed me."[16] Another comes from the Old Testament and the commandment to establish six cities of refuge for the Israelites and others who have "accidentally and unintentionally" killed another person and have to "find protection from the avenger of blood." If said avenger comes looking for the refugee, "the elders of the city must not surrender the fugitive" who must "stay in that city until" he is tried by the people.[17]

Double Standards on Immigration

When immigrants from the island nation of Cuba, just ninety miles from Florida, enter the United States illegally, they may receive privileges not granted to other undocumented groups. Why? Because of the 1966 Cuban Adjustment Act (CAA), which provides for a special procedure under which Cuban natives or citizens and their accompanying spouses and children may get a green card (permanent residence). Congress passed the CAA to encourage Cubans to leave the oppression of their communist country. It was a way to show dictator Fidel Castro in 1966 that the United States did not approve of his regime. The CAA allows Cuban exiles to establish almost immediate naturalization regardless of quotas and visa procedures. As the JournalistsResource.org explains,

> After the fall of the Soviet Union [1991], Cuban migration to the U.S. accelerated: In 1994 alone, 33,000 Cubans were intercepted by the U.S. Coast Guard. In response, U.S. and Cuban governments worked to establish a solution that would prevent Cubans from risking their lives at sea. The result, in 1995, came to be known as the "wet foot, dry foot" policy: Any Cuban who successfully arrives on U.S. soil is accepted; those stopped at sea are repatriated. The policy remains in effect today.[18]

In December 2014, one group of fifteen young people was able to cross the Straits of Florida, a treacherous seaway (sometimes called "refugee soup") between Key West, Florida, and Cuba. They landed their homemade boat safely on American soil at Fort Zachary Taylor State Park in Key West. "They were almost delirious with excitement," wrote Bob Mellis, a retired journalist who was volunteering at the park and met the refugees. He was the first to greet them. "They hugged each other and screamed 'Libre, Libre' to me as I got on my walkie-talkie to call the administration."[19]

Park staff gave the refugees towels to dry off and protect them from the cool weather. Key West police arrived to take charge and, according to Mellis, "were exceedingly kind to the young people." Later in the day, Mellis described the event to park visitors who "were in awe that these young people risked so much to make the 90-mile voyage to our version of freedom."[20]

Cubans who are able to make land are entitled by the "dry foot" policy to lawfully live and work in the United States and within a year can apply for citizenship. According to a Reuters report, "An average of about 36,000–40,000 Cubans arrive each year. . . . Roughly 10,000 arrive without visas each year, smuggled by boat or via the border with Mexico."[21]

"In addition to these arrivals at the U.S. border, thousands of Cubans are granted refugee status each year after applying from Cuba," writes Mary Turck on Aljazeera.com. "In 2013 the U.S. admitted 26,407 Cubans as refugees or asylees. That is nearly one-fourth of the refugee and asylum seeker total admitted that year." In contrast, Turck points out in her article that "more than 50,000 children, mostly from Honduras, Guatemala and Nicaragua, have sought safe haven in the United States" from January to August 2014. "U.S. immigration laws pose almost insurmountable barriers for these Central American youths fleeing gangs, drug lords and threats of death or rape."[22]

However, some changes will help undocumented Central American and Mexican immigrants. In October 2014, the federal government announced that it would provide $9 million to nonprofit organizations that offer legal services for 2,600 children who have immigrated illegally without parents or guardians. The Conference of Catholic Bishops in Washington, DC, and the U.S. Committee for Refugees and Immigrants in Arlington, Virginia, will distribute the funds. In a separate proceeding, California provided $3 million of legal assistance for un-documented children in its state.

Meantime, Americans, especially politicians, are debating the benefits Cubans receive compared to that of other immigrants. Some argue that the CAA should be rescinded—it is unfair and outdated. People have more freedom to travel to and from the island than in the past, so Cubans do not need special incentives to emigrate; they leave in order to take advantage of better economic conditions, the same reason others come to the United States.

Yet, some congressional leaders have vowed to prevent any changes to policies and laws favoring Cuba. They angrily oppose calls for Congress to end the 1960 U.S. trade embargo that bans U.S. exports to and prohibits most imports from Cuba. Supporters of the embargo say it should stand until the Cuban regime takes significant steps to end oppression and establish a democratic government. As of early 2015, few Americans believed that Congress would alter or repeal the CAA or the U.S. trade embargo in the near future.

What Is a Green Card?

If someone has a green card, she or he has a photo identification card with a green background that indicates the right to lawfully live and work in the United States. In other words, that person is a legal permanent resident. Green-card holders are allowed to travel in and out of the country and can request green cards for close family members. But they do not have the benefits of citizenship, such as the right to vote. Before they can become citizens, immigrants with green cards must live in the United States for at least five years prior to the date they file an Application for Naturalization—the beginning of a legal process to obtain U.S. citizenship or nationality.

In spite of opposition, President Obama announced in late December 2014 that some U.S. restrictions on travel to Cuba and banking and commerce constraints would be lifted. New travel regulations were implemented in January 2015. Diplomatic relations were also reestablished, and U.S. Secretary of State John Kerry officially opened the American embassy in Havana on August 14, 2015.

LEARNING TO BE
AN ACTIVIST

··

"As a black student, my rationale for doing the die-in was that structural racism causes not only police brutality, but also the starving of majority black public schools. This is a subtler form of violence."—Will Daniels, Eastern Michigan student activist protesting school closings in urban black communities[1]

Throughout this book, one story after another tells about activists who advocate for or against social, political, environmental, religious, educational, and other causes. These activists have chosen to devote their time and energy to make changes. Sometimes they have been motivated by hurtful or dangerous situations that they or friends or family have experienced. Some find personal meaning in current events, so they are inclined to become activists for a cause. In other cases, they have read about or become aware of injustices and want to protect people's rights or animals' welfare. Some take action because of ideology. These activists, whoever they are, believe they can make a positive difference in their community, state, nation, or world.

To actually become an activist, you have to start somewhere. You could participate for short periods as a volunteer in civic or school activities, which can be an introduction to longer-term activist operations. For example, in New Haven, Connecticut, Isaiah Lee became an activist when he brought Wilbur Cross High School students together in 2012 to protest teacher layoffs. Forty students rallied at city hall and Lee met with New Haven's mayor. "It's important to have young people's perspectives on these issues," Lee told John Micklos Jr. of *Teaching Tolerance* magazine. "We are the ones who are ultimately affected by the decisions made by the authorities." Lee's political activism provided an opportunity to learn "how to research and present an argument, and how to mobilize people on important issues."[2]

Training to be an activist requires some serious thought.

Becoming an Activist

It is common for many people to begin their activism through established organizations; several are listed at the back of this book. If you browse the Internet, you can find hundreds of advocacy groups asking for help. DoSomething.org, for one, has a Teens for Jeans program to collect slightly used jeans for distribution to homeless youth.

Teens participate in many other DoSomething.org campaigns. They collect cell phones for domestic violence programs. They create activity books for hospitalized children. They donate eyeglasses for programs serving needy people. They help older people gain access to the Internet or learn how to use email. They distribute guides that show how to use condoms correctly. They collect books for people in low-income areas. They share small socks that cover thumbs to remind people not to text and drive. Dozens of other teen advocacy projects are described on the DoSomething.org's website, which includes ideas for those who want to get started as an activist.

Some teens attend summer camps like Youth Empowered Action (YEA), sponsored by Earth Island Institute, to learn about activism. YEA camps are located in California, Oregon, and New York for young people ages twelve to seventeen who want to make a difference in the world. As one teenage camper, Griffin, noted, "I gained a ton of confidence, both in my activism skills and my value as a person. If you want to change anything anywhere in the world, come to YEA." Jasmine, another summer camper declared YEA "was the best experience of my life. Thanks for being an inspiration and so supportive and kind to me."[3]

Other groups that provide activist training include Training for Change, Earth Activist Training, League of Education Voters, Highlander Research and Education Center, and Green Corps. In addition, many young adults learn about and become involved in diverse types of activism online. A study by the Intelligence Group, a research organization focusing on youth, pointed out in a 2012 report called *The Casandra Good Guide* that two out of three Millennials believed that "a person on a computer, being aware and spreading the word" was capable of sparking more change than "a person on the street, rallying and protesting."[4] In a 2014 article for *Teen Vogue*, Alexis Manrodt pointed out that "grassroots movements are created through tweets, reblogs, likes, and status updates. . . . This new wave is proving how logging on can seriously impact your community—and the world." However, Manrodt cautioned that "some critics derisively refer to [online activism] as 'slacktivism.'"[5]

In a 2014 *Forbes* article, Brian Honigman agreed that critics "dismiss online activism as lazy, ineffectual and even dangerous to healthy political discourse. They deride large tallies of 'likes,' viral videos views and floods of memes as 'slacktivism,' and doubt their ability to impact the political process."[6]

Still, social media allow people to become advocates for a cause and help pass on information about an issue, which could lead to action. Consider the "# (hashtag) activism" that ensued after the death of Michael Brown, an unarmed eighteen-year-old African American shot and killed by a white police officer in Ferguson, Missouri. After a grand jury decided not to indict the police officer, millions of people responded to #Ferguson on Twitter.

Millions of users also connected to other online sites #ICantBreathe and #EricGarner. The hashtags were reactions to videos of New York police arresting Eric Garner of Staten Island for selling "loosies" (single, unpackaged) cigarettes while on a city sidewalk. Police restrained him with a choke hold (a banned police procedure) and held him face down on the pavement. Garner pleaded eleven times, "I can't breathe" until he was unconscious and soon died. As in the Brown

> ## ! "Armchair Activists"
>
> ● *Armchair activism* is another term for *slacktivism*, which also is known as cyber activism, digital activism, Internet activism, online activism, and email campaigning. These "isms" basically mean that people may support a cause online but will not take substantive offline action. It's a way to feel good about yourself without much effort. As Rosalie Tostevin writes on TheGuardian.com, "It's easy to click, but just as easy to disengage." She adds, "You can change your profile picture [on Facebook] to raise awareness, share videos and articles and keep in touch with charities by liking their pages. Making a difference seems pretty easy in the digital age. But is your contribution any deeper than a click?" In conclusion, she notes that "while the digital age may enhance the power of those that are already active, it can't seem to drag the rest out of their armchairs."[a]

case, a grand jury did not indict the officer, Daniel Pantaleo, who applied the choke hold. After a bystander's video of the incident was posted online, it quickly spread, which led to the hashtags #ICantBreathe and #EricGarner and massive street protests.

The public response spurred action by President Obama. He "requested funding for 50,000 police body cameras, created a task force to get specific recommendations on building trust between communities and law enforcement and invited young leaders to the White House for a meeting in the Oval Office," NBC News reported. In addition, the "Senate passed the Death in Custody Reporting Act with unanimous consent." (The bill had passed the House in 2013.) President Obama signed the act in December 2014. The law requires "law enforcement officials to report deaths of people killed during arrest or in police custody."[7]

Online Activism

In spite of slacktivism critics, numerous young people begin their activism online, hoping to spark change. In fact, one activist movement is actually called SPARK, which involves girls and women ages thirteen to twenty-two "to demand an end to the sexualization of women and girls in media," according to its website. SPARK stands for Sexualization, Protest, Action, Resistance, Knowledge and along with more than sixty partner organizations such as Girls, Inc., supports "the development of girls' healthy sexuality and self-esteem."[8]

With the help of SPARK, teenager Julia Bluhm of Waterville, Maine, began an online petition in 2012 to demand that *Seventeen* include one photo spread that was not digitally retouched. In her petition, Julia wrote, "To girls today, the word 'pretty' means skinny and blemish-free. . . . Here's what lots of girls don't know. . . . Those 'pretty women' that we see in magazines are fake." The online petition received thousands of signatures, crashing SPARK's website. Julia and her friend Izzy Labbe continued their campaign by making a video of interviews with their friends and peers who presented their opinions about the magazine's photos. SPARK members met with *Seventeen* editors, who made no promises about how they would handle photos in the future.[9]

Nevertheless, Julia's petition prompted other actions. SPARK's message resonated at *Vogue*. The magazine adopted a pledge to "not knowingly work with models under the age of 16" and also to "encourage designers to consider the consequences of unrealistically small sample sizes of their clothing, which limits the range of women who can be photographed in their clothes, and encourages the use of extremely thin models." In conclusion, the magazine promised to "be ambassadors for the message of healthy body image."[10]

SPARK's website provides information about other young women who have been part of the SPARK team and how they have been involved. For example, Corrie Fulcher of Ann Arbor, Michigan, "is passionate about combating sexualization in comics as a medium and an industry." Another on the team is Ambar Johnson, twenty, who is concerned about "dismantling the harmful images and feedback of black women in the media." And fifteen-year-old Julia Khan of the San Francisco Bay Area "is particularly passionate about gender equality and representation in the media." Coming from a biracial and multireligious family, Julia understands the significance of cultural identity and the complications behind having multiple ethnic backgrounds.[11]

Online activists also have inspired people to donate to charitable causes, to send aid to victims of natural disasters, and, most important, to leave their comfort zones and participate in an activist group. Some online activists hope to gain the attention of policy makers and elected officials regarding political issues.

One person who became an online political activist was Juan Escalante, at the time a full-time graduate student at Florida State University in Tallahassee. In September 2014, he explained to an MSNBC interviewer that when he was ready to enroll in college in 2007, "[I] received a call from the University of Central Florida asking for a copy of my green card. My mother revealed to me that our immigration case had been closed without appeal due to our lawyer's poor advice, thus leaving us in an immigration limbo." In other words, Escalante and his family were undocumented. He became involved in an online forum DreaAmAct .info, and from that point on his activism has been online. "My goal is to educate individuals on how new technologies can benefit their campaigns." Escalante said,

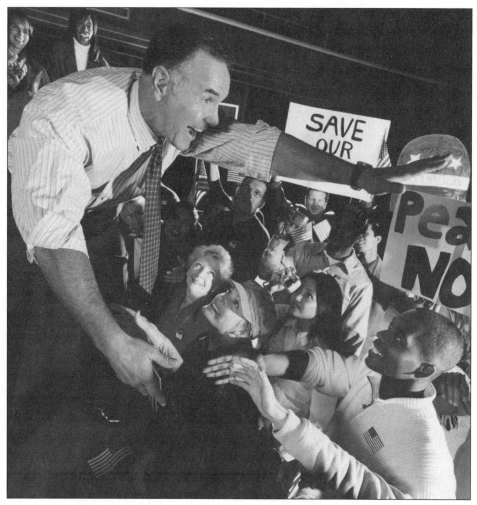

Teenagers often learn how to become activists by working for politicians in campaigns.

One of the most crucial elements of the immigrant rights and reform movements is, and continues to be, personal stories. We need everyone who is impacted by the broken immigration system to wield their personal narrative and struggle as a tool of empowerment for their communities. This means being involved in all levels of government, educating community members about the issue, seeking state or local organization, or being active on social networks—you don't have to be an activist to be involved, you just need the passion to inform and educate others.[12]

Demonstrating

Anyone who has read or seen movies and TV shows about the 1950s through the early 1970s is aware that countless students were involved in boycotts, demon-

A Post from the Past

For some people, activism begins with experiencing and observing injustice. That was the basis for Ron Kovic's (1946–) antiwar campaign. A decorated Marine and Vietnam War veteran, Kovic had volunteered to serve in Vietnam. His first tour was from December 1964 to January 1967. During his second tour in 1968, he was hit with an enemy bullet that severed his spinal column and left him paralyzed. He received a bronze star for his actions in combat. But while being treated in the St. Albans Naval Hospital in New York, he became disgusted with the overcrowded facility and its substandard care and unhygienic conditions. He later reported that rats roamed the building.

After leaving the hospital, Kovic moved to California where he learned about a group of Vietnam veterans who had gone to Washington, DC, to throw away their medals in a protest against their poor health care and disrespectful treatment after coming home from combat. Kovic contacted the group known as Vietnam Veterans Against the War (VVAW) who soon asked Kovic to give a speech at a rally in Pasadena, California. He complied and thereafter spoke often at VVAW protests. He became a dedicated speaker and activist against the war, which incited war supporters. In 1976, he published his book *Born on the Fourth of July* (McGraw-Hill) because, as he wrote,

> I wanted people to understand. I wanted to share with them . . . what I had gone through, what I had endured. I wanted them to know what it really meant to be in a war—to be shot and wounded, to be fighting for my life on the intensive care ward. . . . I wanted people to know about the hospitals and the enema room, about why I had become opposed to the war, why I had grown more and more committed to peace and nonviolence.[b]

A movie by the same title as Kovic's book was directed by Oliver Stone and starred Tom Cruise. It was released in 1989, winning an Academy Award. A paperback version was published in 2005. In the book, Kovic wrote, "I had been beaten by the police and arrested twelve times for protesting the war and I had spent many nights in jail in my wheelchair. I had been called a Communist and a traitor, simply for trying to tell the truth about what had happened in that war, but I refused to be intimidated."[c]

He continued his protests and speaking out about the "tragic and senseless" war in Iraq. He also began to focus on peace efforts and explored nonviolent methods for solving the world's conflicts. As of late 2014, Ron Kovic was still speaking out, expressing outrage that veterans are homeless and sleeping on the streets and not getting the health care they need. As he told a reporter for the *Los Angeles Times*, "What we owe them more than anything is to respect them enough to not squander their lives in wars that make no sense. . . . Yes, we need to be aware of dangers that beset our country around the world. But at the same time, if you can't care for those who wear the uniform and serve and risk their lives, then what kind of country is this?"[d]

strations, marches, sit-ins, and other actions for civil rights. Numerous public protests against the Vietnam War were also common. During more recent history, students have taken part—often for the first time—in diverse demonstrations for or against causes. Some first-time demonstrators become dedicated activists.

One demonstration occurred in Jefferson County, Colorado, in September 2014. Hundreds of students in five high schools near Denver along with some teachers protested a decision by the county's school board to create a committee that would review and change curriculum materials for the Advanced Placement U.S. history course. Some members of the school board (and others across the nation) have objected to the history course as placing too much emphasis on social and economic problems and omitting numerous American icons such as the founding fathers and civil rights heroes. Proposed new materials "'would call for promoting 'positive aspects' of the United States and its heritage'" and "avoid material that would encourage or condone 'civil disorder, social strife or disregard of the law.'" The new curriculum would promote "'citizenship, patriotism, essentials and benefits of the free enterprise system, respect for authority and respect for individual rights,'" according to the *Denver Post*.[13]

Colorado students objected to the attempt to make America seem perfect. At one school they gathered at a busy intersection chanting, "It's our history, don't make it a mystery." They waved signs and shot "selfies on their smartphones. There were cheerleaders in their purple and white uniforms and a student in a black bandana and hoodie claiming an association with the protest network called Anonymous," the *Post* reported.[14] Demonstrations continued for several weeks and the Jefferson County School Board offered a small compromise. They agreed to include administrators, teachers, and students in a review committee.

In December 2014, students staged die-ins at their schools in Detroit, Baltimore, and Philadelphia. They protested the fact that school boards shut down high schools in primarily black areas. For example, on December 17, "Baltimore's school board voted to shut down the first of five schools," George Joseph of the *Nation* magazine reported. Students responded by staging "a die-in, chanting, 'Black lives matter!' and 'the school board has failed us!' The board soon fled. Without missing a beat, the students took the commissioners' chairs and held a community forum on the closures. The next day in an uncoordinated action in Philadelphia, public school student organizers staged a die-in in front of their district building, mourning the 2013 loss of twelve-year-old Laporshia Massey, who died from an asthma attack after being sent home from a school with no nurse on duty."[15]

Joseph explained further,

Like a country after wartime, the United States is home to thousands of empty schools today, standing in ruins. School closures nationwide, which rose to almost 2,000 schools in the 2010–2011 school year, exert a disproportionate impact on urban black communities as recently seen in Philadelphia, Detroit, Baltimore and, most notably, Chicago. During the 2013–2014 school year, for example, Chicago Mayor Rahm Emanuel pushed through the shutdown of an unprecedented fifty-two schools. Fifty-three of the fifty-four schools served elementary school students, 90 percent of them black students, in a district with a 40 percent black population.[16]

For first-time demonstrators, another major motivating issue is a demand for an increase in the federal and state minimum wages. The federal minimum wage is $7.25 per hour, also a minimum in some states. Teens are the most likely to be paid minimum wage or less; they are usually entry-level employees without the skills needed for jobs at higher wages. However, young employees may earn even less. According to the U.S. Department of Labor, "A special minimum wage of $4.25 per hour applies to employees under the age of 20 during their first 90 consecutive calendar days of employment. . . . After 90 days, the Fair Labor Standards Act (FLSA) requires employers to pay the full federal minimum wage."[17]

The U.S. Bureau of Labor Statistics reported, "In 2013, 75.9 million workers age 16 and older in the United States were paid at hourly rates, representing 58.8 percent of all wage and salary workers. Among those paid by the hour, 1.5 million earned exactly the prevailing federal minimum wage of $7.25 per hour. About

1.8 million had wages below the federal minimum. Together, these 3.3 million workers with wages at or below the federal minimum made up 4.3 percent of all hourly paid workers."[18]

In 2013 and 2014, numerous fast-food workers launched rallies and protests to demand wages higher than the federal standard. Their rallying cry was "Fight for 15"—a minimum of $15.00 per hour. One protest was in Flint, Michigan, in September 2014. High school senior Jada Williams, who works at McDonald's, was protesting, even though Michigan had increased its minimum wage from $7.40 to $8.15 per hour. As she prepared for graduation, she told reporter Eric Dresden for MLive.com news that she could not even afford to buy school clothes. Dresden reported that another worker, "Jackie McNeal, 23, works two jobs, with his other paying above minimum wage, but he still struggles to pay the bills for his child and himself. 'I want to see a $15 minimum wage,' he said. 'I really have is-

Fast-food workers become activists when they organize to advocate for an increase in the minimum wage.

sues with paying the bills.'" A seventeen-year-old worker, Sapphire Newby, "was among protesters and said her check from Taco Bell . . . barely pays her phone bill." When protestors blocked a roadway, which is illegal, Newby justified the action, saying, "We have the right to protest and be heard."[19]

In December 2014, fast-food workers as well as other employees receiving minimum wage in nearly two hundred cities participated in rallies and protests under the banner "Fight for 15." The *Wall Street Journal* reported that "fast-food workers in New York walked off their jobs at dozens of restaurants including McDonald's and Burger King." Workers also included a one-minute protest "over recent grand jury decisions not to indict white police officers involved in the deaths of African-American men in both Ferguson, Mo., and New York City." Carlos Robinson, a twenty-three-year-old cook at Burger King, explained to the *Wall Street Journal*, "Overall the people in Ferguson are fighting for their rights, just like the people in fast food are fighting for their rights." Robinson "is struggling on part-time hours and a wage of $7.75 an hour. 'They should be able to pay us a decent wage,'" he said of fast-food employers.[20]

Some states have increased the minimum wage. Connecticut's minimum was $9.15 in 2015, to be increased to $10.10 by 2017, according to the *Hartford Courant*.[21] In San Francisco, the minimum wage will be $15.00 per hour in 2018. Seattle, Washington, set a minimum wage of $15.00, payable in 2017 or as late as 2021, depending on the size of the company or franchise.

Off the Bookshelf

Be a Changemaker: How to Start Something That Matters by Laurie Ann Thompson (Simon & Schuster, 2014) is an excellent book for teens who want to begin their activism. Each of the eighteen chapters in the book includes a profile of a socially conscious young person who has been able to bring about real change in his or her community and/or other part of the world. Along with profiles, the book includes practical ideas for beginning activists such as how to research in order to be informed about an issue, raise funds for a cause, budget to sustain a campaign, recruit supportive adults, and work with the media. Chapters deal specifically with these how-tos, as examples of some titles demonstrate: "Researching Your Big Ideas," "Building Your Dream Team," "Enlisting a Savvy Adult," "How to Sell Well," "Working the Media," and "Covering Your Assets."

A Pipeline Debate

Another issue prompting first-time activists has been the debate over the proposed 1,179 mile Keystone XL Pipeline carrying crude oil from Canada's tar sands across parts of eight states to refineries in Nebraska, Illinois, and Texas. Polls since 2014 have consistently shown that most Americans favor the pipeline. Proponents say building the pipeline would promote U.S. energy independence and create jobs. The U.S. State Department released a report in January 2014 declaring that the Keystone XL would not have a significant environmental impact because whether or not the pipeline is completed, oil from the Canadian tar sands will extracted and sold through other means.

A *New York Times* op-ed contributor Jonathan Waldman wrote in March 2015 that "blocking [the pipeline] won't actually prevent Canada from extracting its tar sands oil. Ours is an energy-thirsty world, and when demand eventually drives up the price of oil, out it will come. . . . Pipelines are the safest way to move oil. They're an order of magnitude more reliable than trains, and trains are an order of magnitude more reliable than trucks."[22]

Opponents of the pipeline declare the project threatens the environment and the vast Ogallala Aquifer because of possible leaks and hazardous oil spills, which could endanger water supplies and human health. The pipeline is of special concern to the Lakota in South Dakota and other tribal members along the pipeline's proposed routes in Washington, Nebraska, and Oklahoma. As activist Winona LaDuke of Minnesota has noted, tribal groups have been campaigning for years against XL. "The Keystone XL Pipeline will transport the dirtiest oil on the planet through the largest freshwater aquifer in the United States, while sustaining the current levels of mass destruction occurring at tar sands extraction sites in Canada," wrote Tara Houska in a January 2015 edition of *Indian Country Today*. She explained, "Tar sands crude is resistant to typical cleanup techniques and requires a cocktail of carcinogenic chemicals just to get it through a pipe. Extraction produces 1.5 barrels of toxic waste for every barrel of tar sands crude and is nearly 20-percent more greenhouse gas-intensive than standard oil."[23]

Tribal groups are not only concerned about risks to health and climate change, but also about treaty violations. Treaties signed hundreds of years ago protect Native American territory and sacred lands, and tribes have the right to give or deny approval of projects that infringe on their territory. Yet their rights appear to be ignored, protesters contend, and thousands of tribal members and their supporters marched in New York City in 2014 to protest the pipeline.

In March 2014, about 1,200 students from across the country rallied in Washington, DC, against the pipeline. Hundreds of these students participated in civil disobedience by using plastic handcuffs to lock themselves to the White House fence, and "[another] group of activists in hazmat suits deployed a giant mock oil spill on the sidewalk as the police began to cordon off the area," according to a *Huffington Post* report.[24] Nearly four hundred students were arrested following the protest. In such cases, students usually receive a citation and a fine.

In January 2015, the U.S. House and Senate passed bills approving construction of the pipeline. However, because of amendments to the Senate bill, both chambers had to agree on a single version, and President Obama had declared earlier that he would veto whatever bill reached his desk. The president did just that hours after he received a bill on February 24, 2015. Proponents in Congress vowed to override the veto, but in the opinion of political pundits there are not enough congressional votes to overturn the veto.

See This Flick

The Normal Heart, which premiered on HBO in May 2014, is an adaptation of the stage play by activist Larry Kramer. This intense film portrays a young man who becomes a dedicated activist due to personal encounters with men dying of what was once called "gay cancer." The story is partly autobiographical and based on real people and situations of the early 1980s. It is told from the perspective of Ned Weeks (played by Mark Ruffalo), a fictional writer and gay activist who tries to raise public awareness of HIV/AIDS but encounters myriad obstacles.

The movie begins at a resort community on Fire Island, off the south shore of Long Island, New York, where gay men are reveling in their sexuality. Suddenly, Craig, one of the men and a friend of Ned Weeks, collapses for no apparent reason. Shortly thereafter back in New York City Craig suffers a seizure and dies. This sets the stage for a crusade by gay activists to learn how to fight and control the virus that is killing gay men.

After Weeks reads a newspaper article about a rare cancer afflicting homosexuals, he visits Dr. Emma Brookner (Julia Roberts), who has seen many patients—all gay men—with the symptoms of this rare infection. Brookner examines Weeks and finds him disease-free. She is concerned about other gay men, however, and asks Ned to help her raise awareness of this disease within the gay community. Ned agrees and arranges a meeting of local gay men who listen to Brookner's theory that the gay cancer is sexually transmitted. But the men at the meeting scoff at the suggestion; they are opposed to abstinence and giving up their sexual freedom.

Weeks and several of his gay friends launch a community organization called Gay Men's Health Crisis (GMHC), hoping to gain recognition from the city government and medical community that research and help are needed to counteract the disease, which has not yet been identified as AIDS. Few people join the GMHC cause and members become increasingly frustrated, often bickering among themselves about tactics. Sometimes they are so full of rage that they attack each other.

As the movie progresses, scenes depict other gay men who are infected and dying. In one highly dramatic episode, Weeks and Dr. Brookner visit a hospital where employees refuse to enter the room of a dying man, and doctors don protective covering before seeing their infected patients. Brookner finds the protection pointless, since she is convinced the disease is contacted through sex.

Weeks continues his efforts with GMHC and gets legal help from his brother Ben (Alfred Molina), a successful lawyer. The brothers, who are close, have a riveting confrontation when Ben cannot totally accept Ned's homosexuality. Weeks vows to never see his brother again.

Weeks turns to a *New York Times* gay reporter Felix Turner (Matt Bommer), asking him to cover the news about the epidemic, now called AIDS, afflicting gay men. But the newspaper editors are not interested in such stories. Weeks and Turner become lovers and the story focuses on their romantic relationship, which has wretched moments when Turner shows symptoms of AIDS. The rest of the film shows Turner's slowly dying and Weeks's efforts to keep him alive. With the help of Dr. Brookner, the two marry in the hospital before Turner dies. Weeks's brother is also at the bedside ceremony and Ben finally sees that Ned and Felix have not had a promiscuous affair; they truly love each other.

Activist Characteristics

Many people who want to be activists have started out by volunteering to advocate for a cause. Characteristics that make a good volunteer also apply to an effective activist: empathy and compassion; self-determination; enthusiasm and energy; commitment; reliability; respect for others' views. Activists also are most effective if they are flexible, open-minded, and ready to learn something new. Other helpful attributes for an activist include the ability to

- focus on the cause for which you are advocating, even though there may be side issues that attract your attention;
- maintain self-control when others deliberately provoke;
- accept that some friends and acquaintances who do not share your concerns may avoid or reject you;
- avoid personal attacks on those who have views that differ from yours;
- perform various routine tasks like writing letters to politicians, government officials, and company executives to ask them to support your cause;
- be outspoken and protest unjust actions, bigotry, and racism;
- persuade others to join your advocacy for a cause;
- plan and organize actions;
- continue your activism even when you are discouraged;
- see obstacles as challenges to overcome; and
- give credit to those who have helped you achieve a goal.

At times, it seems that to be an effective activist you have to be near perfect, but none of us are without flaws. Regardless of shortcomings and obstacles, it is possible to take up a cause and be persistent in trying to bring about positive solutions. Examples include those profiled in this book, such as Brady Kissel of Idaho, Milo Cress of Colorado, Richie Yarrow of Maryland, Zach King of Ohio, Issak Wolfe of Pennsylvania, Jordyn Schara of Wisconsin, Teresa Onstott of Illinois, Aleesa Perez of California, Daisy Coleman of Missouri, and many others. Check out their stories again. They could be inspirations and guides for your particular advocacy.

Glossary

amnesty: a general pardon for offenses against a government

bullhook: a stick with a sharp hook to prod elephants

civil disobedience: refusing to obey governmental demands or laws as a nonviolent protest

conscientious objector: a person who on the basis of conscience refuses to serve in the armed forces

conscription: military draft

coyote: a term for a person who smuggles immigrants into United States

creationism: a theory that God created various forms of life and the world

evolution: in biology, different kinds of living organisms are thought to have developed and diversified from earlier forms during the history of the earth

First Nations: the name to identify Canada's aboriginal or indigenous peoples

genetically modified organisms (GMOs): plants or animals created in laboratories by removing desired genes from a species of plant or animal and transferring them to other species

green card: a permit allowing a foreign national to live and work permanently in the United States

hate crime: a crime motivated by prejudice or intolerance toward an individual's national origin, ethnicity, color, gender, religion, sexual orientation, or disability

hydraulic fracturing: a process to open (fracture) rocks below the earth's surface to inject chemicals and liquids at high pressure to extract natural gas or oil

indigenous people: refers to descendants of people who were inhabitants of a region before their lands were invaded or colonized

militia: citizen (not professional) soldiers who are called out on occasion for duty

organic foods: foods from animals produced without antibiotics or growth hormones and produce grown without chemical pesticides and fertilizers

polygamy: the practice of having more than one spouse at a time

skinhead: often refers to a young person who is a member of a white supremacist group

status quo: the existing state or condition

steroids: organic compounds that have physiological effects on a user

tar sands: sand or sandstone that contains petroleum

Further Reading

Alexie, Sherman. *The Absolutely True Diary of a Part-Time Indian* (New York: Little, Brown, 2009).

Clay, Andreana. *The Hip-Hop Generation Fights Back: Youth, Activism, and Post-Civil Rights Politics* (New York: New York University Press, 2012).

Corrie, Rachel. *Let Me Stand Alone: The Journals of Rachel Corrie* (New York: W.W. Norton, 2008).

Gorant, Jim. *The Lost Dogs: Michael Vick's Dogs and Their Tale of Rescue and Redemption* (New York: Gotham/Penguin, 2010).

Halpi, Mikki. *It's Your World—If You Don't Like It, Change It: Activism for Teenagers* (New York: Simon Pulse, 2004).

Hunter, Zach. *Generation Change: Roll Up Your Sleeves and Change the World* (Grand Rapids, MI: Zondervan/Youth Specialties, 2013).

Lewis, Barbara A. *The Teen Guide to Global Action: How to Connect with Others (Near & Far) to Create Social Change* (Minneapolis, MN: Free Spirit Publishing, 2007).

Regan, Margaret. *The Death of Josseline: Immigration Stories from the Arizona Borderlands* (Boston: Beacon Press, 2010).

Taft, Jessica K. *Rebel Girls: Youth Activism and Social Change across the Americas* (New York: New York University Press, 2010).

Thompson, Laurie Ann. *Be a Changemaker: How to Start Something That Matters* (New York: Simon Pulse/Beyond Words, 2014).

Thorpe, Helen. *Just Like Us: The True Story of Four Mexican Girls Coming of Age in America* (New York: Scribner, 2011, paperback).

Activist Organizations

Advocates for Youth
2000 M Street, NW, Suite 750
Washington, DC 20036
Phone: 202-419-3420
No email address
http://www.advocatesforyouth.org/

Al-Anon Family Group Headquarters
1600 Corporate Landing Parkway
Virginia Beach, VA 23454-5617
Phone: 757-563-1600
wso@al-anon.org
http://www.al-anon.alateen.org/

American Civil Liberties Union
125 Broad Street, 18th Floor
New York, NY 10004
Phone: 212-549-2500
media@aclu.org
https://www.aclu.org/

American Society for the Prevention of Cruelty to Animals
424 E. 92nd Street
New York, NY 10128-6804
Phone: 888-666-2279
publicinformation@aspca.org
https://www.aspca.org/

Animal Legal Defense Fund
National Headquarters
170 East Cotati Avenue
Cotati, CA 94931
Phone: 707-795-2533
info@aldf.org
http://aldf.org/

Beyond Differences
711 Grand Avenue, Suite 200
San Rafael, CA 94901
Phone: 415-256-9095
beyonddifferences@gmail.com
http://www.beyonddifferences.org

By Any Means Necessary (BAMN)
PO Box 7322
Detroit, MI 48207
Phone: 855-275-2266
email@bamn.com
http://www.bamn.com/

Centers for Disease Control and Prevention
1600 Clifton Road
Atlanta, GA 30329-4027
Phone: 800-232-4636
Contact: CDC-INFO
http://www.cdc.gov/

DoSomething.org
19 West 21st Street, 8th Floor
New York, NY 10010
Phone: 212-254-2390
help@dosomething.org
https://www.dosomething.org/

Earth Activist Training
PO Box 170177
San Francisco, CA 94117-0177
Phone: 800-381-7940
earthactivisttraining@gmail.com
http://www.earthactivisttraining.org

Green Corps
1543 Wazee Street, Suite 300
Denver, CO 80202
Phone: 303-573-3865
info@greencorps.org
http://www.greencorps.org/

Hands of Peace
1000 Elm Street
Glenview, IL 60025
Phone: 224-406-5045
abates@handsofpeace.org
http://www.handsofpeace.org/

Highlander Research and Education Center
1959 Highlander Way
New Market, TN 37820
Phone: 865-933-3443
hrec@highlandercenter.org
http://highlandercenter.org/

Humane Society of the United States
2100 L Street, NW
Washington, DC 20037
Phone: 866-720-2676
donorcare@humanesociety.org
www.humanesociety.org

League of Education Voters
2734 Westlake Avenue N
Seattle, WA 98109
Phone: 206-728-6448
info@educationvoters.org
http://educationvoters.org/

National Institute on Drug Abuse
Office of Science Policy and Communications, Public Information and Liaison
Branch
6001 Executive Boulevard
Room 5213, MSC 9561
Bethesda, MD 20892-9561
Phone: 301-443-1124
http://www.drugabuse.gov/

Project RACE
PO Box 2366
Los Banos, CA 93635
Fax: 209-826-2510 (no phone listed)

projectrace@projectrace.com
http://www.projectrace.com/

Rape, Abuse and Incest National Network
1220 L Street NW, Suite 505
Washington, DC 20005
Phone: 202-544-1034
info@rainn.org
https://www.rainn.org/

Seattle Young People's Project
510 Maynard Avenue S
Seattle, WA 98122
Phone: 206-860-9606
info@sypp.org
http://sypp.org/

Sexuality Information and Education Council of the United States
SIECUS NY Office
90 John Street, Suite 402
New York, NY 10038
Phone: 212-819-9770
mrodriguez@siecus.org
http://www.siecus.org/

Southern Poverty Law Center
400 Washington Avenue
Montgomery, AL 36104
Phone: 334-956-8200 or 888-414-7752
No email address
http://www.splcenter.org/

Sparkle Effect
5080 Center Court
Bettendorf, IA 52722
No phone number
info@thesparkleeffect.org
http://www.thesparkleeffect.org/

Students Today Leaders Forever
609 S 10th Street, Suite 103

Minneapolis, MN 55404
Phone: 612-276-2003
info@stlf.net
http://www.stlf.net

Students Working Against Tobacco
Florida Department of Health
Bureau of Tobacco Prevention Program
4052 Bald Cypress Way, Bin C-23
Tallahassee, FL 32399-1743
Phone: 850-245-4144
contact@tobaccofreeflorida.com
http://www.swatflorida.com/

Taylor Hooton Foundation
PO Box 2104
Frisco, TX 75034-9998
Phone: 972-403-7300
info@taylorhooton.org
http://taylorhooton.org/

Teen Activist Project
New York Civil Liberties Union
125 Broad Street
New York, NY 10004
Phone: 212-607-3300
jcarnig@nyclu.org
http://www.nyclu.org/

Teens Turning Green
2330 Marinship Way, Suite 205
Sausalito, CA 94965
Phone: 415-289-1001
info@teensturninggreen.org
http://www.teensturninggreen.org/

Training for Change
PO Box 30914
Philadelphia, PA 19104
Phone: 267-289-2280
info@trainingforchange.org
https://www.trainingforchange.org/

VOX Teen Communications
229 Peachtree Street NE #725
Atlanta, GA 30303
Phone: 404-614-0040
info@voxteencommunications.org
http://www.voxteencommunications.org/

Youth Empowered Action
c/o Earth Island Institute
2150 Allston Way, Suite 460
Berkeley, CA 94704
Phone: 415-710-7351
info@yeacamp.org
http://yeacamp.org/

Youth LEAD
75/12 Ocean Tower II, 15th Floor
Soi Sukhumvit 19
Klong Toey Nua
Wattana Bangkok, 10110
Thailand
info@youth-lead.org
http://youth-lead.org/

Notes

Chapter 1

1. Jane Northrop, "Community Service Spurs Student to Major in Social Activism," *San Jose Mercury News*, May 27, 2014, http://www.mercurynews.com/ci_25845919/community -service-spurs-student-major-social-activism (accessed May 28, 2014).
2. See the Youth Activism Project home page, http://youthactivismproject.org/ (accessed June 15, 2014).
3. Adrian Walker, "Teen Activists Rally for Summer Jobs," *Boston Globe*, February 19, 2014, http://www.bostonglobe.com/metro/2014/02/19/teen-activists-rally-for-summer-jobs-but -will-adults-listen/5Ew6Kc7Er25RCMJJzRi2yK/story.html (accessed May 13, 2014).
4. Tara Holmes, "Making an Impact: Are You an Activist?" Truth-Out.org, May 25, 2014, http://www.truth-out.org/opinion/item/23900-making-an-impact-are-you-an-activist (accessed May 25, 2014).
5. "About," BAMN, n.d., http://www.bamn.com/about-bamn (accessed June 12, 2014).
6. Susan Bell, "Volunteering vs. Activism," DornsifeLive.usc.edu, January 24, 2014, http://dornsifelive.usc.edu/news/stories/1611/volunteering-vs-activism/ (accessed May 13, 2014).
7. Archana Pyati and Amy Reinink, "Bethesda Magazine's Extraordinary Teen Awards," *Bethesda Magazine*, March–April 2014, p. 12, http://www.bethesdamagazine.com/Bethesda -Magazine/March-April-2014/Top-Teens-2014/index.php?cparticle=5&siarticle=4 (accessed June 12, 2014).
8. Pyati and Reinink, "Bethesda Magazine's Extraordinary Teen Awards," p. 5.
9. Pyati and Reinink, "Bethesda Magazine's Extraordinary Teen Awards," p. 10.
10. MBD (Political Blind Spot author), "Major Protests at UND against Racist 'Siouxper Drunk' Anti-Native American Shirts," PoliticalBlindSpot.com, May 16, 2014, http://politicalblind spot.com/major-protests-at-und-against-racist-siouxper-drunk-anti-native-american-shirts/ (accessed June 14, 2014); also see http://www.valleynewslive.com/story/25513115/dozens -turn-out-for-protest-of-siouxper-drunk-shirts (accessed June 14, 2014).
11. Hayley Miller, "LGBT Men Experience High Rates of Street Harassment," *HRC Blog*, June 4, 2014, http://www.hrc.org/blog/entry/lgbt-men-experience-high-rates-of-street-harassment (accessed June 16, 2014).
12. "National Day of Silence (April 17, 2015)," NCTSNet.org, n.d., http://www.nctsnet.org/ resources/public-awareness/national-day-silence (accessed June 20, 2014).
13. James Nichols, "Oregon Students Protest Day of Silence with 'Gay Not OK' Shirts," *Huffington Post*, April 14, 2014, http://www.huffingtonpost.com/2014/04/14/gay-not-ok -shirt_n_5146967.html (accessed June 20, 2014).
14. "*Growing Up LGBT in America*: Key Findings," HRC.org, n.d., http://www.hrc.org/youth/ about-the-survey-report#.U6Brn3bQvXQ (accessed June 6, 2015); also see "Children & Youth," HRC.org, http://www.hrc.org/youth (accessed June 6, 2015).

15. Human Rights Campaign, *Growing Up LGBT in America*, n.d., http://hrc-assets.s3-website -us-east-1.amazonaws.com//files/assets/resources/Growing-Up-LGBT-in-America_Report .pdf (accessed June 6, 2015).

16. Jonathan Rauch, "Red America's Anti-Gay Backlash," *Daily Beast*, June 15, 2014, http:// www.thedailybeast.com/articles/2014/06/15/red-america-s-anti-gay-backlash.html (accessed June 16, 2014).

17. Andrew Knittle, "North Grad Took Own Life after Week of 'Toxic' Comments," *Norman Transcript*, October 10, 2010, http://www.normantranscript.com/headlines/x1477594493/-I -m-sure-he-took-it-personally (accessed July 10, 2014).

18. Morgan Welch, "'Broken Heart Land' Documentary Releases Promotional Trailer," Dot429 .com, May 13, 2014, http://dot429.com/articles/4462-broken-heart-land-documentary -releases-promotional-trailer (accessed July 11, 2014).

19. Nancy Harrington, "How Losing Our Gay, HIV-Positive Son to Suicide Turned Our Family into Activists," *The Blog*, HuffPost Gay Voices, June 16, 2014, http://www.huffingtonpost .com/nancy-harrington/how-losing-our-gay-hiv-positive-son-to-suicide-turned-our-family -into-activists_b_5486252.html (accessed July 10, 2014).

20. Harrington, "How Losing Our Gay, HIV-Positive Son."

21. See Child Labor Education Project, https://www.continuetolearn.uiowa.edu/laborctr/child _labor/about/us_history.html (accessed June 18, 2014).

22. "Are You Eligible to Join the Military?" Military.com, n.d., http://www.military.com/join -armed-forces/join-the-military-basic-eligibility.html (accessed June 21, 2014).

23. What Kids Can Do, "Urban Youth Grow 30,000 Lbs. of Organic Produce to Relieve Hunger," WKCD.org, June 16, 2014, http://www.whatkidscando.org/new/WKCD_UrbanRoots .html (accessed June 21, 2014).

24. What Kids Can Do, "Urban Youth."

---

a. American Youth Congress, "The Declaration of Rights of American Youth," July 4, 1936, H-net.msu.edu, http://h-net.msu.edu/cgi-bin/logbrowse.pl?trx=vx&list=h-us1918-45& month=0307&week=a&msg=K9jayTtAEbZvuThF3ngH%2Bg&user=&pw= (accessed June 10, 2014).

b. "Be Straw Free Campaign," EcoCycle.org, n.d., http://www.ecocycle.org/bestrawfree (accessed June 10, 2014).

c. Charlie Bermant, "Colorado Boy Takes Anti-straw Campaign to Peers in Port Townsend," *Peninsula Daily News*, May 27, 2014, http://www.peninsuladailynews.com/article/20140527/ news/305279993/colorado-boy-takes-anti-straw-campaign-to-peers-in-port-townsend (accessed May 1, 2015).

d. Bermant, "Colorado Boy."

Chapter 2

1. Belinda and Eric, "Youth Activists," AdvocatesforYouth.org, n.d., http://www.advocatesfor youth.org/press-room/meet-our-youth-activists (accessed June 30, 2014).

2. Allison Manning, "Bullied Gay Teen Becomes an Activist," *Columbus Dispatch*, July 29, 2012, http://www.dispatch.com/content/stories/local/2012/07/29/bullied-gay-teen-becomes-an -activist.html (accessed July 3, 2014).

3. "ACLU Warns High School Principal Who Removed Transgender Pennsylvania Student from Prom King Ballot," ACLUPA.org, April 26, 2013, http://www.aclupa.org/news/2013/04/26/aclu-warns-high-school-principal-who-removed-transgender-pen (accessed July 4, 2014).

4. "Frequently Asked Questions," YouthRights.org, n.d., http://www.youthrights.org/issues/drinking-age/frequently-asked-questions/.

5. "Minimum Legal Drinking Age—Pros and Cons," ProCon.org, n.d., http://drinkingage.procon.org/ (accessed July 2, 2014).

6. Sally Kohn, "Can't Hardly Wait," Prospect.org, October 28, 2011, http://prospect.org/article/cant-hardly-wait (accessed June 26, 2014).

7. Jonathan Bernstein, "Good News for Teen Voting," *Washington Post*, November 11, 2013, http://www.washingtonpost.com/blogs/post-partisan/wp/2013/11/11/good-news-for-teen-voting/ (accessed June 26, 2014).

8. "First Nation Teen Told Not to Wear 'Got Land?' Shirt at School," CBC.ca, January 14, 2014, updated January 15, 2014, http://www.cbc.ca/news/canada/saskatchewan/first-nation-teen-told-not-to-wear-got-land-shirt-at-school-1.2497009 (accessed November 17, 2014).

9. Kate Schwass-Bueckert, "'Got Land? Thank an Indian' Shirts Hot Commodity after Controversy, Seller Says," *Toronto Sun*, January 17, 2014, updated January 17, 2014, http://www.torontosun.com/2014/01/17/got-land-thank-an-indian-shirts-hot-commodity-after-controversy-seller-says (accessed November 17, 2014).

10. Tyler Hayden, "UCSB Professor Accused of Assaulting Anti-Abortion Activist," *Santa Barbara Independent*, March 11, 2014, updated March 13, 2014, http://www.independent.com/news/2014/mar/11/ucsb-professor-accused-assaulting-pro-life-activis/ (accessed June 28, 2014).

11. "UCSB Professor Faces Assault Charges after Dispute with Pro-Life Protesters," *Daily Nexus*, March 13, 2014, http://dailynexus.com/2014-03-13/feminist-studies-professor-enters-confrontation-with-pro-life-protestors/ (accessed June 27, 2014).

12. "UCSB Professor Faces Assault Charges."

13. Mary Turck, "Central High School Students, Teachers Read Banned Books, Protesting Arizona Censorship," *Twin Cities Daily Planet*, February 16, 2012, www.tcdailyplanet.net/news/2329/10/22/st-paul-notes-central-high-school-students-teachers-read-banned-books-protesting-ari?print=1 (accessed July 2, 2014).

14. Ted Robbins, "Tucson Revives Mexican-American Studies Program," NPR.org, July 24, 2013, http://www.npr.org/blogs/codeswitch/2013/07/24/205058168/Tucson-Revives-Mexican-American-Studies-Program (accessed June 29, 2014).

15. Molly Driscoll, "World Book Night: Cops Are Called as Idaho Teen Hands Out Challenged Book," *Christian Science Monitor*, April 28, 2014, http://www.csmonitor.com/Books/chapter-and-verse/2014/0428/World-Book-Night-cops-are-called-as-Idaho-teen-hands-out-challenged-book (accessed June 28, 2014).

16. Jay Hathaway, "Handing Out Banned Books," Gawker.com, April 29, 2014, http://gawker.com/parents-call-cops-to-stop-kids-from-handing-out-banned-1569491566 (accessed June 29, 2014).

17. Kimberly Yates, "Are Student Dress Codes a Violation of Civil Rights?" SeattlePI.com, n.d., http://education.seattlepi.com/student-dress-codes-violation-civil-rights-1644.html (accessed July 6, 2014).

18. Jay Sekulow, "Religious Clothing at School," ACLJ.org, n.d., http://old.aclj.org/education/religious-clothing-at-school (accessed July 6, 2014).

19. "Religious Discrimination in Education," Justice.gov, n.d., http://www.justice.gov/crt/spec_topics/religiousdiscrimination/ff_education.php (accessed July 6, 2014).
20. "Religious Discrimination in Education."

a. Marlow Stern, "How Katy Butler, 'Bully' Documentary's Teen Crusader, Was Bullied," March 28, 2012, http://www.thedailybeast.com/articles/2012/03/28/how-katy-butler-bully-documentary-s-teen-crusader-was-bullied.html (accessed July 5, 2014).
b. Donna St. George, "Katy Butler: A New Voice against Bullying," *Washington Post*, March 16, 2012, http://www.washingtonpost.com/local/education/katy-butler-a-new-voice-against-bullying/2012/03/16/gIQAXUPbHS_story.html (accessed July 5, 2014).
c. See the U.S. Census Bureau's "State & County QuickFacts," http://quickfacts.census.gov/qfd/states/00000.html (accessed July 1, 2014).
d. See http://www.thefire.org/spotlight/ (accessed June 30, 2014).
e. Greg Lukianoff, "11 Student and Faculty Victories over Campus 'Free Speech Zones,'" *The Blog*, HuffPost College, September 12, 2013, http://www.huffingtonpost.com/greg-lukianoff/11-student-and-faculty-vi_b_3913959.html#s2879995&title=University_of_Cincinnati (accessed June 30, 2014).
f. *Tinker et al. v. Des Moines Independent Community School District et al.*, argued November 12, 1968, decided February 24, 1969, http://scholar.google.com/scholar_case?case=15235797139493194004&q=Tinker+v.+Des+Moines+Independent+Community+School+District&hl=en&as_sdt=40006&as_vis=1 (accessed July 1, 2014).

Chapter 3

1. Phil Anderson, "Red Ribbon Event Honors Teens Fighting Drug, Alcohol Abuse," *Topeka-Capital Journal*, March 27, 2014, http://cjonline.com/news/2014-03-27/students-honored-red-ribbon-event (accessed July 17, 2014).
2. "What Do Older Teens Say about Alateen—How Alateen Helps," YouTube video, September 4, 2014, http://www.youtube.com/watch?v=KX0nFbAWB2c (accessed July 17, 2014).
3. "What Do Older Teens Say about Alateen."
4. Anderson, "Red Ribbon Event Honors Teens Fighting Drug, Alcohol Abuse."
5. "Fact Sheets—Underage Drinking," CDC.gov, n.d., http://www.cdc.gov/alcohol/fact-sheets/underage-drinking.htm (accessed July 17, 2014).
6. "Alcohol and Other Drug Use," CDC.gov, n.d., http://www.cdc.gov/healthyyouth/alcoholdrug/ (accessed July 17, 2014).
7. See NIDA's "Commonly Abused Drugs Charts" at http://www.drugabuse.gov/drugs-abuse/commonly-abused-drugs/commonly-abused-drugs-chart (accessed July 17, 2014).
8. National Institute of Drug Abuse, "DrugFacts: High School and Youth Trends," DrugAbuse.gov, updated January 2014, http://www.drugabuse.gov/publications/drugfacts/high-school-youth-trends (accessed July 21, 2014).
9. Jordyn Schara, "WI Pill & Drug Disposal," CaseFoundation.org, 2010, http://befearless.casefoundation.org/projects/wi-pill-drug-disposal/jordyn-schara (accessed July 23, 2014).
10. Megan Dobransky, "High School Students Help Pass Landmark Legislation," Enviro Advisory.com, March 2011, http://www.enviroadvisory.com/top_story_High%20School%20Students%20Help%20Pass%20Landmark%20Legislation.shtml (accessed July 24, 2014).

11. U.S. Food and Drug Administration, "Teens and Steroids: A Dangerous Combo," FDA.gov, November 2013, http://www.fda.gov/forconsumers/consumerupdates/ucm373014.htm (accessed July 16, 2014).

12. Don Hooton Jr., response to questionnaire, received by the author July 29, 2014. Subsequent quotes from Hooton are also from this questionnaire.

13. National Institute of Drug Abuse, "DrugFacts."

14. See SWAT Florida's website at http://www.swatflorida.com/ (accessed July 10, 2014).

15. "Get to Know Us," SWATFlorida.com, n.d., http://www.swatflorida.com/get-to-know-us (accessed July 10, 2014).

16. Alessandro Boyd, "Campion College Kicks Butts—School Hosts Anti-Smoking Day to Educate Teens on the Dangers of Smoking," *Gleaner*, March 21, 2014, http://www.jamaica -gleaner.com/gleaner/20140321/news/news4.html (accessed June 6, 2015).

17. "Southeast Teens Are Kicking Butts," *Healthy Living Southeast*, March 20, 2014, http:// www.healthylivingse.org/quitting-tobacco/2014/3/20/southeast-teens-are-kicking-butts (accessed July 9, 2014).

18. American Lung Association, "Tobacco Free Colleges and Universities," Lung.org, May 19, 2014, http://www.lung.org/stop-smoking/tobacco-free-colleges-universities.html (accessed July 10, 2014).

19. Monica Eng, "Chicago High Schoolers to Demand Better Food at Board Meeting," *Chicago Tribune*, March 23, 2010, http://articles.chicagotribune.com/2010-03-23/news/ct-met-cps -students-school-lunch-speech-20100322_1_school-food-food-service-board-meeting (accessed July 13, 2014).

20. Monica Eng, "Healthier Lunches Unpopular with CPS Students," Chicago.cbslocal.com, February 21, 2011, http://chicago.cbslocal.com/2011/02/21/healthier-lunches-unpopular -with-cps-students/ (accessed July 13, 2014).

21. "Teens for Food Justice," StudentsforService.org, n.d., http://www.studentsforservice.org/ get-involved/volunteer/ (accessed May 14, 2014).

22. See the Be Fearless Hub on the Case Foundation's website, http://befearless.casefoundation .org/projects/youth-lead/erin-healy (accessed July 22, 2014).

23. Carol Lawrence, "Occupy Monsanto Starts Campaign on Movement's Anniversary," *Ventura County Star*, September 18, 2012, http://www.vcstar.com/business/occupy-monsanto-starts -campaign-on-movements (accessed July 15, 2014).

24. David H. Freedman, "The Truth about Genetically Modified Food," *Scientific American*, August 20, 2013, http://www.scientificamerican.com/article/the-truth-about-genetically -modified-food/ (accessed July 24, 2014).

25. Ashutosh Jogalekar, "*Scientific American* Comes Out in Favor of GMOs, and I Agree," *Scientific American* (blog), September 6, 2013, http://blogs.scientificamerican.com/the-curious -wavefunction/2013/09/06/scientific-american-comes-out-in-favor-of-gmos/ (accessed July 24, 2014).

26. "SIECUS: Fact Sheet," SIECUS.org, October 2009, http://www.siecus.org/index.cfm ?fuseaction=Page.ViewPage&PageID=1193 (accessed July 14, 2014).

27. Douglas Kirby, Summary of *Emerging Answers 2007: Research Findings on Programs to Reduce Teen Pregnancy and Sexually Transmitted Diseases* (Washington, DC: The National Campaign to Prevent Teen and Unplanned Pregnancy, 2007), 15–16.

28. Ryan Holman, "Danny Sparks: Sex Education Activist," Advocate.com, March 10, 2010, http://www.advocate.com/society/activism/2010/03/10/sex-ed-student-turns-teen-activist (accessed July 14, 2014).

29. See the blog of CREATE council members Adrian Nava and Scarlett Jimenez at http://www
.nationalpartnership.org/blog/general/youth-activism-for-sex-education.html (accessed August 31, 2015).
30. The link to Scarlett's testimony is found at http://www.nationalpartnership.org/blog/general/
youth-activism-for-sex-education.html (accessed August 31, 2015).

---

a. "Temperance Movement," HowStuffWorks.com, February 27, 2008, http://history.howstuff
works.com/american-history/temperance-movement.htm (accessed July 22, 2014).
b. U.S. Department of Health and Human Services, *The Health Consequences of Smoking—50 Years of Progress: A Report of the Surgeon General* (Atlanta, GA: U.S. Department of Health and Human Services, Centers for Disease Control and Prevention, National Center for Chronic Disease Prevention and Health Promotion, Office on Smoking and Health, 2014), http://www.surgeongeneral.gov/library/reports/50-years-of-progress/fact-sheet.html (accessed July 13, 2014).
c. Associated Press, "Supreme Court Clears Way for California Ban on Gay Conversion Therapy," FoxNews.com, June 30, 2014, http://www.foxnews.com/politics/2014/06/30/supreme
-court-clears-way-for-california-ban-on-gay-conversion-therapy/ (accessed July 13, 2014).

Chapter 4

1. "Teen 'Rape Victim,' Jada, Bravely Fights Back against Internet Trolls and Victim Blaming," *Huffington Post UK*, July 17, 2014, http://www.huffingtonpost.co.uk/2014/07/17/jadapose-american-girl-rape-victim-viral-_n_5594899.html (accessed July 26, 2014).
2. "National Survey on Teen Relationships and Intimate Violence," NORC.org, n.d., http://
www.norc.org/Research/Projects/Pages/survey-on-teen-relationships-and-intimate-violence
.aspx (accessed April 28, 2015).
3. Catherine Mijs, "Teen Survivor of Brutal Sexual Assault Speaks Out at Solano Event," *Contra Costa Times*, April 10, 2014, http://www.contracostatimes.com/breaking-news/ci_25538934/
teen-survivor-brutal-sexual-assault-speaks-out-at (accessed August 4, 2014).
4. Associated Press, "Maryville Man Accused of Rape in Daisy Coleman Case Pleads Guilty to Child Endangerment," *New York Daily News*, January 9, 2014, http://www.nydailynews.com/
news/national/college-student-accused-maryville-rape-case-charged-child-endangerment
-article-1.1571171 (accessed August 1, 2014).
5. CNN staff, "4 More School Employees Charged in Steubenville Rape Case," CNN.com, updated November 26, 2013, http://www.cnn.com/2013/11/25/justice/ohio-steubenville-rape
-case/ (accessed July 30, 2014).
6. Mark Gillispie, "Steubenville Schools Chief Accused of Destroying Evidence in Rape Investigation," *Huffington Post*, May 23, 2014, http://www.huffingtonpost.com/2014/05/23/
michael-mcvey_n_5382894.html?utm_hp_ref=steubenville-rape (accessed July 31, 2014).
7. Travis Gettys, "Georgia Teens Indicted for Brutal Post-Prom Rape That Left Unconscious Victim Hospitalized," RawStory.com, July 8, 2014, http://www.rawstory.com/rs/2014/07/08/
georgia-teens-indicted-for-brutal-post-prom-rape-that-left-unconscious-victim-hospital-ized/ (accessed July 30, 2014).
8. "Nearly Half of Colleges Have Not Investigated Sexual Violence Reports," RAINN.org, July 14, 2014, https://www.rainn.org/nearly-half-of-colleges-have-not-investigated-sexual
-violence-reports (accessed August 7, 2014).

9. Kristen Lombardi, "A Lack of Consequences for Sexual Assault," PublicIntegrity.org, February 10, 2010, updated July 14, 2014, http://www.publicintegrity.org/2010/02/24/4360/lack-consequences-sexual-assault-0 (accessed July 29, 2014).

10. Krystyna Biassou, "Oklahoma State under Fire after Sexual Misconduct Allegations," *USA Today*, December 19, 2012, http://college.usatoday.com/2012/12/19/oklahoma-state-under-fire-after-sexual-misconduct-allegations/ (accessed July 29, 2014).

11. "Former Oklahoma State Student Pleads Guilty to Sexual Battery Charges," KOCO.com, September 20, 2013, http://www.koco.com/news/oklahomanews/around-oklahoma/former-osu-student-to-enter-plea-in-sexual-assault/22040368#!bpY1pc (accessed July 29, 2014).

12. Jennifer Steinhauer, "Senators Offer Bill to Curb Campus Sexual Assault," *New York Times*, July 31, 2014, http://www.nytimes.com/2014/07/31/us/college-sexual-assault-bill-in-senate.html?_r=0 (accessed August 3, 2014).

13. George Will, "George Will: Colleges Become the Victims of Progressivism," *Washington Post*, June 6, 2014, http://www.washingtonpost.com/opinions/george-will-college-become-the-victims-of-progressivism/2014/06/06/e90e73b4-eb50-11e3-9f5c-9075d5508f0a_story.html (accessed August 4, 2014).

14. Lisa Reed, "A College Rape Survivor Responds to George Will's 'Coveted Status' Remarks," MediaMatters.org, June 10, 2014, http://mediamatters.org/print/blog/2014/06/10/a-college-rape-survivor-responds-to-george-will/199658 (accessed August 5, 2014).

15. Jenny Wilkinson, "Sexually Assaulted at UVA," *New York Times*, April 5, 2015, http://www.nytimes.com/2015/04/05/opinion/sunday/sexually-assaulted-at-uva.html?_r=1 (accessed April 27, 2015).

16. Wilkinson, "Sexually Assaulted at UVA."

17. "The Women's Program," OneInFourUSA.org, n.d., http://oneinfourusa.org/thewomensprogram.php (accessed August 2, 2014).

18. "The Men's Program," OneInFourUSA.org, n.d., http://oneinfourusa.org/themensprogram.php (accessed August 2, 2014).

19. "About Us," SAFERCampus.org, n.d., http://safercampus.org/about-us (accessed July 30, 2014).

20. "Trafficking in Persons Report 2011," State.gov, n.d., http://www.state.gov/j/tip/rls/tiprpt/2011/164220.htm (accessed July 29, 2014).

21. "Human Trafficking," FBI.gov, n.d., http://www.fbi.gov/about-us/investigate/civilrights/human_trafficking (accessed July 29, 2014).

22. See the Rights4Girls website, http://www.rights4girls.org/#!trafficking-of-girls/cthj (accessed July 27, 2014).

23. Mary Beth Marklein, "168 Children Rescued from Sex Trafficking, FBI Says," *USA Today*, June 23, 2014, http://www.usatoday.com/story/news/nation/2014/06/23/fbi-trafficking-sex-children/11271829/ (accessed August 5, 2014).

24. Marklein, "168 Children Rescued."

25. "Human Trafficking Prevention Month Raises Awareness of Enforcement and Victim Assistance Efforts," *News Blog*, FBI.gov, January 10, 2014, http://www.fbi.gov/news/news_blog/human-trafficking-prevention-month-raises-awareness-of-enforcement-and-victim-assistance-efforts (accessed August 6, 2014).

26. Stephanie Chuang and Liza Meak, "From Child Sex Slave to Activist: Berkeley Woman Breaks Chains of Human Trafficking," NBCBayArea.com, December 31, 2012, http://www.nbcbayarea.com/investigations/From-Sex-Slave-to-Activist-How-a-Berkeley-Woman-is-Using-Her-Past-to-Help-Others—184471481.html (accessed August 4, 2014).

27. Chuang and Meak, "From Child Sex Slave to Activist."
28. "Mission & History," GEMS-Girls.org, n.d., http://www.gems-girls.org/about/mission-history (accessed May 13, 2014).
29. Saskia de Melker, "Filmmakers Explore Sex Trafficking Abuses in 'Tricked' Documentary," PBS.org, February 1, 2014, http://www.pbs.org/newshour/updates/meet-filmmakers-behind-human-trafficking-documentary-tricked/ (accessed August 6, 2014).
30. de Melker, "Filmmakers Explore Sex Trafficking Abuses."
31. Danielle Douglas, "How I Tell My Sex Trafficking Survivor Story," *The Blog*, HuffPost Impact, December 12, 2013, http://www.huffingtonpost.com/danielle-douglas/how-i-tell-my-sex-trafficking-survivor-story_b_4427388.html (accessed August 6, 2014).

a. Carol Kuruvilla, "16-Year-Old Houston Girl Speaks Out after Purported Photos of Her Rape Go Viral," *New York Daily News*, July 10, 2014, http://www.nydailynews.com/news/crime/houston-teen-speaks-rape-viral-article-1.1861897 (accessed July 26, 2014).
b. "#IAMJADA—Jada Speaks Out," MSNBC.com, n.d., http://www.msnbc.com/ronan-farrow-daily/watch/-iamjada-jada-speaks-out-304563780002 (accessed July 26, 2014).
c. Alexandra Brodsky, Dana Bolger, and NationAction, "Want Colleges to Protect Students from Sexual Assault? Take Action to Give Title IX Teeth," *Nation*, July 8, 2014, http://www.thenation.com/blog/180558/want-colleges-protect-students-sexual-violence-take-action-give-title-ix-teeth# (accessed August 2, 2014).
d. Rachel Lloyd, *Girls Like Us: Fighting for a World Where Girls Are Not for Sale, an Activist Finds Her Calling and Heals Herself* (New York: HarperCollins, 2011), p. 45.
e. "The Victims," PolarisProject.org, n.d., http://www.polarisproject.org/human-trafficking/overview/the-victims?gclid=CN6qjPuri8ACFbTm7Aodp0gAlQ (accessed April 28, 2015).

Chapter 5

1. Elizabeth Hernandez, "Boulder Teen Activist Leads Initiative to Sow Seeds of Hope for Environment," *Daily Camera*, April 19, 2014, www.dailycamera.com/news/boulder/ci_25600219/boulder-teen-activist-leads-initiative-sow-seeds-hope (accessed August 30, 2014).
2. Marisa McNatt, "Teens Say 'Environment' Is Top Concern," Earth911.com, February 25, 2010, http://earth911.com/news/2010/02/25/teens-say-environment-is-a-top-concern/#comments (accessed August 30, 2014).
3. "The History of Greening Forward," GreeningForward.org, n.d., http://greeningforward.org/the-history-of-greening-forward/ (accessed August 12, 2014).
4. Steve Orr, "Georgia Teen Brings Eco Message to Rochester," *Democrat & Chronicle*, April 4, 2014, http://www.democratandchronicle.com/story/news/2014/04/21/charles-orgbon-environmental-earth-day/7968575/ (accessed August 12, 2014).
5. Ben Whitford, "Native American Activism: Environmental Issues Take Priority," *Ecologist*, n.d., http://www.theecologist.org/News/news_analysis/1942396/native_american_activism_environmental_issues_take_priority.html (accessed September 1, 2014).
6. Whitford, "Native American Activism."
7. Coast Salish Sea Tribes and Nations, "Coast Salish Nations Unite to Protect Salish Sea," *Indian Country*, February 17, 2014, http://indiancountrytodaymedianetwork.com/2014/02/17/coast-salish-nations-unite-protect-salish-sea (accessed September 2, 2014).

8. Ben Block, "Climate Change Activists Pour into D.C.," worldwatch.org, updated September 1, 2015, http://www.worldwatch.org/node/6027 (accessed September 1, 2015).

9. Moms Clean Air Force, "Texas Teen Tackles Air Pollution and Wins!" MomsCleanAirForce .org, September 13, 2012, http://www.momscleanairforce.org/texas-teen-tackles-air -pollution-and-wins/ (accessed August 20, 2014).

10. Moms Clean Air Force, "Texas Teen Tackles Air Pollution and Wins!"

11. Katherine Ellison, "An Inconvenient Lawsuit: Teenagers Take Global Warming to the Courts," *Mother Jones*, May 10, 2012, http://www.motherjones.com/environment/2012/05/ alec-loorz-global-warming-lawsuit (accessed August 31, 2014).

12. United States Court of Appeals for the District of Columbia Circuit, *Alec L., et al. v. Gina McCarthy, et al.* (accessed June 5, 2014).

13. Megan Claflin, "Rally on the Rails," PTLeader.com, December 18, 2013, http://www .ptleader.com/news/education/rally-on-the-rails-port-townsend-high-school-students-to/ article_98a9a812-6775-11e3-be9a-001a4bcf6878.html (accessed August 14, 2014).

14. Responses to questionnaire from Ewan Shortess, received by the author June 13, 2014.

15. Responses to questionnaire from Ewan Shortess, received by the author June 13, 2014.

16. Responses to questionnaire from Ewan Shortess, received by the author June 13, 2014.

17. Carolyn Thompson, "35 Years after Toxic Waste Site Spurred Environmental Reform, Residents Sue over Illnesses," *USA Today*, November 2, 1013, http://www.usatoday.com/story/ money/business/2013/11/02/suits-claim-love-canal-still-oozing-35-years-later/3384259/ (accessed August 19, 2014).

18. "Teen Fights for Toxic Waste Cleanup," PBSLearningMedia.org, n.d., http://www.pbs learningmedia.org/resource/envh10.sci.life.eco.superfund/teen-fights-for-toxic-waste -cleanup/ (accessed August 20, 2014).

19. Jared Saylor and Debra Mayfield, "A Toxic Inheritance," Earthjustice.org (first published in the Spring 2014 issue of the *Earthjustice Quarterly Magazine*), http://earthjustice.org/ features/a-toxic-inheritance (accessed August 22, 2014).

20. Paldon Dolma, "It's Easy Being Green," *YCteen*, September–October 2011, http:// www.ycteenmag.org/topics/activism/It%E2%80%99s_Easy_Being_Green.html?story_ id=NYC-2011-09-14 (accessed August 30, 2014).

---

a. Gaylord Nelson, "How the First Earth Day Came About," EnviroLink.org, n.d., http:// earthday.envirolink.org/history.html (accessed August 13, 2014).

b. "What Is the Difference between Weather and Climate?" NOAA.gov, n.d., http://ocean service.noaa.gov/facts/weather_climate.html (accessed August 13, 2014).

c. Katy Lederer, "The Near Thing Which Must Not Be Named," *Tampa Bay Times*, May 3, 2015, p. 4P.

d. Carl Hiaasen, *Scat* (New York: Alfred A. Knopf, 2009), p. 185.

Chapter 6

1. Elora West, response to questionnaire, received by the author October 2014.

2. See Last Chance for Animals' "Mission Statement," http://www.lcanimal.org/index.php/ about-lca/mission-statement (accessed May 3, 2015).

3. Lou Wegner, response to questionnaire, received by the author October 2014. Unless stated otherwise, subsequent quotes from Lou are also from this questionnaire.

4. Angela Lutz, "Meet the Teen Animal Activist Who Took Two Shelter Dogs to Prom," Dogster.com, February 21, 2014, http://www.dogster.com/lifestyle/dog-rescue-adoption-kids-against-animal-cruelty-actor-lou-wegner-shelter-dogs-prom (accessed October 22, 2014).

5. "'Simpsons' Producer Dies at 59," SamSimonFoundation.com, n.d., http://www.samsimonfoundation.com/news.asp (accessed October 14, 2014).

6. "Farm Animal Cruelty," ASPCA.org, n.d., https://www.aspca.org/fight-cruelty/farm-animal-cruelty (accessed October 16, 2014).

7. JeffRincon, "What Actually Happens to Animals in Factory Farms," *Teen Ink*, n.d., http://www.teenink.com/opinion/all/article/434978/What-Actually-Happens-to-Animals-in-Factory-Farms/ (accessed May 4, 2015).

8. "Timeline of Major Farm Animal Protection Advancements," HumaneSociety.org, September 8, 2014, http://www.humanesociety.org/issues/confinement_farm/timelines/timeline_farm_animal_protection.html?credit=web_id275813364 (accessed October 16, 2014).

9. See the Humane Farming Association's website, http://www.hfa.org/ (accessed October 16, 2014).

10. "Undercover Investigations," MercyforAnimals.com, n.d., http://www.mercyforanimals.org/investigations.aspx (accessed October 16, 2014).

11. Matt Rice, "Breaking News: Nestlé Makes Sweeping Animal Welfare Policy Change Following MFA Investigation," MFAblog.org, August 21, 2014, http://www.mfablog.org/breaking-news-nestle-makes-sweeping-animal-welfare-policy-change (accessed October 16, 2014).

12. "Teen Tracks," AAWL.org, n.d., https://aawl.org/teen-tracks (accessed May 4, 2015).

13. Samarrah Stephan, "Service Day at AAWL," *Teen Track Times*, Fall 2014, p. 2; also see https://aawl.org/sites/default/files/teen-tracks-december-2014.pdf (accessed May 4, 2015).

14. "Our Story," OPHRescue.org, 2014, https://ophrescue.org/aboutus (accessed October 14, 2014).

15. "Children—At-Risk Youth," GentleBarn.org, n.d., http://www.gentlebarn.org/children/at-risk-youth.html (accessed October 14, 2014).

16. See the Circus Protest website, http://circusprotest.com/about_us.html (accessed October 19, 2014).

17. "Circuses and Performing Animals," BornFree.org, n.d., http://www.bornfree.org.uk/campaigns/zoo-check/circuses-performing-animals/ (accessed September 1, 2015).

18. Deborah Nelson, "The Cruelest Show on Earth," *Mother Jones*, November–December 2011, pp. 48+, http://www.motherjones.com/environment/2011/10/ringling-bros-elephant-abuse (accessed October 13, 2014).

19. "Cockfighting," ASPCA.org, n.d., https://www.aspca.org/fight-cruelty/cockfighting (accessed May 4, 2015).

20. "Cockfighting," HumaneSociety.org, n.d., http://www.humanesociety.org/issues/cockfighting/ (accessed October 23, 2014).

21. Steve Williams, "Cockfighting: It's Illegal So Why Is It Still Happening in the United States?" Care2.com, April 28, 2014, http://www.care2.com/causes/cockfighting-its-illegal-so-why-is-it-still-happening-in-the-united-states.html (accessed October 19, 2014).

a. Elora West, responses to questionnaire, received by the author October 2014.

b. Jim Gorant, *The Lost Dogs: Michael Vick's Dogs and Their Tale of Rescue and Redemption* (New York: Gotham Books/Penguin, 2010), p. 126.

c. "Truth about Blackfish," SeaWorld.com, n.d., http://seaworld.com/truth/truth-about-blackfish/ (accessed April 29, 2015).

Chapter 7

1. Bill Moyers and Zack Kopplin, "Fighting Creeping Creationism," BillMoyers.com, March 1, 2013, http://billmoyers.com/episode/full-show-fighting-creeping-creationism/ (accessed September 13, 2014).

2. "The ACLU and Freedom of Religion and Belief," ACLU.org, n.d., https://www.aclu.org/religion-belief/aclu-and-freedom-religion-and-belief (accessed September 24, 2014).

3. Heather L. Weaver, "Don't B-SHOCked: Settlement Shows Public Schools Can't Proselytize," ACLU.org, January 24, 2012, https://www.aclu.org/blog/religion-belief/dont-b-shocked-settlement-shows-public-schools-cant-proselytize (accessed September 24, 2014).

4. Weaver, "Don't B-SHOCked."

5. "Intelligence Briefs," *Intelligence Report* (of the Southern Poverty Law Center), Fall 2014, p. 11.

6. Cavan Sieczkowski, "Baptist Church Gets a Big Surprise While Protesting Wilson High School," *Huffington Post*, June 9, 2014, http://www.huffingtonpost.com/2014/06/09/westboro-baptist-church-wilson-high-school_n_5473009.html (accessed September 24, 2014).

7. "Florida Schools Forced to Allow Satanic Church Access to Its Young Students," 21st-CenturyWire.com, September 19, 2014, http://21stcenturywire.com/2014/09/19/florida-schools-forced-to-allow-satanic-church-access-to-its-young-students/ (accessed September 25, 2014).

8. Robyn Pennacchia, "Santorum Wants to Classify 'Secularism' as a Religion," *Death and Taxes*, September 9, 2014, http://www.deathandtaxesmag.com/227833/santorum-wants-to-classify-secularism-as-a-religion/ (accessed September 25, 2014).

9. "Religion and Prayer in U.S. Public Schools," ReligiousTolerance.org, n.d., http://www.religioustolerance.org/ps_pra9.htm (accessed September 22, 2014).

10. Rachel K. Jones and Jenna Jerman, "Abortion Incidence and Service Availability in the United States, 2011," *Perspectives on Sexual and Reproductive Health*, March 2014, no page. See "Highlighted Research Articles," http://www.guttmacher.org/sections/by-type.php?type=article (accessed September 9, 2014).

11. Ellyn Fortino, "Reproductive Rights Advocates Demand Repeal of Illinois' Abortion Notification Law," ProgressIllinois.com, April 3, 2014, http://www.progressillinois.com/quick-hits/content/2014/04/03/youth-reproductive-rights-advocates-demand-repeal-abortion-notificatio (accessed September 8, 2014).

12. Fortino, "Reproductive Rights Advocates."

13. Susan Tyrrell, "Pro-Life Teenagers Brave below Freezing Temps to Rally against Abortion," LifeNews.com, December 13, 2013, http://www.lifenews.com/2013/12/13/pro-life-teenagers-brave-below-freezing-temps-to-rally-against-abortion/ (accessed September 8, 2014).

14. Kevin Murphy, "Kansas Abortion Clinic Reopens Four Years after Doctor's Murder," Reuters.com, April 4, 2013, http://www.reuters.com/article/2013/04/04/us-usa-abortion-kansas-idUSBRE93305020130404 (accessed September 9, 2014).

15. Allison Yarrow, "The Abortion War's Special Ops," *Newsweek*, August 20, 2014, http://www.newsweek.com/inside-covert-abortion-war-265866 (accessed September 9, 2014).

16. Kimberly Winston, "Jessica Ahlquist, Teenage Atheist, Wins Case to Remove Prayer Banner from Cranston High School," *Huffington Post*, January 14, 2012, http://www.huffingtonpost.com/2012/01/14/judge-prayer-banner-high-school_n_1205627.html (accessed September 5, 2014).

17. Winston, "Jessica Ahlquist, Teenage Atheist."

18. Michael Stone, "After Threats and Harassment, NC Teen Abandons Atheist Group," Patheos .com, February 26, 2014, http://www.patheos.com/blogs/progressivesecularhumanist/2014/02/ after-threats-and-harassment-nc-teen-abandons-atheist-group/ (September 23, 2014).

19. Stone, "After Threats and Harassment."

20. See http://www.legis.state.la.us/lss/lss.asp?doc=631000 (accessed September 11, 2014).

21. Katherine Weber, "Teen Activist Continues Fight against Creationism in La. Classrooms," *Christian Post*, January 16, 2013, http://www.christianpost.com/news/teen-activist-continues -fight-against-creationism-in-la-classrooms-88387/ (accessed September 3, 2014).

22. Moyers and Kopplin, "Fighting Creeping Creationism."

23. Moyers and Kopplin, "Fighting Creeping Creationism."

24. Moyers and Kopplin, "Fighting Creeping Creationism."

---

a. See http://caselaw.lp.findlaw.com/scripts/getcase.pl?court=US&vol=319&invol=624 (ac- cessed September 5, 2014).

b. Jill Filipovic, "Five Years after Dr. Tiller's Murder, Abortion Clinics Remain at Risk," *Cosmo- politan*, May 30, 2014, http://www.cosmopolitan.com/politics/news/a6998/dr-tiller-murder/ (accessed September 21, 2014).

c. See the PBS website, http://www.pbs.org/wgbh/nova/evolution/intelligent-design-trial.html (accessed April 29, 2015).

d. Liesl Dargar, "Essay: My Fight as a Child of Polygamy" (reprinted in *The Polygamy Blog* by Nate Carlisle), *Salt Lake Tribune*, August 2, 2013, http://www.sltrib.com/sltrib/blogs polygblog/56678985-191/family-liberties-polygamy-speak.html.csp (accessed September 17, 2014).

Chapter 8

1. Michael Rose, "The Girl Who Transformed the Paper Crane into the Symbol for Peace and Hope," *Huffington Post*, August 20, 2013, http://www.huffingtonpost.com/michael-rose/the -girl-who-transformed-the-paper-crane_b_3787670.html (accessed September 30, 2014).

2. Janet Penn, interviewer, "Growing Up in the Shadow of 9/11: America's Youth Speak Out on How This Grim Defining Moment Changed Them Forever," Youth LEAD, Inc., n.d., www .youthleadonline.org/GrowingUpInTheShadowOf9-11.pdf (accessed October 2, 2014).

3. Penn, "Growing Up in the Shadow of 9/11."

4. Penn, "Growing Up in the Shadow of 9/11."

5. Alex Kane, "Young New York City Muslims Speak Out on How Islamophobia Impacts Daily Life," Mondoweiss.net, August 15, 2013, http://mondoweiss.net/2013/08/young-new-york -city-muslims-speak-out-on-how-islamophobia-impacts-daily-life (accessed September 1, 2015).

6. Kane, "Young New York City Muslims."

7. Ben Norton, Tyra Walker, Anastasia Taylor, Alli McCracken, Colleen Moore, Jes Grob- man, and Ashley Lopez of CodePink, "There Is No Future in War: Youth Rise Up, a Manifesto," CommonDreams.org, September 12, 2014, http://www.commondreams.org/ views/2014/09/12/there-no-future-war-youth-rise-manifesto (accessed October 2, 2014).

8. "Americans Don't Want a Ground War on ISIS," *The Compass* (RWC blog), January 12, 2015, http://www.realclearworld.com/blog/2015/01/americans_dont_want_an_all-out_assault_on _isis_110900.html (accessed March 10, 2015).

9. John LaForge, "Three U.S. Anti-War Activists Sentenced to Long Prison Terms for Non-violent Action," GlobalResearch.ca, February 19, 2014, http://www.globalresearch.ca/three-u-s-anti-war-activists-sentenced-to-long-prison-terms-for-nonviolent-action/5369641 (accessed April 29, 2015).

10. LaForge, "Three U.S. Anti-War Activists Sentenced."

11. Associated Press, "Court to Hear Sabotage Appeal of 85-Year-Old Nun, Activists," Wate.com, March 11, 2015, http://wate.com/2015/03/11/court-to-hear-sabotage-appeal-of-85-year-old-nun-activists/ (accessed April 29, 2015).

12. Alex Kane, "Assault on Gaza Fuels Surge of Civil Disobedience in Protest of Israeli Actions," Mondoweiss.net, July 29, 2014, http://mondoweiss.net/2014/07/assault-disobedience-protest (accessed October 7, 2014).

13. Kane, "Assault on Gaza."

14. U.S. Department of Defense, "Conscientious Objectors," May 31, 2007, p. 2, www.dtic.mil/whs/directives/corres/pdf/130006p.pdf (accessed October 9, 2014).

15. "Conscientious Objection and Alternative Service," SSS.gov, n.d., https://www.sss.gov/consobj (accessed October 9, 2014).

16. "Youth Programs," American Friends Service Committee, n.d., http://www.afsc.org/program/youth-programs (accessed October 4, 2014).

17. "Interfaith Understanding Propels Innovative 'Hands of Peace' Program," UCC.org, August–September 2008, http://www.ucc.org/ucnews/augsep08/interfaith.html (accessed October 5, 2014).

18. "Interfaith Understanding."

19. "Interfaith Understanding."

20. "Interfaith Understanding."

21. Brian L. Cox, "'Hands of Peace' Brings Teens Together Here," *Chicago Tribune*, February 12, 2014, http://articles.chicagotribune.com/2014-02-12/news/ct-tl-ns-0704-winnetka-peace-picnic-20130701_1_north-shore-teenagers-gretchen-grad-palestinians (accessed October 3, 2014).

22. See https://www.globalpeace.org/united-states (accessed September 1, 2015).

23. See http://www.peacejam.org/action.aspx (accessed October 4, 2014).

24. See http://www.seedsofpeace.org/mission (accessed October 4, 2014).

25. Nell Gluckman, "Emotions Run High at Seeds of Peace Camp in Maine amid Israeli-Palestinian Conflict," *Bangor Daily News*, August 9, 2014, http://bangordailynews.com/slideshow/emotions-run-high-at-seeds-of-peace-camp-in-maine-amid-israeli-palestinian-conflict/ (accessed October 5, 2014).

26. Gluckman, "Emotions Run High."

27. Gluckman, "Emotions Run High."

28. "Camp Plants Seeds of Peace in Israeli and Palestinian Teens," NBCNews.com, August 5, 2014, http://www.nbcnews.com/watch/nightly-news/camp-plants-seeds-of-peace-in-israeli-and-palestinian-teens-315400259676 (accessed October 3, 2014).

a. Friends of Peace Pilgrim, comp., *Peace Pilgrim: Her Life and Work in Her Own Words* (Santa Fe, NM: Ocean Tree Books, 1992), p. 26; see also identical version in pdf at PeacePilgrim.org (accessed September 29, 2014).

b. Craig and Cindy Corrie, eds., *Let Me Stand Alone: The Journals of Rachel Corrie* (New York and London: W. W. Norton, 2008), 200.

c. Roberta Seid, "Rachel Corrie's Dreams: The (Self) Deceit of Rachel Corrie," *Commentary* magazine, n.d., http://www.commentarymagazine.com/viewarticle.cfm/the—self—deceit-of-rachel-corrie-11453?page=all (accessed October 10, 2014).

d. Lee Kaplan, "Op-Ed: Rachel Corrie's Case Is Back in Court," *Arutz Sheva*, May 12, 2014, http://www.israelnationalnews.com/Articles/Article.aspx/14991#.U3Ic4XZ8HXQ (accessed May 13, 2014).

e. Jonathan S. Tobin, "Rachel Corrie Was No Peace Activist," *Commentary* magazine, August 28, 2012, http://www.commentarymagazine.com/2012/08/28/rachel-corrie-was-no-peace-activist-israel-palestinians-terrorism/ (accessed October 10, 2014).

Chapter 9

1. Melissa Stern, "Locals Fight Back against Hate Group," Fox4KC.com, November 11, 2013, fox4kc.com/2013/11/09/locals-fight-back-against-hate-group/ (accessed September 1, 2015).

2. "Hate Crime," Justice.gov, n.d., http://www.justice.gov/crs/hate-crime (accessed October 24, 2014).

3. "Nearly Two-Thirds of Hate Crimes Went Unreported to Police in Recent Years" (press release), BJS.gov, March 21, 2013, http://www.bjs.gov/content/pub/press/hcv0311pr.cfm# (accessed October 25, 2014).

4. Allana Akhtar, "Sikh Students Hold Rally against Hate Crimes," *Michigan Daily*, September 26, 2013, http://www.michigandaily.com/news/speak-against-hate-holds-rally-diag (accessed October 31, 2014).

5. Stern, "Locals Fight Back."

6. Stern, "Locals Fight Back."

7. Robert Richardson, "Civil Rights Activists Rally against Recent Klan Propaganda," ABC3340.com, June 23, 2014, http://www.abc3340.com/story/25850718/civil-rights-activists-rally-against-recent-klan-propaganda (accessed October 27, 2014).

8. Kimber Williams, "'Teach-In against Hate' Counters Graffiti with Support and Education," Emory.edu, October 17, 2014, http://news.emory.edu/stories/2014/10/er_teach_in_against_hate_coverage/campus.html (accessed October 31, 2014).

9. Jamelle Bouie, "Don't Expel Members of Sigma Alpha Epsilon. Educate Them. Show Them What Their Words Mean," *Slate*, March 10, 2015, http://www.slate.com/articles/news_and_politics/politics/2015/03/university_of_oklahoma_expels_two_students_and_disbands_sigma_alpha_epsilon.html (accessed March 15, 2015).

10. Madison Jackson in *Stop the Hate: Youth Speak Out* (Beachwood, OH: Maltz Museum of Jewish Heritage, March 2014), p. 11; also see www.maltzmuseum.org/stop-the-hate/winners-2014/ (accessed November 17, 2014).

11. Jackson, in *Stop the Hate*, p. 11.

12. Rebekah Rae, "Young Teen Activist Challenges Racial Stigmas," JRN.com, February 14, 2014, http://www.jrn.com/kmtv/news/Young-Teen-Challenges-Race-245594421.html (accessed November 12, 2014).

13. See http://www.adcmich.org/cyber-12 (accessed May 5, 2015).

14. See http://www.adcmich.org/news (accessed October 28, 2014).

15. "Youth and Student Rights," NYCLU.org, n.d., http://www.nyclu.org/issues/youth-and-student-rights (accessed October 28, 2014).

16. "National Youth Leadership Mission," ADL.org, n.d., http://regions.adl.org/dc/programs/national-youth-leadership.html (accessed October 28, 2014).

17. "Programs Overview," NCCJ.org, n.d., https://www.nccj.org/nccj-programs-overview-all (accessed October 28, 2014).

18. Michael Stoops, ed. *Vulnerable to Hate: A Survey of Hate Crimes and Violence Committed against Homeless People in 2013.* A report by the National Coalition for the Homeless (Washington, DC: National Coalition for the Homeless, June 2014), p. 4.

19. Stoops, *Vulnerable to Hate*, pp. 8, 10.

20. Stoops, *Vulnerable to Hate*, pp. 5, 8.

21. Associated Press, "Navajo Leader, Mayor to Meet over Homeless Killings," *Huffington Post*, July 24, 2014, http://www.huffingtonpost.com/2014/07/24/navajo-leader-homeless -killings_n_5616838.html (accessed October 30, 2014).

22. Mark Guarino, "Teenagers, Social Media, and Terrorism: A Threat Level Hard to Assess," *Christian Science Monitor*, May 4, 2013, http://www.csmonitor.com/USA/Justice/2013/0505/ Teenagers-social-media-and-terrorism-a-threat-level-hard-to-assess (accessed November 4, 2014).

23. Guarino, "Teenagers, Social Media, and Terrorism."

24. Guarino, "Teenagers, Social Media, and Terrorism."

25. Will Fellows, "Former Skinhead Shares His Life after Hate," *Wisconsin Gazette*, December 30, 2010, http://www.wisconsingazette.com/wisconsin-gaze/former-skinhead-shares-his-life -after-hate.html (accessed November 3, 2014).

26. Fellows, "Former Skinhead Shares His Life after Hate."

27. "A 'Recovering Skinhead' on Leaving Hatred Behind," NPR.org, April 7, 2010, http://www .npr.org/templates/story/story.php?storyId=125514655 (accessed November 14, 2014).

28. "A 'Recovering Skinhead.'"

29. Frank Meeink and Jody M. Roy, *Autobiography of a Recovering Skinhead: The Frank Meeink Story as Told to Jody M. Roy* (Portland, OR: Hawthorne Books, 2010), p. 151.

30. "A 'Recovering Skinhead.'"

31. "A 'Recovering Skinhead.'"

a. "Hate and Extremism," SPLCenter.org, n.d., http://www.splcenter.org/what-we-do/hate -and-extremism (accessed April 30, 2015).

Chapter 10

1. Jason Bergman, "My Thoughts on Newtown: Americans Have to Learn That They Cannot Take Advantage of Their Freedoms," StageofLife.com, January 23, 2013, http://www .stageoflife.com/Default.aspx?tabid=72&g=posts&t=8570 (accessed December 2, 2014).

2. Meredith Bennett-Smith, "15-Year-Old Maryland Girl Argues against Gun Control in Viral Testimony," *Huffington Post*, April 10, 2013, updated April 11, 2013, http://www .huffingtonpost.com/2013/04/10/15-year-old-gun-control-video-sarah-merkle_n_3055740 .html (accessed November 21, 2014).

3. Matt Howard, "Firearm Safety Act—One Year Impact on the State of Maryland," WMDT .com, October 7, 2014, updated October 14, 2014, http://www.wmdt.com/story/26731040/ firearm-safety-act-one-year-impact (accessed November 21, 2014; page no longer available).

4. KelseyAN, "Life after Newtown: Why Schools Are Better Off without Guns," StageofLife .com, February 1, 2013, http://www.stageoflife.com/Default.aspx?tabid=72&g=posts&t=8826 (accessed November 21, 2014).

5. Children's Defense Fund, *Protect Children Not Guns* (Washington, DC: Children's Defense Fund, 2013), pp. 4–7, 24; also see http://www.childrensdefense.org/campaigns/protect-children-not-guns/ (accessed September 1, 2015).

6. "2014 Toll of Gun Violence," GunViolenceArchive.org, n.d., http://www.gunviolencearchive.org/tolls/2014 (accessed February 12, 2015).

7. Law Center to Prevent Gun Violence, *Regulating Guns in America: A Comprehensive Analysis of Gun Laws Nationwide* (San Francisco, CA: Law Center to Prevent Gun Violence, March 2014), pp. 3, 6; also see http://smartgunlaws.org/wp-content/uploads/2014/10/RGIA-For-Web.pdf (accessed November 20, 2014).

8. Dave Cullen, "The Depressive and the Psychopath," *Slate*, April 20, 2004, http://www.slate.com/articles/news_and_politics/assessment/2004/04/the_depressive_and_the_psychopath.html (accessed November 24, 2014).

9. EmiliaCristy, "My Thoughts on Newtown: Don't Fight Fire with Fire," StageofLife.com, January 23, 2014, http://www.stageoflife.com/Default.aspx?tabid=72&g=posts&t=8567 (accessed November 21, 2014).

10. Gslangner, "Newtown: A Harsh Reality America Has to Face," StageofLife.com, January 27, 2013, http://www.stageoflife.com/?tabid=72&g=posts&t=8601 (accessed December 2, 2014).

11. Bergman, "My Thoughts on Newtown."

12. Winwinhh, "My Thoughts on Newtown: The Rifle—My Companion and Another's Weapon," StageofLife.com, January 1, 2013, http://www.stageoflife.com/Default.aspx?tabid=72&g=posts&t=8814 (accessed December 3, 2014).

13. "Essays about Gun Control," StageofLife.com, n.d., www.stageoflife.com/gundebate.aspx#Gun Control (accessed December 2, 2014).

14. Megan Garvey, "Transcript of the Disturbing Video 'Elliot Rodger's Retribution,'" *Los Angeles Times*, May 24, 2014, http://www.latimes.com/local/lanow/la-me-ln-transcript-ucsb-shootings-video-20140524-story.html?track=rss&utm_source=twitterfeed&utm_medium=twitter (accessed November 29, 2014).

15. Allison Griner, "Gun Control, Gun Rights Advocates Push Dueling Ballot Measures in Washington," *Washington Post*, August 4, 2014, http://www.washingtonpost.com/blogs/govbeat/wp/2014/08/04/gun-control-gun-rights-advocates-push-dueling-ballot-measures-in-washington/ (accessed November 19, 2014).

16. Griner, "Gun Control."

17. Michael Kruse, "Fear at FSU," *Tampa Bay Times*, November 21, 2014, p. 5A. Also Mark Schlueb and Stephen Hudak, "FSU Shooter Myron May Feared 'Energy Weapon,' Heard Voices, Thought Police Were Watching Him," *Orlando Sentinel*, November 21, 2014, http://www.orlandosentinel.com/news/breaking-news/os-fsu-shooting-myron-may-update-20141121-story.html#page=2 (accessed November 23, 2014).

18. Kathleen McGrory, "A Difficult Day of Emotions on FSU Campus Following Deadly Shooting," *Miami Herald*, November 20, 2014, http://www.miamiherald.com/news/state/florida/article4039995.html (accessed November 23, 2014).

19. Ari N. Schulman, "What Mass Killers Want—and How to Stop Them," *Wall Street Journal*, November 8, 2013, http://online.wsj.com/articles/SB10001424052702303309504579181702252120052 (accessed November 24, 2014).

20. Tom Junod, "Why Mass Shootings Keep Happening," *Esquire*, October 24, 2014, www.esquire.com/news-politics/a30024/mass-shooters-1014/ (accessed September 1, 2015).

21. Brian Mann, "Will Upstate NY Cops, Sheriffs Enforce Gun Control Laws?" North CountryPublicRadio.org, August 14, 2014, http://www.northcountrypublicradio.org/news/

story/22532/20130814/will-upstate-ny-cops-sheriffs-enforce-gun-control-laws (accessed November 30, 2014).

22. Doug Wyllie, "PoliceOne's Gun Control Survey: 11 Key Lessons from Officers' Perspectives," PoliceOne.com, April 8, 2013, http://www.policeone.com/Gun-Legislation-Law-Enforcement/articles/6183787-PoliceOnes-Gun-Control-Survey-11-key-lessons-from-officers-perspectives/ (accessed December 1, 2014).

23. D.K., "Trigger Happy," *Democracy in America* (blog), *Economist*, August 15, 2014, http://www.economist.com/blogs/democracyinamerica/2014/08/armed-police (accessed December 1, 2014).

24. D.K., "Trigger Happy."

25. Wesley Lowery, "How Many Police Shootings a Year? No One Knows," *Washington Post*, September 8, 2014, www.washingtonpost.com/news/post-nation/wp/2014/09/08/how-many-police-shootings-a-year-no-one-knows/ (accessed April 30, 2015).

26. Mike Males, the Center on Juvenile and Criminal Justice, "Who Are Police Killing?" CJCJ.org, August 26, 2014, http://www.cjcj.org/news/8113 (accessed December 25, 2014).

27. Simon Moya-Smith, "Who's Most Likely to Be Killed by Police?" CNN.org, December 24, 2014, http://www.cnn.com/2014/12/24/opinion/moya-smith-native-americans/index.html?hpt=hp_t3 (accessed December 25, 2014).

28. Lowery, "How Many Police Shootings a Year?"

a. "About Us," NRA.org, n.d., http://home.nra.org/home/document/about (accessed November 23, 2014).

b. Alan Berlow and Gordon Witkin, "Gun Lobby's Money and Power Still Holds Sway over Congress," PublicIntegrity.org, May 1, 2013, http://www.publicintegrity.org/2013/05/01/12591/gun-lobbys-money-and-power-still-holds-sway-over-congress (accessed November 23, 2014).

c. "Part I: Teens and Gun Statistics—Survey Results," StageofLife.com, n.d., http://www.stageoflife.com/gundebate.aspx (accessed November 22, 2014).

d. "Speeches," FBI.gov, n.d., http://www.fbi.gov/news/speeches/hard-truths-law-enforcement-and-race (accessed February 13, 2015).

Chapter 11

1. NBC News Bay Area, "Undocumented SJ Man and Sen. Feinstein Call for Immigration Reform," NBCBayArea.com, December 20, 2012, http://www.nbcbayarea.com/news/local/Undocumented-SJ-Man-and-Sen-Feinstein-184274941.html (accessed December 21, 2014).

2. Arturo Garcia, "Teen Activist: 'I Feel Betrayed' by Boehner after Immigration Talk at Diner," RawStory.com, November 13, 2013, http://www.rawstory.com/rs/2013/11/13/teen-activist-i-feel-betrayed-by-boehner-after-immigration-talk-at-diner/ (accessed May 13, 2014).

3. Ricardo Ramirez, "Seven Children Arrested Advocating for Immigration Reform," FIRM news release, April 30, 2014, http://www.fairimmigration.org/category/press-release/ (accessed May 25, 2014).

4. Ramirez, "Seven Children Arrested."

5. Ramirez, "Seven Children Arrested."

6. "10 Myths about Immigration," Tolerance.org, Spring 2011, http://www.tolerance.org/immigration-myths (accessed January 2, 2015).

7. "Issue Brier: Criminalizing Undocumented Immigrants," ACLU.org, February 2010, https:// www.aclu.org/files/assets/FINAL_criminalizing_undocumented_immigrants_issue_brief _PUBLIC_VERSION.pdf (accessed January 2, 2015).

8. Robert P. Jones, Daniel Cox, Juhem Navarro-Rivera, E. J. Dionne Jr., and William A. Galston, "What Americans Want from Immigration Reform in 2014," Brookings.edu, June 10, 2014, http://www.brookings.edu/research/reports/2014/06/10-americans-immigration-reform -2014-survey-panel-call-back (accessed December 22, 2014).

9. Jones et al., "What Americans Want."

10. Roberto G. Gonzales and Veronica Terriquez, "Who and Where the DREAMers Are, Revised Estimates," ImmigrationPolicy.org, October 16, 2012, http://www.immigrationpolicy.org/ issues/DREAM-Act (accessed December 22, 2014).

11. President Barack Obama, "Remarks by the President in Address to the Nation on Immigration," WhiteHouse.gov, November 20, 2014, http://www.whitehouse.gov/issues/ immigration/immigration-action# (accessed December 22, 2014). Subsequent quotes by President Obama come from this speech.

12. Daniel González, "Farmers, Laborers Caught in Middle of Migrant Debate," *USA Today*, July 29, 2013, http://www.usatoday.com/story/news/politics/2013/07/29/farm-immigration -debate/2595697/ (accessed December 29, 2014).

13. Lauren Smiley, "Farm Confessional: I'm an Undocumented Farm Worker," ModernFarmer .com, November 6, 2013, http://modernfarmer.com/2013/11/farmworker-confessional/ (accessed December 29, 2014).

14. Smiley, "Farm Confessional."

15. Smiley, "Farm Confessional."

16. Matthew 25:35, English Standard Version.

17. Joshua 20:2–6, New International Version.

18. "Cuban-Americans: Politics, Culture and Shifting Demographics," JournalistsResource.org, last updated December 18, 2014, http://journalistsresource.org/studies/government/immigration/cuban-americans-politics-culture-demographics# (accessed December 31, 2014).

19. Bob Mellis, "Refugees," *Tampa Bay Times*, Floridian, January 4, 2014, p. 5; also see "Coming to America . . . Today," *RV Rolling On* (blog), December 9, 2014, http://robertsmellis .blogspot.com/2014/12/coming-to-americatoday.html (accessed January 4, 2015).

20. Mellis, "Refugees" and "Coming to America."

21. David Adams and Tom Brown, "Cuban Perks under Scrutiny in U.S. Immigration Reform," Reuters.com, February 8, 2013, http://www.reuters.com/article/2013/02/08/us-usa -immigration-cuba-idUSBRE9170F920130208 (accessed December 31, 2014).

22. Mary Turck, "US Embrace of Cuban Refugees Underscores Hypocrisy on Immigration," Aljazeera.com, August 26, 2014, http://america.aljazeera.com/opinions/2014/8/cuban -refugees-centralamericanmigrantsimmigrationdeportation.html (accessed December 31, 2014).

---

a. See "Anarchist Exclusion Act" at http://eng.anarchopedia.org/Anarchist_Exclusion_Act (accessed April 30, 2015).

b. "Immigration Act [1907]," HistoryCentral.com, n.d., http://www.historycentral.com/ documents/immigrationact.html (accessed May 7, 2015).

c. Mario Orellana, "Niño," *The Blog*, HuffPost Teen, September 24, 2013, http://www .huffingtonpost.com/mario-orellana/teen-immigration-story_b_3984514.html (accessed December 21, 2014).

d. *CBP Border Security Report*, December 19, 2014, http://www.cbp.gov/sites/default/files/documents/FINAL%20Draft%20CBP%20FY14%20Report_20141218.pdf (accessed January 1, 2015).

Chapter 12

1. George Joseph, "Black Lives Matter—at Schools, Too," TheNation.com, January 19, 2015, http://www.thenation.com/article/195321/black-lives-matter-school-too# (accessed January 21, 2015).
2. John Micklos Jr., "From Awareness to Action," *Teaching Tolerance*, Spring 2012, p. 40; see also http//www.tolerance.org/sites/default/files/general/Awareness.pdf (accessed May 6, 2015).
3. See the YEA home page at http://yeacamp.org/ (accessed January 10, 2015).
4. See *The Casandra Good Guide* report at http://www.cassandra.co/wp-content/themes/trendcentral/pdfs/MediaMemo.pdf (accessed May 6, 2015).
5. Alexis Manrodt, "The New Face of Teen Activism," *Teen Vogue*, April 2014, http://www.teenvogue.com/my-life/2014-04/teen-online-activism (accessed May 6, 2015).
6. Brian Honigman, "How Tumblr Is Changing Online Activism," *Forbes*, February 18, 2014, http://www.forbes.com/sites/citi/2014/02/18/how-tumblr-is-changing-online-activism/ (accessed January 15, 2015).
7. Shaquille Brewster, "After Ferguson: Is 'Hashtag Activism' Spurring Policy Changes?" NBC News.com, December 12, 2014, http://www.nbcnews.com/politics/first-read/after-ferguson-hashtag-activism-spurring-policy-changes-n267436 (accessed January 16, 2015).
8. "About Us," SPARKSummit.com, n.d., http://www.sparksummit.com/about-us/ (accessed January 12, 2015).
9. Austin Considine, "Saying 'No' to Picture Perfect," *New York Times*, May 16, 2012, http://www.nytimes.com/2012/05/17/fashion/saying-no-to-picture-perfect.html?_r=0 (accessed January 12, 2015).
10. Eric Wilson, "*Vogue* Adopts a 16-and-Over Modeling Rule," *On the Runway* (blog), *New York Times*, May 3, 2012, http://runway.blogs.nytimes.com/2012/05/03/vogue-adopts-a-16-and-over-modeling-rule/?_r=1 (accessed January 13, 2015).
11. "The SPARKteam," SPARKSummit.com, n.d., http://www.sparksummit.com/sparkteam/ (accessed January 12, 2015).
12. Alicia Maule and Traci G. Lee, "A Grad Student by Day, Online Activist by Night," MSNBC.com, September 22, 2014, http://www.msnbc.com/msnbc/grad-student-day-online-activist-night (accessed January 15, 2015).
13. Jesse Paul, "Jeffco Students Protest Proposed 'Censorship' of History Curriculum," *Denver Post*, September 22, 2014, http://www.denverpost.com/news/ci_26582843/jeffco-students-skip-classes-protest-censorship-history-curriculum?source=infinite (accessed September 1, 2015).
14. Jesse Paul, "Jeffco Students Walk Out of 5 High Schools in School Board Protest," *Denver Post*, September 23, 2014, http://www.denverpost.com/news/ci_26588432/jeffco-high-school-students-plan-walk-out-their (accessed September 1, 2015).
15. Joseph, "Black Lives Matter."
16. Joseph, "Black Lives Matter."

17. "eLaws—Fair Labor Standards Act Advisor," DOL.gov, n.d., http://www.dol.gov/elaws/faq/esa/flsa/003.htm (accessed January 30, 2015).

18. See the report at http://www.bls.gov/cps/minwage2013.pdf (accessed January 30, 2015).

19. Eric Dresden, "Minimum Wage Protest at Flint McDonald's Ends with 25 Taken into Police Custody," MLive.com, September 24, 2014, http://www.mlive.com/news/flint/index.ssf/2014/09/flint_police_take_25_into_cust.html (accessed January 30, 2015).

20. Melanie Trottman, "Low-Wage Workers Stage Strikes and Protests over Pay," *Wall Street Journal*, December 4, 2014, http://www.wsj.com/articles/low-wage-workers-stage-strikes-and-protests-over-pay-1417713773 (accessed February 2, 2015).

21. Mara Lee, "Fast Food Workers, Union Activists Push for Higher Wages," *Hartford Courant*, December 4, 2014, http://www.courant.com/business/hc-fight-for-15-20141204-story.html (accessed January 16, 2015).

22. Jonathan Waldman, "Don't Kill Keystone XL. Regulate It," *New York Times*, March 6, 2015, http://www.nytimes.com/2015/03/06/opinion/dont-kill-keystone-xl-regulate-it.html?ref=topics&_r=0 (accessed May 6, 2015).

23. Tara Houska, "Houska: Obama to Veto Keystone XL Pipeline Bill, but Will He Reject Permit?" *Indian Country Today*, January 27, 2015, http://indiancountrytodaymedianetwork.com/2015/01/27/houska-obama-veto-keystone-xl-pipeline-bill-will-he-reject-permit-158882 (accessed February 7, 2015).

24. Jamie Henn, "Hundreds of Students Arrested at White House Protesting Keystone XL," *The Blog*, HuffPost Green, March 2, 2014, http://www.huffingtonpost.com/jamie-henn/keystone-xl-protest_b_4886208.html (accessed February 7, 2015).

a. Rosalie Tostevin, "Online Activism: It's Easy to Click, but Just as Easy to Disengage," *Media and Tech Network* (blog), *Guardian*, March 14, 2014, http://www.theguardian.com/media-network/media-network-blog/2014/mar/14/online-activism-social-media-engage (accessed January 15, 2015).

b. Ron Kovic, *Born on the Fourth of July* (New York: Akashic Books, 2005), pp. 16–17.

c. Kovic, *Born on the Fourth of July*, p. 17.

d. Steve Lopez, "Forty Years after 'Fourth of July,' Ron Kovic Still Speaking Up against War," *Los Angeles Times*, November 8, 2014, http://www.latimes.com/local/california/la-me-1109-lopez-kovic-20141109-column.html (accessed February 9, 2015).

Selected Bibliography

Books

Boggs, Grace Lee with Scott Kurashige. *The Next American Revolution: Sustainable Activism for the Twenty-First Century* (Berkeley: University of California Press, 2012, paperback).

Chomsky, Aviva. *Undocumented: How Immigration Became Illegal* (Boston: Beacon Press, 2014, paperback).

Lloyd, Rachel. *Girls Like Us: Fighting for a World Where Girls Are Not for Sale: A Memoir* (New York: Harper/HarperCollins, 2012, paperback).

Martin, Cortney M. *Do It Anyway: The New Generation of Activists* (Boston: Beacon Press, 2010, paperback).

Shaw, Randy. *The Activist's Handbook: Winning Social Change in the 21st Century*, 2nd ed. (Berkeley and Los Angeles: University of California Press, 2013).

Shragg, Eric. *Activism and Social Change: Lessons for Community Organizing*, 2nd ed. (North York, Ontario, Canada: University of Toronto Press, 2013).

Willis, Laurie, ed. *Extremism* (Farmington Hills, MI: Greenhaven Press, 2011).

Articles

Eichenwald, Kurt. "The Bible So Misunderstood It's a Sin," *Newsweek*, January 2–January 9, 2015, pp. 26–41.

Eichenwald, Kurt. "Take Two Slugs and Call Me in the Morning," *Newsweek*, November 7, 2014, pp. 26–28.

Flannery, Mary Ellen. "The Kids Are All Right: Meet the Next Generation of Social Justice Activists," *NEA Today*, Spring 2014, pp. 42–44.

Long, Cindy. "Still Separate, Still Unequal?" *NEA Today*, Spring 2014, pp. 31–39.

Lynas, Mark. "Why GMOs Are Not Evil," *Tampa Bay Times*, May 3, 2016, p. 4P.

Potok, Mark. "Back to the Border," *Intelligence Report*, Winter 2014, pp. 27–33.

Troutt, David Dante. "Imagining Racial Justice in America," *The Nation*, December 29, 2014, pp. 17–19.

Index

About the Author

Among the 120 books by **Kathlyn Gay** are nonfiction titles focusing on social and environmental issues, culture, and history. She also has written books about science, communication, sports, and other topics. She notes, "Because of the extensive research required when writing nonfiction, the learning opportunities abound." In addition, she feels rewarded by being able to collaborate on some book projects with family members who are scattered across the United States.

Some of Kathlyn's works have received starred reviews in *Booklist* and have been selected as Books for the Teen Age by the New York Public Library, awarded "Outstanding Book" by the National Council for Social Studies and National Science Teachers' Association, selected for "notable books for young people" by the American Library Association, and listed on *VOYA*'s Nonfiction Honor List. *School Library Journal* declares Gay's books are "well-organized, thoughtful presentations." A Kirkus reviewer writes that her books contain "lively, effective quotes." "Well researched, supported by facts" is a *Booklist* description.

Kathlyn also has published hundreds of magazine features, stories, and plays, and she has written and contributed to encyclopedias, teachers' manuals, and textbooks. She is the author of a number of titles in the It Happened to Me series: *Epilepsy* (2002, with Sean McGarrahan), *Cultural Diversity* (2003), *Volunteering* (2004), *Religion and Spirituality in America* (2006), *The Military and Teens* (2008), *Body Image and Appearance* (2009), *Living Green* (2012), *Bigotry and Intolerance* (2013), and *Divorce* (2014).